New perspectives on technical
editing

NEW PERSPECTIVES ON TECHNICAL EDITING

Edited by

Avon J. Murphy
Murphy Editing and Writing Services

Baywood's Technical Communications Series
Series Editor: CHARLES H. SIDES

Baywood Publishing Company, Inc.
AMITYVILLE, NEW YORK

Baywood Publishing Company, Inc.
26 Austin Avenue
P.O. Box 337
Amityville, NY 11701
(800) 638-7819
E-mail: baywood@baywood.com
Web site: baywood.com

Library of Congress Catalog Number: 2009029860
ISBN 978-0-89503-394-9 (cloth : alk. paper)
ISBN 978-0-89503-410-6 (epub)
ISBN 978-0-89503-409-0 (epdf)
ISBN 978-0-89503-411-3 (mobi)
http://dx.doi.org/10.2190/NPO

Library of Congress Cataloging-in-Publication Data

New perspectives on technical editing / edited by Avon J. Murphy.
        p. cm. -- (Baywood's technical communications series)
    Includes bibliographical references and index.
    ISBN 978-0-89503-394-9 (cloth : alk. paper)
 1. Technical editing.   I. Murphy, Avon Jack.
    T11.4.N487   2009
    808'.0666--dc22

                                                    2009029860

Table of Contents

CHAPTER 1

Introduction

Avon J. Murphy

Now is an exciting time to be involved in technical editing, whether you are a practitioner, a teacher, or a student. Consider the following developments:

- The widespread adoption and adaptation of the levels of edit concept, enunciated most familiarly by Van Buren and Buehler [1], tells editors and clients alike that this technical editing business is complex and deserves careful planning and management.
- Job advertisements typically stress the responsibilities and challenges of editing positions in today's workplace.
- In day-to-day work environments, technical communicators fulfill such editorial roles as developmental editors, copyeditors, and proofreaders. You can choose the type of work that best suits your temperament and skills.
- Technical editing involves closely working with other individuals, sometimes in a one-on-one arrangement, sometimes in a team environment.
- The editor is the gatekeeper of quality for information products developed by the client or team. For many editors, this central responsibility makes the work particularly rewarding.
- A corpus of high-quality research has evolved and grown during the past 30 years.

As used in this book, *technical editing* refers to the planning, analysis, restructuring, and language changes made to other people's technological or scientific documents in order to make them more useful and accurate for their intended audiences. The effective technical editor enjoys paying rigorous attention to nuance and detail, finessing the intricacies of language, and negotiating with

1

http://dx.doi.org/10.2190/NPOC1

authors. Note that our scope excludes *revising*, which involves changing one's own writing, a related but very different activity that lacks the elements of negotiation and seeing documents through the eyes of someone besides the original author.

PURPOSE

New Perspectives in Technical Editing is designed, first, to help you better understand the discipline by examining multiple ways of approaching technical editing. Like other maturing disciplines, technical editing is rich enough that we can look at it through various critical lenses, gaining a deeper understanding as we shift from one lens to another. Each contributor in this volume takes a particular fruitful approach to thinking about the field, offering informed, highly personal research findings, interpretations, and recommendations. The chapters, all strong contributions to the research literature, together constitute a varied and balanced combination of ways of viewing the depth and possibilities of technical editing.

The collection is designed to help you take action. We hope that after reading the essays, you will have the resources to

- Add more value to your organization as you edit with greater efficiency, closer attention to the exact environment within which you work, and expanded awareness of processes that can bring you success versus those that can get you into trouble.
- Effectively support technical editing within your work environment.
- Teach the subject with understanding and rigor.
- Apply and add to the body of research literature on technical editing.

The audience for this book includes teachers and students in upper-division and graduate technical communication courses, researchers, and practicing editors, all of whom want to go beyond the rehashing of commonplaces and gain an understanding of the depth and rich diversity of approaches to technical editing. The writing style for this diverse audience, even when a contributor is discussing theoretical issues, is straightforward and readable. We discuss issues, trends, and best practices; we do not target readers looking for step-by-step tutorials on daily editing procedures.

Note: If you are teaching a technical editing course, you will find that this book complements a textbook such as Carolyn Rude's *Technical Editing* [2]. You could well have your students follow the textbook for its straightforward how-to advice and exercises and then delve into *New Perspectives in Technical Editing* for supplementary reading that will further develop their skill sets and suggest areas for individual research.

THE ESSAYS

The contributors are recognized editing authorities who exercise considerable independence of judgment and creative speculation. The sequence of their chapters within the collection is basically from the general to the more particular. Each chapter includes

- Introduction to the perspective
- History and review of the specialized literature
- Where we stand today and the future
- Special approaches and concerns, best practices, and tips
- References

Research within the field of technical editing is coming into its own. But how can you best pursue that research? Researcher Angela Eaton argues that our understanding and practice will reach their full potential only with greater involvement in research by both practitioners and academics. Pointing out how much past research has been anecdotal, she recommends that you instead follow such methodologies as the case study, meta-analysis, textual analysis, survey, and experiment. She looks into the strengths, flaws, and fine points of these approaches. The uses of the various approaches become concrete with her analyses of specific research projects on such topics as the levels of edit, the effect of editing on the final quality of a document, gender bias, electronic editing, the use of editorial guidelines, and editorial comments. Eaton makes a strong case that we must continue to expand our research and provides the tools to do so.

To understand current practices and the future of technical editing, you must understand its past. Professor emeritus and historical scholar Thomas L. Warren provides hints in his engaging interpretation of historical trends in our field. Focusing on what he terms the Beginning Period, the Middle Period, and the Modern Period, Warren teases us with questions about when editing as we now define it really began, why early authors allowed editors to make changes on their own, how different environments in different times led to changing mixes of generalist and specialist editors, to what degree such factors as rationalism and user-focused psychology brought changes to editing, and how research methodologies and educational initiatives are shaping the student of editing in new ways. His sweeping investigation brings us to the inescapable conclusion that technical editing is becoming more complex. If you enjoy historical mysteries, this chapter is for you.

You may well know Carolyn D. Rude for her frequently adopted textbook [2]. But now she looks at technical editing from the perspective of a master teacher addressing fellow teachers. Drawing upon both her own experience and feedback from teachers using her textbook, she reflects on the value of the editing course within the technical communication curriculum, the evolution of the course in response to changing environments, effective teaching methods (including the use of electronic tools), and possible ways to set up the course. She makes clear that the effective instructor thinks well beyond clever class exercises and stories from the trenches when developing and teaching the modern technical editing course.

Michelle Corbin addresses difficult and sometimes controversial issues that affect technical editors within today's various organizational structures. Working from practices and trends within both her own workplace and other organizations, she challenges you to make a strong case for editorial resources, dissects the present-day scenarios for editors, offers advice on building a smart career track, and details possible future writing environments. This might be an excellent chapter for human resources specialists to read.

A seasoned professional, Jean Hollis Weber offers insights into the complex art of copyediting. She argues for not only the copyeditor's pivotal role in quality control, but also the extent to which copyediting on the job stretches to include activities associated with other types of editing. You'll find a full bag of tools for avoiding doing the wrong things with grammar, smoothing out the copyeditor-author relationship, and taking advantage of the changing rules and new opportunities in copyediting online material.

Computer tool guru Geoffrey J. S. Hart places modern editing within the context of increasingly rapid technological change. Reminding us that technical editing remains what it long has been, he shows the subtle ways in which computers have changed the rules by which we edit. He introduces possible editorial solutions to new problems caused by non-linear and nonverbal content, communal creation of information, and single sourcing. Refreshingly, Hart shares with you his optimism that technology is not replacing the technical editor.

Barbara Gastel provides a thorough grounding in what it means to be a science editor. If you're not familiar with the field, you might be surprised by the number of niches that she describes within science editing. She persuasively demonstrates the importance of specialized ethical requirements, medical publication standards, and certification for many practitioners. If you're just moving into science editing, consider the many sources of education listed in the chapter. Look particularly at the details on the activities, services, and publications of the Council of Science Editors, in which Gastel has been deeply involved.

Longtime journal editor George F. Hayhoe, working from his experience within STC and the Institute of Electrical and Electronics Engineers as well as other research, scrutinizes what it takes to edit a technical journal. His close-up details show the complexity of the task in the many editorial and production roles that various people fill, the strict recordkeeping that keeps the operation going, and the intricate interpersonal relationships that ensure long-term viability. He prepares you to grapple with difficult, often controversial issues, such as the place of acceptance rates and citation frequency in determining a journal's value, second-language authors, and the political chemistry within a journal published by one kind of organization versus that within one published else-where. If you want specific hints about how to keep records, ensure you have enough content to put out issues, and prepare for a new editor, you'll find them here.

Finally, the annotated bibliography, compiled by Avon J. Murphy and Thomas L. Warren, presents critical summaries of approximately 100 significant books, articles, and other resources for today's technical editor. While the References sections of individual chapters contain resources appropriate to the perspectives in those chapters, the bibliography approaches the research literature from a broader perspective.

You'll note some fruitful overlap among chapters. Both Barbara Gastel and George Hayhoe, for example, go into the editing of professional journals. But their contexts differ greatly: whereas Gastel is sorting out career paths open to science editors, Hayhoe is laying out explicit, often day-to-day details for the editor of any type of professional journal. Similarly, several authors look at such areas as the nature of technical editing, the future of our discipline, the levels of edit, and electronic tools within the contexts of their chapters. And you'll find frequent mention of people who have contributed significantly to the practice of and research on technical editing, including Mary Fran Buehler, Donald W. Bush, Michelle Corbin, David Dayton, David K. Farkas, Judith A. Tarutz, and Lola M. Zook.

We hope that the essays in this volume serve to enrich the growing body of literature on technical editing. We invite your feedback and continued discussion.

REFERENCES

1. R. Van Buren and M. F. Buehler, *The Levels of Edit* (2nd ed.), Jet Propulsion Laboratory, Pasadena, California, 1980.
2. C. D. Rude, *Technical Editing* (4th ed.), Pearson Longman, New York, 2006.

CHAPTER 2

Conducting Research in Technical Editing

Angela Eaton

Defining *research*, like defining other terms in our field, isn't easy. The definition is complicated by the evolution of quantitative and qualitative research methods, and by differing views of how knowledge is created—positivism and feminism for two. I define *research* as an effort to understand a topic by conducting a systematic inquiry.

The importance of research differs greatly between academic and practitioner spheres. Academics are indoctrinated early in the importance of research. PhD programs require one to four research courses, and we teachers know that tenure-track positions at research-intensive institutions expect that 40% of our time will be spent on research, the first or second criterion considered for tenure. In a 2003 survey of members of the Association for the Teachers of Technical Writing, when respondents were asked how they want to see the field of technical communication evolve, one of the top three themes represented was "the need to develop our own knowledge base by conducting more empirical research focused on practitioners and users and building theories from it" [1, p. 138].

Practitioners, however, differ more widely in their perception of the nature and importance of research. Some read the research literature and use it in their practice. Some conduct their own studies and present them at professional meetings and conferences. Some publish in the journals. Others rarely notice research at all.

Ultimately, however, for the field of technical editing to grow and improve, we need both practitioner participation in and increased academic involvement in editing research. Without publication, the immense professional knowledge

http://dx.doi.org/10.2190/NPOC2

practitioners have accumulated over their careers is passed on only through mentoring, or, if the practitioner has taught a class, to thirty or sixty students a semester. But publishing that knowledge, and even better, conducting research on that knowledge to enhance it, shares it as widely as possible—to the thousands of subscribers to the journal it's published in and to anyone who finds references to the article in online databases.

This chapter introduces research methods useful in studying technical editing and provides summaries of research studies performed, in hopes of inspiring academics and practitioners to read, support, and ultimately perform technical editing research. This chapter discusses practitioner research, case studies, meta-reviews and meta-analysis, textual analysis, surveys, and experiments and quasi-experiments. This chapter introduces their purposes, describes their most important strengths and weaknesses, and provides examples of studies that use them.

Naturally, these aren't all the research methods that exist—ethnographies, focus groups, and historical studies have not been included in this chapter, for example—but those described here have all been applied to technical editing research. Now, obviously, one book chapter can only introduce research methods. To undertake a project, additional reading will be necessary. Any of the references cited in each section provides a good starting place. I have used many of them in my graduate Introduction to Research Methods and Quantitative Research Methods classes for PhD students at Texas Tech University.

PRACTITIONER RESEARCH—
OR ANECDOTAL RESEARCH?

Most of the methods presented here are healthy ones, with a long history of use in social science and technical communication. One of the few methods whose legitimacy is hotly argued is anecdotal research, occasionally called "practitioner research." *Anecdotal research* is simply a description of what one person or company did in a given situation; practitioner research has been defined as "basically a report, or story, of how an individual handled a particular writing problem or situation" [2, p. 584]. It is often confused with the case study, a more sophisticated, robust methodology that is planned before the event and collects data to examine the event, often incorporating multiple methods for data triangulation (described in the next section).

Both quantitative and qualitative researchers have disapproved of anecdotal research. MacNealy, in her *Strategies for Empirical Research in Writing*, cautions researchers that a good case study "consists of more than a retrospective or anecdotal report on some procedure or event" [3, p. 196]. Qualitative researchers also do not hold that personal experience alone should be declared research and are quite clear in describing the creation of a theoretical framework and multimodal methods of data collection [4].

In anecdotal research, there is little if any evidence that any research was actually conducted or any data collected. The term *practitioner research* is a misnomer, and a denigrating one, because it implies—strongly—that practitioners cannot perform any other type of research.

In terms of usefulness, anecdotal research is one step more helpful than personally fumbling through a new situation, simply because it is the benefit of someone else's experience. In my research class, I refer to the results as "cup of coffee articles," because they're useful, but only as useful as having a cup of coffee with someone, chatting about his or her experience. Anecdotal research is, of course, more common in new fields and in developing fields, as technical communication as a whole is. The problem is that it makes up such a large amount of the "research" that we have. Examine any conference proceedings, and you will see a great number of such articles. (For a review of 20 years of conference proceedings from the early years of technical communication, see [5].) In terms of the goals of research, of building a body of knowledge that we can all benefit from, these anecdotes are only small steps forward, one group or person and experience at a time, vaguely described. We need to concentrate on larger steps. In discussing research in this chapter, I have not included any anecdotal research.

CASE STUDY

A *case study* is a common qualitative method used across disciplines, "a carefully designed project to systematically collect information about an event, situation, or small group of persons or objects for the purpose of exploring, describing, and/or explaining aspects not previously known or considered" [3, p. 197]. MacNealy categorizes it as one of the two major qualitative methods, along with ethnography; it can be differentiated from ethnography by its narrow focus on a small group and typically a short time span. Case studies "are the preferred strategies when the 'how' or 'why' questions are being posed, when the investigator has little control over events, and when the focus is on a contemporary phenomenon within some real-life context" [6, p. 1]. Yin, in his helpful *Case Study Research: Design and Methods*, further classifies case studies into explanatory, exploratory, and descriptive; they can also be grouped by whether they contain one or multiple cases [6]. Generally, however, they provide deep detail of one specific situation.

The strengths of the case study include that it can be conducted by one or more people in their own workplace, making it an excellent first study for a new researcher [3]. Case studies are often used early in a topic's development, before the important variables are known, but Yin argues that they can be used at any point. Case studies can be used to provide potential hypotheses that can be tested with a follow-up study.

As for weaknesses, both Yin and MacNealy mention that case studies aren't necessarily well respected; MacNealy thinks they aren't well respected because simplistic anecdotal reports are often labeled case studies, diluting the strength of the method. Additionally, because they are in-depth explorations of one situation, their results do not necessarily generalize well to other situations [3, 7], but Yin labels this traditional critique as one of the "traditional prejudices against the case study methodology," and he urges a rethinking of it [6, p. 10]. Case studies have been accused of being subject to bias because they are often conducted by one person [3]. Additionally, the costs involved, such as in transcription of interviews, can be high.

Case studies need to be pre-planned and have data gathered as the event or project evolves, not gathered from memory after it is completed [3]. This data is often gathered using multiple methodologies [6, 7]; Yin recommends collecting information from physical artifacts, interviews, documents, archival records, direct observations, and participant observations. The steps in a case study are to define the problem; to carefully choose the participants or location, usually because they are very unusual or very typical; to plan and test the methods of collecting data before data collection begins; to collect data systematically in a way that the data can be examined by others (such as by transcribing interviews rather than just taking personal notes); to verify conclusions by having another researcher examine the data; and to present conclusions tentatively [3]. Yin's book provides multiple designs for single and multiple case studies and in Chapter 2 explains the use of theory within the case study.

The case study has a long tradition in sociology and anthropology and is currently used frequently in business, psychology, medicine, and political science [7]. Technical communication's most famous case studies are probably those written by Odell and Goswami in the early 1980s about writers' choices in content, style, and conveying commands and requests [3]. The two case studies discussed in this chapter include a group's revision of their levels of edit and an exploration of six editors' practices while editing client documents.

Revising the Levels of Edit

Los Alamos National Laboratory's writing and editing group began revising the levels of edit they used as part of a quality improvement project. Their goals were to "simplify the editing process, focus editing on improving technical clarity, and ensure that value was added in editing" [8, p. 1].

Their survey of 100 authors and their seventy editors revealed that authors frequently misunderstood what the levels entailed, and editors occasionally did; they determined that three factors drove how the authors chose the level of edit: audience, cost, and turnaround time.

They then created a matrix of all the errors contained in the old levels of edit (included in their proceedings article), analyzed the effect of those errors on clarity, and found that with the exception of glaring errors, which affected all audiences, the effect of the errors on clarity was very audience-dependent. They redesigned three levels of edit based on their matrix and passed the levels to the editors for critique; the editors suggested that more errors be included.

After refining the checklist, renaming the levels, and determining which errors would be fixed by the editors and which would be queried to the author, two and a half years later, they created three levels of edit—the proofreading edit, grammar edit, and full edit—and defined them in terms of what the authors could understand. They created a checklist that showed all the items that were checked within each level and a diagnostic table that provided recommendations for the appropriate editing level based on the genre of document to be edited and the audience who would read it.

They then created training documents for the editors that spelled out in more detail the changes to be made, essentially adding style guide entries to the checklist from the levels of edit. They had a small group of editors use the training documents and then refined them, and then trained all 70 editors on the new checklists and refined them even further. The editors were also asked to note how long it took to edit documents under the revised system, making possible accurate estimates.

As a result of the revision, authors could choose the appropriate level of edit more easily with the diagnostic chart and full checklist, editors liked the very clear description of what is contained in each level of edit, and authors and editors appreciated fewer levels. New editors were also found to be trained faster with the checklist/style guide hybrid.

Studying Six Editors Editing

Bisaillon undertook a study of editors editing after noting that North American and European editing and revision researchers have studied self-editing but have "rarely" studied professional editing and noted that descriptions of professional editors' work have "to date have been described only rather sketchily" [9, pp. 295, 318, 319]. She notes that her study contributes by researching professional editors in natural editing tasks, as part of their work day, unlike other studies which created an artificial task for the editor to accomplish.

Bisaillon studied six professional part-time and full-time editors, two men and four women, half of whom had less than 4 years' experience and half of whom had more than 12 years of experience. She filmed the editors for 2 hours in their workplace, either a professional or home office, while editing for a client. After the filming, a researcher conducted a retrospective verbalization by scrolling through the edited document with the editor sitting nearby and asked about the reason for each change while being audiotaped. The editor then participated in a semi-structured interview about his or her professional experience. The videotapes, edited documents, and audiotapes were then coded by recording every action the editor took and examining the actions for strategies.

She found that errors were corrected either automatically, as with grammar or punctuation problems (57% of the time), or by using a problem-solving strategy. Problem-solving strategies included rereading (5% of the strategies used) and reflection (10%), immediate search (22%), postponement of solution (4%), and a tentative solution (less than 1%).

She examined the effectiveness of the various strategies by examining their outcome. Automatic correction was effective 98.22% of the time and did not result in a solution less than 2% of the time and was then postponed. Reflection was effective 76% of the time, and rereading was effective 69% of the time. Immediate search was effective 53% of the time. Postponed search's effectiveness varied. More experienced authors used reflection more often, and inexperienced authors used immediate search more often.

The author then discussed solutions, in contrast to the problem-solving strategies above. Immediate solutions included no modification 6%, revision 62%, and rewriting 6%. Postponed solutions included suggestions to the author, slightly more often than 1% of the time, postponement of a decision (no percentage was provided), and doing nothing, 24% of the time. Overall, she believes editing is a linear process, because the editors she observed looked back through the document only six times in all.

META-REVIEW AND META-ANALYSIS

Every research project should begin with a review of the literature—a search for relevant articles that results in a summary of what research has been performed before, which becomes the opening paragraphs to the research article. These literature reviews help establish why the new study is necessary and how it continues building on what is already known; it also shows the researcher's preparation.

Another type of literature review is what I call a *meta-review*—a more extensive, systematic review of the literature that describes how the articles were searched for, indicates how they were included or excluded from the groups of articles examined, and then summarizes the results of their findings—including where they conflict, where they support each other, and what work yet needs to be done. Within medical contexts, they're simply called review articles, a clinical review [10], or a Cochrane review [11]. These meta-reviews can stand alone as individual articles.

A *meta-analysis* is a step beyond the meta-review. It incorporates all the same steps but then examines the group of studies as if they were each a participant in a larger study: each study's results become data for the meta-analysis [12]. Meta-analyses help counter bias by including multiple groups gathered in multiple ways and analyzing them as one; one theorist remarks that there should be at least six studies performed on the same topic before a meta-analysis can be performed [3]. While useful, meta-analysis can very rarely be performed in technical editing research, because the questions and measures used in each study often vary so widely.

Meta-reviews do not involve reanalyzing data as meta-analyses do. They are excellent projects for new researchers, because they provide a very thorough overview of what has been done and increase the researcher's familiarity with the databases, journals, and research methods of the field. If the researcher is very new, he or she may benefit from partnering with a more advanced researcher for that person's advanced methodological knowledge for the critique of the studies. If constructed carefully, a dissertation's first chapter can become a meta-review.

To conduct a meta-review, choose your topic for research. This sounds easier than it sometimes is, because the same topic can appear under different search terms depending on the field. What we think of as "editing," for example, might be found under "peer review" in education, but that's not the same as "peer review" in academic articles, which often incorporates editing but is actually the review process for acceptance in a journal. As a result, it's very important to keep a log of the search terms used and the databases searched for writing up the meta-review (a useful habit in itself). As articles are included or excluded during the search, keep careful records of the criteria for admission. At the end of the search, review all the articles to make sure they conform to the final criteria. Finally, read and summarize all of the relevant articles. Note their methodologies and any mistakes in implementation that might endanger the quality of the results. Note the variables and themes they study, and how they were measured or explored. Examine the results and conclusions carefully, and determine if the researchers missed any aspects or misinterpreted their results. Finally, note their individual calls for future research, included in the conclusions, usually as the last few paragraphs, and see what needs to be studied next. Then attempt to provide the reader with an overview of all the relevant research done to date. Two examples of meta-reviews done on editing research follow.

Effects of Technical Editing on Article Quality

Wager and Middleton conducted a meta-review of the effects of technical editing in biomedical journals. They define technical editing widely, as "any processes applied to articles between acceptance and publication that were designed to improve accuracy or clarity or impose a predefined style" [10, p. 2821].

The authors conducted a systematic review of the literature by searching 14 databases, searching nine individual journals, searching the Internet, and contacting individual researchers [11]. To be included, studies had to report original data and compare at least two groups, and any study examining readability or comprehension had to use typical readers of the journal. Two researchers independently evaluated whether the study fulfilled the selection criteria and resolved conflicting evaluations through discussion. The measures used in the studies were too different for the authors to compare them statistically as a meta-analysis, so they compared them descriptively.

Overall, they found that there is some evidence that technical editing does improve article quality. Two studies reported improved readability—although the articles still received ratings in the difficult category—and shorter length as a result of technical editing and peer review, and a third reported significantly improved quality in four of 34 categories. Two studied the effects of technical editing or peer review, and each was found to improve article reporting quality by approximately 60%. A study following the implementation of stricter editorial policies resulted in 20 areas of no change, 12 areas improved, and four worsened. Two articles found that editorial policies reduced errors in abstracts, and three found that editing reduced errors in citations.

However, many of the studies had multiple methodological flaws, such as not using enough participants or articles to detect changes, using unvalidated measures, having a large loss of participants or a low response rate, or failing to report inter-rater reliability (a measure of reliability of the classification of data between coders). The author's main conclusion was "there has been little rigorous research to show which processes can improve accuracy or readability the most, or if any have harmful effects" [11, p. 2].

Effects of Peer Review on Article Quality

A 2002 study conducted an extensive search of the literature and reviewed the results of 19 studies examining the effects of peer review on articles submitted to biomedical journals [13, 14]. A formal meta-analysis wasn't possible because the data collected and questions to be answered differed too greatly.

The researchers noted the "remarkably few well-designed studies" [14, p. 2785] they found. By far, the majority of the studies had design problems that endangered the usefulness of their results or they found no significant difference. Of the nine studies examining the effect of blinding identity in peer review, five found no difference and the other four were methodologically flawed, having small confidence intervals or inappropriately masking identity [13]. Two studies that examined submission checklist effectiveness were split in their findings. A study that implemented a statistical checklist found it to be beneficial, but the results may not generalize widely because of the small size and setting of the study, while the other study did not find a benefit to providing a checklist. Two studies examining the effect of training reviewers were also split. One resulted in increased inter-rater reliability and the other found no effect; the design of both was questioned by the authors. A study examining reviewer bias found no evidence of bias, but the study had a relatively low response rate. A study examining the effect of review on validity found no result, but the sample was small.

Few studies found positive effects with relatively sound designs. Using the Internet to allow reviewers to communicate benefited the authors and did not impact the quality of reviews, while calling reviewers to remind them a review is due lengthened the time they took to return it and shortened the time they spent on it. Two studies found that peer review can improve report quality, although the authors point out that those studies are in atypical journals that are well funded.

The researchers concluded that "given the widespread use of peer review and its importance, it is surprising that so little is known of its effects. However, the research needed to address these questions would require a well-funded and coordinated effort involving several sectors of the scientific community as well as the cooperation of large numbers of authors and editors, and the methodological issues in conducting proper studies of the subject are daunting" [14, p. 2785].

TEXTUAL ANALYSIS

Textual analysis has been defined as the systematic selection and investigation of "oral, written, or graphic materials that have been produced in *natural* situations for a particular audience and purpose" and the method "to describe and interpret the characteristics of a recorded or visual message" [3, p. 123; 15, p. 225]. Word choice, text organization, publication venue, genre components— any segment of a text can be analyzed [16]. As in meta-reviews, choosing the pieces to be analyzed needs to be thoughtfully performed and recorded. The method is commonly used by linguists, anthropologists, psychologists, mass communication researchers, and educational researchers [3].

Depending on the author describing the technique, content analysis, discourse analysis, rhetorical analysis, and syntactic analysis can all be included or differentiated from textual analysis; purists will insist on the distinctions, but essentially, each of these methods can analyze the text's audience, purpose, surface features, style, rhetorical strategies, meaning, and the relationship among them [17]. Most frequently, the texts are analyzed by creating classifications for the parts of interest and then coding the data—number and type of metaphors used, instances of authors making or not making editorial changes, distance between nouns and verbs (see [17] for a thorough treatment).

Benefits of textual analysis are many. It can be performed anywhere, no matter where the texts were developed [3]. The researcher doesn't bias the results by interacting with the texts, unlike how a researcher can bias a participant's behavior by his or her presence. Textual analysis studies unstructured materials, so unlike survey questions, coding schemes are generated from what is found [15]. It is useful for longitudinal studies, and it enables the study of people, organizations, and civilizations that do not currently exist or are difficult to observe by examining the texts they have left behind [3]. Weaknesses include that it is very time-intensive and can be difficult to do; for example, creating a coding scheme that is reliable across coders is very difficult.

To conduct a textual analysis, the researcher should determine the concept to be investigated and define it carefully, choosing to follow or revise others' definitions from the literature. The texts should be carefully identified and chosen, and random sampling can be used to keep the amount of analysis to an achievable level. A classification scheme in which each piece of data can be placed in only one category is then developed or borrowed, and the data is coded. Ideally, two coders are used to code at least 10% of the data (and frequently more than 10%) and inter-rater reliability is calculated (the necessity of this step is argued by researchers, but empirical researchers state that it is necessary) [3].

Gilbert and others conducted a textual analysis, studying the peer review process by examining all the manuscripts submitted in 1991 to *JAMA: The Journal of the American Medical Association*. They researched gender bias, defined as "the differential handling of a manuscript based on the gender of the author, editor, or reviewer" [18, p. 139]. They reviewed all of the statistics associated with the manuscript—eight variables in all, including manuscript assignment, the editor's selection of reviewers, the editor's rating of reviewer performance, reviewer turnaround time, content reviewer recommendations, statistical reviewer recommendations, manuscript rejection rates without further review, and manuscript acceptance rates.

They determined that bias exists in the review process for biomedical journals. Female editors, despite more often being part-time at *JAMA*, handled nearly twice as many manuscripts as the male editors. Male reviewers helped male editors more often than they did female editors, but female reviewers were equally likely to help female or male reviewers. Female editors received more articles from female corresponding authors significantly more often, but that may be due to research specialization.

Female editors summarily rejected articles significantly more often than male editors did; however, the researchers could not tell if female editors received worse manuscripts initially. For articles that were sent out for review, there was no significant difference in rejection rates between genders.

As for reviewer behavior, male reviewers took significantly longer to return manuscripts than female reviewers. Female editors rated reviewers significantly lower than did male editors, no matter the gender of the reviewer.

The researchers acknowledge that a number of factors that affect acceptance were beyond the scope of the study: "these data include manuscript load at the time of the final decision, priority or originality of the topic, length of the manuscript, institutions with which the authors are affiliated, whether the study found negative or positive results, study sample size, whether the manuscript was solicited, and inventory level for that category at the time of presentation at a manuscript meeting" [18, p. 142].

SURVEYS

Having become widely used in the United States beginning in the 1930s [19], *surveys* may be the most widely implemented research methodology known, and in my experience, the majority of editing research has been conducted through surveys [20-22]. They are extremely common, but they're also quite difficult to write well. They can be conducted on paper, online, by phone, or in person; online administration has the benefit of being able to have respondents automatically skip questions or answer questions just for a subsection of the population, while paper administration can reach a larger audience and depends less on respondents' technological skills.

Surveys are best used in obtaining information that can be described in quantitative terms from large groups of people [3]. They are a commonly known and commonly accepted methodology, can usually be administered quickly, and can be used to generalize to a much larger group than is surveyed. A survey has ecological validity, "asks questions of real people in real situations" [23, p. 625], and costs less than other methods to achieve the same purposes, but it is not always inexpensive.

Surveys are not generally good at getting at the deep detail of individual situations. One of the ways I help my graduate students think about when to choose surveys versus interviews or case studies is whether they can define the term or not. For terms that can be defined well, surveys can usually be conducted fruitfully. For terms that are more difficult to define, such as *persuasiveness* or *quality*, surveys can be difficult (but not impossible) to write. Another problem unavoidable in surveys is that they report what people *think* they believe or do, which does not necessarily correspond perfectly to what they do, and can be affected by memory and what the respondents think is desirable in society or to the researcher. They can be affected by who chooses to answer versus who chooses not to participate, which can introduce bias [23], and have been subject to low response rates [24-29]. Respondents often don't have much time to answer them, limiting the number of questions that can be asked, and they can also take a lot of time to code accurately for the researcher, especially if poorly designed.

Conducting a survey proceeds as you might expect: select a topic, determine who should answer the questions, draft the questions, test them, administer the survey, and analyze the results. However, a few of these steps—determining who should answer the questions, drafting them, and testing them—are much more difficult than they first appear (for an excellent introduction to writing surveys, see [30]).

A Survey of Editors' Use of Electronic Editing

In 1999, Dayton conducted a survey of the Society for Technical Communication members' use of electronic editing [20]. He invited STC members who identified themselves in the writer-editor category via mail (because not all members had a valid e-mail address), plain-text e-mail, and HTML e-mail, resulting in a 59% response rate and 580 respondents.

Dayton found that respondents who edited others were split in approximate thirds: those who edited electronically very frequently/often, occasionally, and never/rarely. Those who edited electronically usually blended hardcopy editing into their practice at some phase—to check final formatting or complex figures, or to develop an idea of the overall document during an initial reading. No significant difference in editing mode was found by gender, industry, age group, or type of document or editing [20, p. 193]. The variables that were most strongly associated with choice of mode were the mode of documents the editors most often received, the distance from their authors, personal preference, and the amount their job emphasized editing.

For those who rarely or never edit electronically, 74% edited on paper because they preferred it, 59% did so because the genres they were editing influenced them to edit on paper, and approximately 50% mentioned that their authors preferred hardcopy edits. Nearly 75% rated themselves as satisfied with their current method of editing. An interesting result is that only 11% used software that included tracking changes, and another 10% made changes in an electronic file but kept track of them on a hardcopy file. Of participants, 44% had written their own macro or software to automate some editing tasks. Other topics examined included what software and tools respondents used, their industry, whether they have experienced computer-related health problems, and even the size of the monitor they used.

Editing from the Author's Point of View

Eaton and others undertook a survey of 449 authors who had participated in the editing process [21]. Participants were invited in three ways: by members of the Society for Technical Communication's Technical Editing Special Interest Group (STC SIG), who were asked by the researchers to invite the three authors they edit the most frequently; through Society for Technical Communication international chapters' listservs; and through other listservs and newsletters for non-native speakers of English.

The online survey asked authors about their preferences in the editing process. They were asked when they meet with an editor, what mode they prefer to be edited in (electronic, on paper, in person, or a combination), how frequently they are edited, how much of their writing is edited, and if they are edited as a matter of policy or by their request.

Respondents were also asked to define editing, characterize the editorial relationship, describe positive and negative experiences, and identify the style of editorial comment they typically followed. Participants were asked how likely they were to accept editorial comments based on the hierarchical position of the editor and the topic of the comment. The survey also built on an earlier article that recommended certain syntactic styles of writing editorial comment, empirically examining whether the article's recommendations were supported by the authors' behavior.

The responses to the answers were then compared by whether the authors were native or non-native speakers of American English to determine if cultural differences existed for author preferences [22]. Significant differences were found in preference for editing mode, how much copyediting their writing experiences, what comments they usually follow, and how obligating they found certain styles of comments.

EXPERIMENTS AND QUASI-EXPERIMENTS

Experiments and *quasi-experiments* attempt to determine the effect of one or more variables on another variable, such as the effect of a certain teaching method on student learning, or the effect of a new editing mode on the responses of authors [31, 32]. The most common design is to compare two groups on some outcome variable; one group can be a control group, which receives no treatment, or both groups can be experimental and receive some sort of treatment. The outcomes are then examined to see if there are significant differences between the groups using statistics such as the *t*-test, chi-square, ANOVA, or Kruskal-Wallis test.

Because experiments try to determine the effect of specific variables on an outcome, all other variables that might make a difference in the situation are controlled as carefully as possible, including randomly assigning participants into a group, also called a "condition." Quasi-experiments differ from experiments in that they are administered to intact groups in a real setting, most popularly students in classes, so their participants are not randomly assigned [31]. A quasi-experiment trades some of the control of the variables found in a laboratory experiment for a more naturalistic situation in which to test.

In trying to control for extraneous variables having an effect on the outcome, experimental and quasi-experimental researchers look for two kinds of threats which might make the results unusable. Internal validity threats include history, which means an event occurring during the experiment or in the group's past affects their responses; maturation, in which a change in the participants, such as becoming more tired or older, is causing the effect instead of the treatment; testing, in which the first administration of a test changes the outcomes on a second test; instrumentation, in which a change in how something is measured or in the person taking the measurement is responsible for the effect; statistical regression, in which people chosen for an extreme score vary naturally away from that score; selection, in which a bias in how groups were chosen is responsible for the effect seen; and mortality, in which members leaving the study differently for different groups somehow changed the results [31]. Quasi-experimental researchers also make an extra effort to show that their groups were equal before treatment to help make up for the fact that they were not randomly assigned [12].

External validity threats might make the study difficult to generalize to other situations, which is usually the primary goal of the study [33]. These threats include nonrepresentativeness, in which the groups studied do not correspond to the group the researcher hopes to generalize to (like freshmen in psychology classes generalizing to the entire adult population), and artificiality, in which the test was so unusual that the effects observed are likely not to be replicated in other settings [34].

The main benefit of experiments and quasi-experiments is the ability to establish a causal relationship [3]. Additionally, experiments and quasi-experiments provide a high level of certainty about the results, an ability to use statistics on the data to determine whether an effect is significant or not, and an ability to test hypotheses.

Experiments and quasi-experiments can be criticized for not having enough environmental validity [2], the idea that the same treatment might not have the same effect outside of the laboratory. Quasi-experiments evolved from experiments for just this reason—to try to make them more valid outside the laboratory. Naturalness of the study is at the other end of a continuum with control; the more control the researcher has over the environment, the less valid the method may be in the "real world" with other variables affecting the treatment. The less control, however, the more difficult it is to tell if the variable being studied is really having an effect or not. The same continuum can be seen in usability testing arguments between testing, say, a software program in the field—such as a busy office—rather than in a quiet lab.

Experiments and quasi-experiments can be difficult to implement when there are only a small group of people, documents, or situations to test in, because they depend in part on seeing if there are differences across groups. For a group of five and five, for example, the change has to be dramatic to be detected.

The basic process for conducting an experiment is to determine the topic of interest, identify the independent variable, such as being a member of the control group or treatment group, and the dependent variable, such as the score on a test. Then, the researcher must determine the treatment, choose the participants either randomly or in a quasi-experimental fashion, and administer the treatment. At the end, the researcher evaluates the differences between the groups. For a classic overview of various experimental and quasi-experimental designs, plus an excellent and concise description of threats to internal and external validity, see Campbell and Stanley [31].

Experiment on Editing Effectiveness

This study was a series of three experiments to test "standard editing procedures" which the researchers defined as "the use of editing guidelines, such as those provided by Strunk and White, together with the editor's intuition about what will be clear and acceptable to the reader" [35, p. 1].

Four editors revised four one-page documents (a guarantee, a description of Workers' Compensation from an employee manual, the first page of an automotive insurance policy, and a consent for surgery form), to be tested on members of the general public, who were recruited from the researcher's acquaintances and people in Laundromats and paid $3 USD for a half-hour's participation.

In the first experiment, twelve participants received two originals and two revisions, a scenario for each document about why they were reading it, and a list of six questions to be answered using the information in the document. No significant differences were found by age, gender, education, or similar experience. For two of the four revised documents, readers answered significantly more questions correctly.

The second experiment was conducted on the problematic car insurance policy to determine where the readers had trouble using a reading protocol. New participants were given the original or the revised policy and asked to read the document and then answer the six questions, but unlike in the previous experiment, they were asked to verbalize their thought processes as they read and answered questions into a tape recorder. Two batches of protocols were conducted with revisions after each, and the protocols conducted did not identify any new problems.

In the third experiment, they administered the final documents and six test questions to 12 new participants, as in the first study. Participants made significantly fewer errors with the final revision than with the original or with the intervening revision.

Studying Authors' Preferences for Text or Voice Comments

This experiment examined the differences in author adoption of comments and perceptions of the editors when receiving comments in text or in recorded voice comments embedded in a document using software the authors created [36].

Twenty authors in computer science, all working on manuscripts of grant proposals and articles that were close to being ready for review, were paired with 20 editors they suggested. Editors read the document completely and then edited the manuscripts either in text or by voice for an hour; the researchers then altered the comments so that authors received comments half in voice (read by the editor) and half in text in the same document. Authors then revised their text for an hour in response to the comments and filled out surveys on reviewer's personal aspects and editing mode preferences. The editors evaluated the revisions on a 7-point scale for responsiveness.

Comments divided into mechanics, style, organization, substance, purpose/ audience, and other (figures and so on); substance comments were significantly the most frequent, followed by style. Overall, there was no significant difference in the number of problems communicated between voice and text modes. Voice comments had significantly more words than the typed comments—2.5 times as many. Voice reviewers made significantly more comments than text reviewers in all categories but substance. Authors significantly preferred to receive audience/purpose and style comments in voice and significantly preferred receiving mechanics comments in writing. However, the study failed to find a significant difference in author responsiveness between the written and voice comments, and reviewers rated author's responsiveness to their comments on average as only a 4.6 on a 7-point scale.

The comments were then coded by two coders for politeness, assuming mitigated comments are more polite than unmitigated comments. Text comments had significantly more direct unmitigated language (an average of 7 comments per paper in voice and 16 in keyboarding), and voice had significantly more mitigated comments (an average of 21 versus 11 per paper).

When assessing the editors' competence, personal integrity, and likeability, there was no significant difference between modes except those receiving comments in text rated their editors as having significantly less personal integrity than editors using voice, which is particularly surprising because participants chose their own reviewers.

RECOMMENDATIONS

Overall, the state of editing research, in the sense of research being a systemic inquiry into a topic, is patchy and dated. By patchy, I mean that the studies rarely build upon each other, and studies that ideally would be the beginning of a longitudinal study, like Dayton's survey of the adoption of electronic editing, are not repeated later. Dayton himself points out study results like his are "time stamped" and, therefore, not likely to be the same in another few years [20, p. 201]. For example, in 1999, when he collected his data, only 11% of his respondents were using track changes features in their software. Is that statistic still accurate?

We also simply have a shortage of research. The majority of the literature on editing is recommendations from experts, and much of it is older, although we might call it "classic"—just observe the dates of the seminal articles in the bibliography in this book. The 1970s and 1980s are nearly as represented as the 1990s and 2000s.

The few research studies we have published in the last ten years are interesting, and many are well designed, but the field is confronting challenges shared by researchers in all social sciences and those unique to technical editing. The challenges shared by all researchers in the social sciences include a lowered response rate to surveys, difficulty obtaining participants and participant worksites to be a part of studies, and exceptionally busy practitioners who do not have much time to contribute as researchers or as participants.

In addition, technical editing, and technical communication as our greater field, has its own research challenges. First, being a younger field has its challenges. Our field is made up of two generations: those who do and those who do not have degrees in technical communication. Those who don't have degrees in technical communication likely learned the research methods involved in their specialty, which could be computer science, biology, literature, or any of a number of fields, and which may or may not assist in technical editing research. For those who have an undergraduate degree in technical communication, the program may or may not have included any research methods training. Today, the most common research methods class for undergraduates is usability testing; it's unlikely that many programs offer any training in the methods described here. Even for master's degrees, methods classes are often optional.

Academics also face challenges from the age of the field; we have two major generations, also: those who are in their fifties and sixties, tenured, and helping to administer their programs and departments, and those in their thirties and forties, on the tenure track and just a few years after tenure, who are moving into administration. Because editing is offered at nearly every school and is one of the first classes included in any program's offerings, many of the editing courses are taught by the first generation of technical communication faculty. When a program hires new faculty members, they are often looking for the newer, more cutting-edge specialties they likely don't already have—new media, online communication, cross-cultural communication. Established programs usually have editing covered, so they don't have a strong need to hire someone who teaches editing, which makes new graduates less inclined to study editing. More established academics are also very often busy with program administration, which means that those who are most likely to teach editing don't have much time to conduct research.

And if someone has enough time and the training to undertake a research project, conducting research itself as an endeavor is challenging. For everyone, conducting research is time-intensive—really time-intensive. It's likely that making the argument for how time spent conducting research is relevant to their job responsibilities is an issue for practitioners.

All these challenges aside, we need to be a field that reads, supports, and conducts research on a regular basis.

Read Research

Reading research literature has its own challenges. First, research in editing can be difficult to locate due to being published in journals from different fields. For example, the meta-reviews described in this article were published in *JAMA* as summaries and by the Cochrane Library as full reports. Secondly, one database doesn't necessarily include every journal that publishes editing research. And finally, reading research necessitates a basic understanding of it, and not everyone has that background.

Solutions to these issues of reading research are already underway. Geoff Sauer, an assistant professor at Iowa State University, has addressed the lack of a single index for finding technical editing and technical communication articles by creating the EServer Technical Communication Library, which seeks to "to provide tech comm practitioners, students, teachers and managers a comprehensive single location from which to access the complete body of knowledge in our field" [37]. As for the research background, the Society for Technical Communication annual conference has frequently hosted a session called "Introduction to Research" to help attendants better evaluate the presentations they are hearing. There are also many articles in the literature to assist practitioners in becoming more familiar with research methods (for example, [2]).

Can we do more? Quite possibly. Ideally, the next step would be researching if and how practitioners use research and how they hope to. That data could help inform the field about needed improvements, such as additional sessions at conferences, promotion of research articles, or additional short-term training.

Support Research

Supporting research as a field is a necessity. Professional association membership is an excellent start, because the dues from the membership support research funding and include a subscription to the organization's research publications. Practitioners also need to promote research in their workplace. Examining journal articles and conference proceedings ought to become a natural part of problem solving.

Making connections between graduate programs and workplaces is also an important step. Graduate students are looking for research sites, and workplaces can benefit from free research. The connections also don't have to be local, since graduate students are generally mobile after they finish coursework and can conduct research nearly anywhere.

Perform Research

But the most important task we need to accomplish as a field is to conduct more research within technical editing. This task differs for graduate students and new faculty and practitioners.

Graduate Students

There's no doubt that your graduate program is already preparing you for your research career. Do, however, be careful to take as wide a variety of research courses as you can. It's too easy to avoid qualitative or quantitative methods—gain experience with every method. You may be certain at this moment about where your research agenda will take you, but that may change. Many faculty members are studying something completely different than they were in the first five years of their career; make sure you have the methodological tools for whatever topic intrigues you.

Don't forget about conducting research with a faculty member when you're still learning about procedures. And don't limit yourself to faculty members within your program. If someone in the field is doing exciting work, introduce yourself through e-mail or at conferences and ask if you can be of assistance. There aren't too many faculty members who have so much help that they couldn't use a little more. Generally, technical communication is a friendly, helpful community. Feel free to volunteer.

Practitioners

For practitioners to begin their own research projects, some methods are better for beginners than others. The case study and meta-review are particularly good beginning projects that can lead to larger projects later.

To find a topic, it's likely that you will want to research a problem that you are currently experiencing, but don't limit yourself, for any issue that piques interest is fair game. To find timely ideas, note that every article ends with a call for research which provides underdeveloped aspects of the topic, and professional organizations often post research objectives either as part of their Web page or as part of their research funding opportunities. And one of the (few) benefits of having underdeveloped research is that there is no area that couldn't benefit from a bit more. Examining a longstanding issue, such as the value added by editing, or whether editors ought to be brought into the editorial process early [38] is always possible.

If you are nervous about your research background, don't hesitate to work with someone who has had methods training. There are companies who specialize in conducting research, but it may be more satisfying and revealing to conduct it yourself with the assistance of a faculty member. In the least, it would be worth e-mailing someone who has conducted a similar study or someone who teaches methods courses in a PhD program, and ask if he or she could assist you in reviewing your design. Oftentimes, if a methods class is going on, the instructor would be delighted to use the design as an opportunity for class discussion. Additionally, students are often looking for paper, thesis, and dissertation topics, and faculty are looking for studies; someone might be willing to do the project for you.

Professional advice is invaluable. In reviewing articles for this chapter, I came across a readability analysis of original research articles published in the *Annals of Internal Medicine*, a competitive, peer-reviewed clinical medical journal. The authors chose to use the Gunning Fog Index and the Flesch Reading

Ease Index to evaluate the readability of the articles, which they call "well-validated" [39, p. 121] but have been severely criticized in technical communication research for being inaccurate. The study was deeply flawed, and even the authors acknowledged it. Specifically, they mentioned "although both indexes have been validated in other media, no readability formula has been validated in medical writing. Both the Gunning and Flesch scores are based on sentence and word length. One might then conclude that these indexes are not valid for medical writing, since medicine's jargon includes words from Latin and Greek (eg 'erythema') instead of Anglo-Saxon (eg 'red skin'), as well as neologisms (eg 'esophogastroduodenoscopy'). . . . Furthermore, the effect of acronyms on the readability of medical writing may be minimized by these indexes, which treat them as one-syllable words" [39, p. 121]. Professional assistance from within technical communication would have avoided this gaffe.

CONCLUSION

The last step in increasing the knowledge base of the field is to share what you have found—present it at a professional organization's chapter meeting; present it at a local, regional, or national conference; publish it in *Intercom, Technical Communication*, or any of our other journals. If nothing else, publish it on a Web page and list it in the tc.eserver.org database. To ensure that our field grows based on thoughtful research instead of isolated personal experience, we need to put a priority on research.

REFERENCES

1. D. Dayton, The Future of Technical Communication According to Those Who Teach It, *Proceedings of STC's 51st Annual Conference,* Society for Technical Communication, Arlington, Virginia, pp. 134-139, 2004.
2. P. Goubil-Gambrell, A Practitioner's Guide to Research Methods, *Technical Communication, 39*, pp. 582-591, 1992.
3. M. MacNealy, *Strategies for Empirical Research in Writing*, Longman, New York, 1999.
4. J. Maxwell, *Qualitative Research Design: An Interactive Approach* (2nd ed.), Applied Social Research Methods Series, Vol. 41, Sage Publications, Thousand Oaks, California, 2005.
5. M. MacNealy, Research in Technical Communication: A View of the Past and a Challenge for the Future, *Technical Communication, 39*, pp. 533-551, 1992.
6. R. Yin, *Case Study Research: Design and Methods* (3rd ed.), Applied Social Research Methods Series, Vol. 5, Sage Publications, Thousand Oaks, California, 2003.
7. J. W. Creswell, *Qualitative Inquiry & Research Design: Choosing Among Five Approaches* (2nd ed.), Sage Publications, Thousand Oaks, California, 2007.

8. J. Prono, M. DeLanoy, R. Deupree, J. Skiby, and B. Thompson, Developing New Levels of Edit, *Proceedings of the 45th Annual STC Conference,* Society for Technical Communication, Arlington, Virginia, pp. 436-440, 1998.
9. J. Bisaillon, Professional Editing Strategies Used by Six Editors, *Written Communication, 24,* pp. 295-322, 2007.
10. E. Wager and P. Middleton, Effects of Technical Editing in Biomedical Journals: A Systematic Review, *JAMA, 287,* pp. 2821-2824, 2002.
11. E. Wager and P. Middleton, Technical Editing of Research Reports in Biomedical Journals, *Cochrane Database of Systematic Reviews,* 2007, Issue 2. Art. No.: MR000002. DOI: 10.1002/14651858.MR000002.pub2.
12. J. M. Lauer and J. W. Asher, *Composition Research: Empirical Designs,* Oxford University Press, Oxford, 1988.
13. T. Jefferson, M. Rudin, S. B. Folsey, and F. Davidoff, Editorial Peer Review for Improving the Quality of Reports of Biomedical Studies, *Cochrane Database of Systematic Reviews,* 2007, Issue 2. Art. No.: MR000016. DOI:10.1002/14651858.MR000016.pub3.
14. T. Jefferson, P. Alderson, E. Wagner, and F. Davidoff, Effects of Editorial Peer Review: A Systematic Review, *JAMA, 287,* pp. 2784-2786, 2002.
15. L. R. Frey, C. H. Botan, and G. L. Kreps, *Investigating Communication: An Introduction to Research Methods* (2nd ed.), Allyn and Bacon, Boston, 2000.
16. C. Geisler, *Analyzing Streams of Language: Twelve Steps to the Systematic Coding of Text, Talk, and Other Verbal Data,* Pearson Longman, New York, 2003.
17. L. R. Frey, C. H. Botan, P. G. Friedman, and G. L. Kreps, *Interpreting Communication Research: A Case Study Approach,* Prentice Hall, Upper Saddle River, New Jersey, 1992.
18. J. Gilbert, E. Williams, and G. Lu, Is There Gender Bias in *JAMA*'s Peer Review Process? *JAMA, 272,* pp. 139-142, 1994.
19. F. J. Fowler, Jr., *Survey Research Methods* (4th ed.), Applied Social Research Methods Series, Vol. 1, Sage Publications, Thousand Oaks, California, 2009.
20. D. Dayton, Electronic Editing in Technical Communication: A Survey of Practices and Attitudes, *Technical Communication, 50,* pp. 192-205, 2003.
21. A. Eaton, P. E. Brewer, T. C. Portewig, and C. R. Davidson, Examining Editing in the Workplace from the Author's Point of View: Results of an Online Survey, *Technical Communication, 55,* pp. 111-139, 2008.
22. A. Eaton, P. E. Brewer, T. C. Portewig, and C. R. Davidson, Comparing Cultural Perceptions of Editing from the Author's Point of View, *Technical Communication, 55,* pp. 140-166, 2008.
23. C. Plumb and J. H. Spyridakis, Survey Research in Technical Communication: Designing and Administering Questionnaires, *Technical Communication, 39,* pp. 625-638, 1992.
24. N. M. Bradburn, Presidential Address: A Response to the Nonresponse Problem, *Public Opinion Quarterly, 56,* pp. 391-397, 1992.
25. E. de Leeuw and W. de Heer, Trends in Household Survey Nonresponse: A Longitudinal and International Comparison, in *Survey Nonresponse,* R. M. Groves, D. A. Dillman, J. L. Eltinge, and R. J. A. Little (eds.), John Wiley & Sons, New York, pp. 41-54, 2002.

26. E. L. Dey, Working with Low Survey Response Rates: The Efficacy of Weighting Adjustments, *Research in Higher Education, 38*, 215-227, 1997.

27. J. R. Fraenkel and N. E. Wallen, *How to Design and Evaluate Research in Education* (7th ed.), McGraw-Hill, New York, 2009.

28. T. W. Smith, Trends in Non-Response Rates, *International Journal of Public Opinion Research, 7*, pp. 157-171, 1995.

29. C. G. Steeh, Trends in Nonresponse Rates, 1952-1979, *Public Opinion Quarterly, 45*, pp. 40-57, 1981.

30. D. A. Dillman, *Mail and Internet Surveys: The Tailored Design Method* (2nd ed.), John Wiley & Sons, Inc., New York, 2000.

31. D. T. Campbell and J. C. Stanley, *Experimental and Quasi-Experimental Designs for Research*, Houghton Mifflin Company, Boston, 1963.

32. T. D. Cook and D. T. Campbell, *Quasi-Experimentation: Design & Analysis Issues for Field Settings*, Houghton Mifflin Company, Boston, 1979.

33. J. H. Watt and S. A. van den Berg, *Research Methods for Communication Science*, Allyn and Bacon, Boston, 1995.

34. D. Charney, Experimental and Quasi-Experimental Research, in *Research in Technical Communication*, L. J. Gurak and M. M. Lay (eds.), Ablex Publishing Corp., Stamford, Connecticut, pp. 111-130, 2002.

35. J. H. Swaney, C. J. Janik, S. J. Bond, and J. R. Hayes, *Editing for Comprehension: Improving the Process through Reading Protocols*, Technical Report No. 14, The Document Design Project, American Institutes for Research, Washington, DC, 1981.

36. C. M. Neuwirth and others, Distributed Collaborative Writing: A Comparison of Spoken and Written Modalities for Reviewing and Revising Documents, *Proceedings of SIGCHI Conference on Human Factors in Computing Systems: Celebrating Independence*, ACM Press, New York, pp. 51-57, 1994.

37. Available online at: http://tc.eserver.org

38. D. Haugen, Editors, Rules, and Revision Research, *Technical Communication, 38*, pp. 57-64, 1991.

39. J. C. Roberts, R. H. Fletcher, and S. W. Fletcher, Effects of Peer Review and Editing on the Readability of Articles Published in Annals of Internal Medicine, *JAMA, 272*, pp. 119-121, 1994.

CHAPTER 3

History and Trends in Technical Editing

Thomas L. Warren

Identifying trends in technical editing is like identifying trends in any activity. There is a great deal of speculation and opinion involved in saying this or that is true both historically and currently. The approach in this essay is a mix of pointing to the literature and guesswork.

People have been changing text for a long time by adding to it, deleting from it, or modifying it. In the early days, it was the author who revised the text before sending it to the printer or copyist, but once it reached the printer or copyist, someone hired by the printer (a *learned collaborator*) or someone else edited it. Malone [1] describes a complex and complicated system of getting text correctly printed in the printing houses of 16th-century Europe. Printers faced three major problems with scholarly texts in scholarly languages such as Latin. First, in-house employees could usually handle the proofreading of texts in their native languages, but when the language was not native to the proofreader, the printer had to subcontract proofreading to scholars fluent in the text's language in order to get truly accurate text. The emphasis for printers of texts that could be sold to the public, as Malone points out, was a correct text when compared to the manuscript. A printer's reputation and sales depended on the accuracy of their printed texts.

The second major problem was content. The printer realized that the author knew what the text meant, but the compositors and proofreaders did not. Therefore, another set of eyes should evaluate the author's content to ensure a measure of accuracy—defined loosely as a faithful reproduction of the author's work. Still, changes and modifications were limited to proofreading and not

29

http://dx.doi.org/10.2190/NPOC3

content editing. However, when a proofreader encountered a questionable passage, it was helpful if that person knew something about the content. Having learned collaborators do this work introduced even more problems for the printer: What happens when the learned collaborator changes the author's content? After all, the authors of the early books rarely saw their work until it was published.

Third, because accuracy of texts also relies on common agreement as to spelling, grammar, and style, the proofreader needed a resource that identified those common agreements. Prior to widely accepted dictionaries and grammars, texts showed a variety of grammatical structures as well as inconsistent spellings, reflecting, no doubt, the author's own inconsistencies. After Johnson [2] and Lowth [3] produced popularly accepted references, texts could be made more consistent, and such consistency added to the text's appearance of accuracy. But was the work done by proofreaders and learned collaborators before and after widespread acceptance of the standard references really editing? The actual term *edit* does not appear until 1793 (although the *Oxford English Dictionary* [*OED*] identifies 1791 as the date), well after Johnson and Lowth. Before 1783, we had tasks done by the proofreader at three levels: matching text that had been typeset to the original manuscript; ensuring that grammar, spelling, and usage conformed to the accepted standards; and, occasionally, correcting perceived errors in content. As Malone suggests, printers were doing such proofreading on through the 17th and 18th centuries[1] where we would see the work as a combination.

Unfortunately, not many examples of authors' revised texts from earlier centuries have come down to allow us to speculate on the principles used to make textual changes other than proofreading corrections. There is also a paucity of manuscripts marked by printers and proofreaders. We can compare manuscripts (when we have them) with printed editions, but those content additions, deletions, and modifications were usually done by the printer. What we do know is that printers in the late 19th and early 20th centuries began producing lists of things to check when making a manuscript consistent before printing. According to Howell [4], these led in turn to more expanded versions that evolved into what we know today as style manuals. Even a standard style manual such as *The Chicago Manual of Style* [5, p. xiii] began as a one-page printer's guide to typographic consistency.

Almost from the beginning of what we call journalism, a very important person was the one who not only reviewed the text but also assigned space for it in the publication. These journalism *editors* made sure that the text was as correct as possible before being sent for printing. For these situations, they used some fundamental reference works—dictionaries, grammars, style manuals, and so forth. They also modified text to fit the space available by eliminating content,

---

[1] A researcher needs to determine why printers changed from only proofreading to editing content.

usually starting at the end of the text. While it would be interesting to speculate how much editors changed content, no manuscripts survive that would settle this issue. But faced with temptations similar to those of Malone's learned collaborators, it is quite possible that journalism editors allowed their personal views and those of the publisher to influence content changes.

To begin to understand what a technical editor is and does through time, let's look first at the term's history.

DEFINITIONS

The American Heritage Dictionary relates *edit* to written materials, newspapers and magazines, and film production. For our needs, this is what the dictionary says about the word's history:

> Word History: The word *edit* is often cited as an example of back-formation. In other words, *edit* is not the source of *editor*, as *dive* is of *diver*, the expected derivational pattern; rather, the reverse is the case. *Edit* in the sense "to prepare for publication," first recorded in 1793, comes from *editor*, first recorded in 1712 in the sense "one who edits." There is more to the story, however. *Edit* also comes partly from the French word *éditer*, "to publish, edit," first recorded in 1784. In the case of *edit*, two processes, borrowing and back-formation, occurred either independently or together, perhaps one person originally taking *edit* from French, another from *editor*, and yet a third from both [6].

Edition, we find elsewhere, derives from *edit*:

> 1551, "act of publishing," from L. *editionem* (nom. *editio*) "a bringing forth, producing," from stem of *edere* "bring forth, produce," from *ex-* "out" + *-dere*, comb. form of *dare* "to give" (see *date* (1). Meaning "form of a literary work" is from 1570. "It is awkward to speak of, *e.g.* 'The second edition of Campbell's edition of Plato's *"Theœtetus"*'; but existing usage affords no satisfactory substitute for this inconvenient mode of expression" [OED]. *Edit* is 1791, probably as a back-formation of *editor* (1649), which, from its original meaning "publisher" had evolved by 1712 a sense of "person who prepares written matter for publication;" specific sense in newspapers is from 1803. *Editorial* "newspaper article by an editor" is Amer.Eng. 1830. Hence, *editorialize* (1856), "introduce opinions into factual accounts" [7].

When we turn to the *OED*, we find for *editor*:

> One who edits.

> **1.** The publisher of a book (cf. Fr. *éditeur*).

> **1649** BP. HALL *Cases Consc.* I. v. (1650) 33 Otherwise some Interloper may perhaps underhand fall upon the work at a lower rate, and undoe the first editor.

2. One who prepares the literary work of another person, or number of persons for publication, by selecting, revising, and arranging the material; also, one who prepares an edition of any literary work.

1712 ADDISON *Spect.* No. 470 1 When a different Reading gives us..a new Elegance in an Author, the Editor does very well in taking Notice of it. **1725** POPE *Notes on Shaks.* (J.), This nonsense got into all the editions by a mistake of the stage editors [8].

Nevertheless, the activity described is to prepare the material for publication. That suggests more than proofreading galley against the original manuscript. The editor would mark the text for additions, deletions, and modifications to make it consistent as well as mark it for the printer to typeset and print. One major difference between editing then and now is that only rarely did the marked text return to the author for review. Rather, the marked text went to the compositor for correction, and then for printing. Such a practice today would invite severe criticism.

It is tempting to see Malone's learned collaborators as contributing to the content, and it must have been difficult for them to resist the temptation to add or modify content especially because the author typically did not see the changes until the work was published.

Another interesting example of an even earlier editing was the work done by the monk Volmar on the books by Saint Hildegard (d. 1179):

The form her revelations took was characteristic of Hildegard—not the sloppy, spontaneous babblings of the typical illiterate seer but a lengthy, convoluted text, *Scivias*, composed by Hildegard with excruciating exactitude over ten years and copyedited with bulldog tenacity by Volmar, whose Latin was better than hers [9, p. 79].

It is not unreasonable to assume that there were other medieval instances where one person proofread and edited another's work, especially if the subject was controversial.

Questions arise: What motivated an editor to mark changes in the author's work before handing it over to a compositor? Likewise, what sort of training would this person have had to allow him to know what to change? And why (if they did) did the authors permit content changes that they learned of after the text was printed? These are some of the research questions waiting to be answered. What we do know is that sometime during the late 18th and early 19th centuries, editors as we would understand them plied their trade. Perhaps it was an easy transition from producing an edition of an older work such as Shakespeare to manipulating the text of a contemporary author.

When product information began to appear, we find as we did before, those who prepared the text (writers, authors) and those who reviewed it and added, deleted, or modified content (editors). In the early days of product information, the editing model normally followed was that of a newspaper. At a newspaper, the motivation for including a journalistic news story rested primarily with the gatekeeper (or editor). This person judged the newsworthiness of what the writer produced. Since the appearance of product information, however, the people charged with reviewing the text of an author have added concern for the user of that information to a concern for language, spelling, and style.

What follows is an overview of three indistinct periods of editing history based on what editors and others have had to say about editors' work. The periods are indistinct because there are no clear-cut lines or specific events that mark the transition from one to the next. However, they are roughly divided into the Beginning Period, to 1975; the Middle Period, 1975 to 1990; and the Modern Period, 1990 to the present.

THE BEGINNINGS

Along with the emergence of technical writers during the early years of World War II, we find other people who functioned in the role of technical editor. In the late 1950s and early 1960s, understanding who was an editor focused on two central areas: the requirements necessary to be a technical editor and the activities associated with being a technical editor. Several papers from that period argue that the technical editor must have extensive language skills, while others argue that technical training is most important. Bezanson's 1959 article [10] is typical of the articles from this period that stress language skills. His how-to article emphasizes the language aspects of editing. The editor should be concerned with syntax, paragraph structure, punctuation, and other mechanical issues, organization, and conformance to the structure of the traditional technical document. He makes no mention of keeping the reader of the document in mind while making these changes. Likewise, all additions, deletions, or modifications are supported by the editor's experience rather than any set of communication theories or standards.

One year later, Lytel [11] offers a much more extensive discussion of what the editor should be doing. Lytel separates the surface features of a communication from the meaning the communication carries. As for the kinds of texts, the editor is reviewing such materials as brochures, marketing presentations, proposals, reports, and other similar publications. He does emphasize that the editor must have a *feel*, as he calls it, for the reader. His editor is trained at the bachelor level in neither the engineering sciences nor the liberal arts exclusively. Rather, he would like to see editors studying general science as well as journalism. Should they go to graduate school, they should continue this emphasis on general science and journalism, and they should gain experience in a technical field of their choice.

To extend Lytel's argument, the editor needs to understand the meaning of the text, and that involves knowing the subject matter. He further broadens the activities that editors are expected to perform from word mechanic to administrator. Editors, in his view, supervise other specialists including writers, artists, and printers, so the editor must be knowledgeable in all phases of production. Thus, Lytel's editor knows general science as well as applied journalistic principles that follow specific standards.

These two articles show the range found in the early literature that explains who an editor is, what an editor does, and how an editor prepares. The next year, 1961, sees the publication of an early book devoted to technical communication in business and industry: Emerson Clarke's *A Guide to Technical Literature Production* [12], in which he devotes a chapter to "The Editorial Function." Clarke is one of the early commentators who stress the professionalism of being a technical editor. While the editor's role is a supporting one (much as the symphony conductor's role is secondary to the music and, in some cases, to the musicians), one of the editor's goals is to enhance the technical documentation department's reputation. For Clarke, the technical editor is a person who has a very broad knowledge base. For example, the technical editor must know military specifications, especially those relating to publication requirements; know how to use art work effectively; recognize and encourage good writing; understand budgets; and be a teacher. On top of these traits, the editor needs to have a firm understanding of the workings of the language.

Clarke's metaphor is the editor as musical conductor, controlling all phases of document production in the same way that a conductor of the orchestra controls the musicians while offering an interpretation of the music. Harold Osborne [13] also makes that comparison. And there is the famous musical metaphor used in W. Earl Britton's essay [14] explaining technical writing by comparing technical documents to bugle calls and non-technical documents to classical music: a bugle call has a single meaning that you had better understand perfectly while classical music has multiple interpretations usually determined by the conductor.

We can summarize the technical editor in the Beginning Period as someone who works much as a newspaper editor works: needing language skills as well as having some understanding of content. That editor can expect to control production, enhancing the reputation of both the department and the authors while remaining in the background.

Nelson Briggs addresses these requirements and the subsequent focus of the editor's work in a pair of 1967 essays [15, 16], in which he contrasts the editor-writer as specialist with the editor-writer as generalist. His view of the technical editor-writer who is a specialist is that this person will have a difficult time staying busy, especially in smaller companies. Briggs sees the evolution of the general technical editor-writer as occurring naturally from the 1930s to the time of his article. This editor-writer is a non-specialist who is capable of writing well, editing well, and handling well a wide variety of document types. Briggs sees the 1940s as a transition period from this generalist to the specialist that finally emerged in the 1950s. He further sees the 1960s as a time when there is pressure for the editor-writer to return to non-specialized work. His metaphor for the editors-writers is the tribe, which he sees as collections of generalists, each of which functions separately, often with overlapping of activities. Tribes are not teams, he argues, because the team is a tightly knit group of coordinated specialists. Because Briggs understands documentation as cyclical, he sees difficulties in documentation teams made up of specialists. Tribes do not have specialists who only write, or edit, or do layout, and so forth. Rather, each member of the tribe is capable of handling each function as required by the project. He suggests that the emphasis in documentation changed beginning as early as the 1960s, when the type of documentation also changed.

The non-specialist approach to editing and writing is a much more efficient use of company resources if there are multiple types of publications such as brochures, reports, and monographs. If the editor-writer provides service to other departments within the company, the non-specialist route again is preferable. Briggs summarizes the choices between a department made up of specialists and a department made up of generalists by asking, "Do you need a vertical capability or a horizontal capability or both?" [15, p. 16] The manuals approach (that is, the specialists approach, as described by Walton [17]) reflects vertical capability; the multiple-genre or horizontal approach requires generalists.

The Beginning Period is also characterized by the emergence of several important authors who started writing about technical editing. Lola Zook in 1975 edited an STC anthology [18] that included important papers by Mary Fran Buehler [19], Eva Dukes [20], and Alberta Cox [21]. The profile of the technical editor that emerges from this anthology, and especially from these papers, is an editor who has both technical knowledge and linguistic knowledge that are applied to the materials. This recognition of the dual needs is one characteristic that suggests that technical editing has moved to a new period.

In looking at the publications of the Beginning Period, we see that many of the descriptions of what an editor or writer does are based on personal and anecdotal experience and very few on empirical research. Vernon Root [22], however, reports on one of the early (1968) studies that relied on questionnaires to identify job titles, knowledge requirements, duties, and so forth. He sent out almost 1,500 questionnaires to companies representing 17 disciplines and had a 26% return rate. Of the 394 replies, he received 206 completed questionnaires (56%), of which 188 replies (91%) indicated that the company had no technical publications groups as such.

What he discovered from the remaining questionnaires was that the people identified as writers or editors fit into 25 job patterns. He found that editing involved policy editing, textual editing, writing and editing, and illustration editing. Within publication groups, he found managers, editing managers, publication engineers, writers-editors, and copyeditors. What is interesting in his results is that different people had editing functions that were primary and secondary. For example, managers did policy edits as their only editorial function; editing managers did policy edits as a primary function and text editing as a secondary function. Text editing and illustration editing for the editing managers became primary at the second or third editing pass of the material. This division of labor into primary and secondary activities as well as multiple passes of the material anticipates *The Levels of Edit* [23] concept developed in the 1970s and also underscores a recognition that technical editing played an important role in the company's products or services.[2]

Representing the opposite view to Briggs' tribe is Thomas Walton [17], who describes the technical editor-writer as a specialist in his 1968 book on writing technical manuals. This approach, in Briggs' terms, represents the specialization of the job, something he rejects. However, in Walton's view the technical manuals publication group, or team, would include writers, catalogers, editors, illustrators, artists, typists, and production staff because of the requirements for producing complex technical manuals. Each specialist would work on a particular aspect of the manual. Rarely would such a specialist work in a different area: Parts list people, for example, did parts lists for their 20 or 30 years with the company, but again, as with so much of the early literature, Walton is presenting his own views and experiences as examples of what large technical manual departments should be rather than using the results of questionnaires or surveys. Nonetheless, his views are important when we try to understand how large technical document departments functioned at that time.

Technical communication publications in the various journals and magazines from the beginning tend to be a recitation of personal experiences and "what works for me" explanations. These are quite valuable to the technical communication community, because they replace different kinds of training— academic or on-the-job. Such publications and the related conference presentations were invaluable to two major groups within the community: those who were new to the community and those who, although experienced, had problems they could not solve. While there is nothing inherently wrong with the anecdotal approach, the theory of the community that would form the basis of the discipline's body of knowledge could not develop in such a way that you could draw generalizations from it [25].

---

[2] A later study (1983) by Zook [24] asked questions of 63 editors, editor/managers, and managers relating to technical editing. While her questions and results did not parallel Root's, they do give some insight into where technical editing has been, where it is now, and where it is going.

With the exception of Root's article, the basis for the articles and books appearing during this early period is rationalism: "I the author have years of experience editing and will share my tips and tricks with new editors." The articles almost become textbooks for on-the-job training. The problem for the new editor is to decide if what the article says is only the author's example and is not necessarily applicable to his or her situation, or offers precepts to be followed. Most of these reports are to be found in the proceedings of the various STC conferences. Even in the STC magazines at the time, a large percentage of the articles are based on personal experience rather than on research taken from other sources. The main exception is the Root study of job titles and duties.

Another problem facing the new technical editor wanting to learn the field is just what body of knowledge exists for technical editing, and what should the trainees' reaction to it be? When a body of knowledge relies on the experience of others shared through various platforms, that body of knowledge is slow to grow, because the presenter's experiences are not quite the same as the readers' or listeners'. These experiences cannot be used for generalizations that carry the potential of being applied to a wide variety of circumstances. Yet this is how most disciplines develop their bodies of knowledge. In the next period, we will begin to see more empirical research that readers or listeners can modify for their own activities. (For example, developments in understanding how communication theory will apply to both writing and editing situations spur renewed interest—and a theoretical basis for writing and editing decisions—in focusing on the user.)

Another major change begun in the Beginning Period and carrying though the later ones is the definition of quality. The standards used to define quality in the beginning days of writers and editors were the material's accuracy, organization, and literacy—meaning grammatical, lexicographical, and stylist accuracy when compared to recognized standards such as traditional grammars, accepted dictionaries, and adopted style manuals. Later, as we shall see, the focus shifts from this definition to one that focuses on the user of the document. The editor must consider the user first and foremost—but that all comes later.

Editors in the beginning had to be generalists in their own right (despite what Walton would have), especially if the writers were specialists in one type of document such as training manuals. They had to know military and other specifications to be able to ensure that the document was accurate and conformed to the prevailing requirements. They also had to know what the document type was, what parts were required, and what the finished product looked like. Academically, they probably had some sort of editing course (usually a journalism one) or a course in English composition as well as a technical specialty. They were still expected to know the subject of the content even though they rarely questioned it.

THE MIDDLE PERIOD

The key trend of the Middle Period was to impose a structure on the process. In addition, it was a time when technical communicators were becoming more and more conscious of communication theory. We also find at this time a shift in focus to include much more concern for the reader. Before, editors received a manuscript and applied all the editing tools and knowledge they had—usually restricted only by the time available for editing. With the introduction of editing strategies such as *The Levels of Edit* [23], a process was in place to structure their work. Originally devised as an accounting process to enable editing groups to charge for their work, the structures quickly became the center of editing education as well as company and independent editing groups. Academics welcomed such structures because it made teaching editing a more realistic process. Editing could now be closer to the other professions (such as law, medicine, dentistry, and accounting) because the client has choices as to the services desired. For company editing groups as well as independent editors, time and budget were still factors, but now the client could specify just what was needed to be done and the editor could give a close estimate of time and costs. The Middle Period saw the continued rise of the major influencers of editing practice: Eva Dukes, Lola Zook, Frank Smith, Don Bush, and, of course, Mary Fran Buehler.

The Middle Period also saw an increase in publications relating to technical editing—especially, textbooks. The appearance of anthologies of articles from *Technical Communication* and STC's annual conference, such as the Zook anthology [18], evidently did well, because in 1994 STC published another collection of articles on editing from *Technical Communication* and non-STC journals edited by Charles Kemnitz [26]. Other anthologies from this period include Jim Shaw's [27] for teachers of in-house courses in writing and editing and Caroline Rude's [28] for academics teaching technical editing. Another resource for teachers was David Farkas' monograph [29]. They all focused attention on how one does technical editing—best practices and approaches. But one difference to be noted is that almost all the "reports" relied on supporting materials rather than just personal experience. That is, the author also tied the material to what others have said about a similar topic. The result is that we see in the Middle Period a movement toward research-based understanding of how communication works.

Again in the Middle Period, rationalism more than other research forms dominates the literature. But the papers begin to show an increase in citation of empirical research to justify authors' suggestions. For example, Mary Fran Buehler [19] and Nelson A. Briggs [30] published essays in which they look ahead to research that goes beyond the personal experience. Buehler, for example, identifies patterns in editing based on language and rhetoric. Her references provide additional information for readers to use when examining their own editing processes. Later, we will find her approach is quite common when researchers are examining how editing works. For example, Dragga and Gong's book [31] concentrates on the rhetorical aspects of editing.

As technical editors became more aware of communication as a process, based no doubt on the Shannon and Weaver [32] communication model that emphasizes the role of the receiver of the message, they turned their attention to understanding just who that reader is for the document that they are editing. What information does that reader need and how accessible is it in the document? Even early textbooks on report writing emphasize the role the reader plays for the writer when preparing a document. As we will see emerging from this period, the editor takes on a new role, advocate for the reader, and edits accordingly.

Even Briggs' 1969 essay [30] invokes Martin Buber's "I-Thou" and "I-It" [33] in describing what should be the relationship between the editor and the author. Previously, the editor's interaction with writers relied on the editor's sense of courtesy and humaneness to guide that relationship. With more and more theories of communication being applied to editing, researchers are exploring and explaining other relationships. For example, accommodation theory as well as theories that help you manage relationships such as constructivism theories are frequently found in the literature. See, for example, the papers by Giles, Coupland, and Coupland [34], and by Nicotera [35].

Also, more interest in cognitive and behavioral psychology added to a focus on the user of the document to provide the editor with a solid starting point: Does the construction help or hinder the user's access to information? Editors can use reader expectations as cognitive schema into which will fit the new information.

During this period, we see editors beginning to specialize—yet again. The specialties include copyeditors, production editors, tagging editors, and so forth. The change can be attributed to advances in technology as well as a cyclical return to the tribe and the non-tribe situation that Briggs [15, 16] described.

THE MODERN PERIOD

The Modern Period finds the published papers moving away even more from the personal experiences of the editor to using support from research (that is, using a reference style citing other studies). Also, it makes possible explaining to clients why certain editing changes are done—other than the position of "I know best." For example, editors can rely on research about how the mind works to argue for additions, deletions, or modifications of the text. Discoveries about literacy levels and how the levels relate to the written text as presented can increase the understanding of both the authors and the editors in their search for ways to present the information in an accessible form for the user. Authors begin to use resources in other areas such as cognitive psychology, communication theory, and empirical research into reading habits. Also, better understanding of workplace culture and the implications for having an editing group available for engineers and others is receiving attention in the literature.

As we enter the 21st century, more and more empirical studies appear that help to explain how editors work. Hayes and Chenoweth [36], for example, examine the role of working memory in editing tasks. Their study examines what the authors call *language bursts* by which writers and editors prepare text. They find that restricting working memory has an impact on writing performance. The point is that studies such as this one give insight into how the cognitive part of the editing process works. This is not to say that there were no attempts previously to understand how editors work. But studies such as this one provide evidence to support assertions concerning editing strategies.

We can gain further insight into how editors solve problems when editing texts by consulting, for example, a study by Jocelyne Bisaillon [37], who identifies strategies used by six technical editors while editing. She identifies the steps in editing as (1) reading for comprehension and evaluation, (2) detecting problems, (3) solving problems, and (4) rereading to make final valuations. When editors detect problems, she writes, they will have anticipated potential problems and compared an item in the text with the knowledge base stored in their memory. When problem-solving, editors read, reflect, and search for solutions. The value of this study when compared to any similar paper focusing on anecdotal reports is that the reader can extrapolate conclusions with more confidence because the paper represents six views as opposed to one.

A significant advance for the professionalism of technical editing is the appearance in the Modern Period of courses that teach editing. Such courses are offered by colleges and universities as well as companies that offer editing seminars. My focus here is on how colleges and universities respond to the need for such courses.

Parallel trends evolve in technical editing as a profession and in teaching technical editing in academic settings, because instructors in technical communication programs follow the lead of what is happening in the profession itself. So, having looked at the profession, I now turn to the academic preparation of technical editors and focus on training in the classroom as well as textbooks available for the instructor to use.

The trends in undergraduate education move from looking at the technical communicator as a combination writer and editor, requiring that they have both skills, to looking at the two activities as separate. In their graduate programs, students study communication skills, and they also study more theory than do their undergraduate colleagues.

For example, the undergraduate editing course introduced at Oklahoma State University in the late 1970s was required for the B.A. in technical writing and emphasized production editing training with minimal copyediting training. Students learned skills needed to produce a mechanical—in this case, mechanicals for a flyer, brochure, and newsletter. They were to identify and work with a client (who would pay for supplies and high DPI printing for the paste-up). Generally, they took the client's materials and edited them for each assignment, but the emphasis in the course was on the mechanical.

After a separate graduate course was introduced in 1983, the undergraduate course changed to strictly copyediting and the graduate course became the production editing course. The reasoning was that by 1983 most entry-level technical communicators with bachelor degrees could now rely on newly-emerging graphic arts departments to produce the mechanicals while those with graduate degrees would be supervising departments that included graphic artists and would have to understand production more thoroughly.

In the 1990s, when desktop publishing became widespread in both industry and academia, graduate students no longer needed the specialized knowledge required to produce mechanicals. Other areas of need replaced production editing—in the case of OSU, that was document production project management. For undergraduates, technology meant choices between editing hard copy and electronic copy—both found when the students did their internships and were hired.

We also added a separate graduate course called Styles and Editing to focus on technical communication style and copyediting. Students in that course spend most of their time learning to be copyeditors, addressing many of the problems that copyeditors face such as working with clients and resolving complex language issues. Combining both style and copyediting in a single class parallels the trend in editing to involve more theory in copyediting—both to explain additions, deletions, or modifications to authors, and to further the editor's understanding of how communication works. So graduate students get project management and copyediting theory training, both of which are valued by internship sponsors and future employers.

The editing textbooks available in the late 1970s and early 1980s were few and far between. Teachers were forced to look to journalism and graphic arts for books about how to copyedit. For example, an early (1973) book that some used was Harry McNaughton's *Proofreading and Copyediting: A Practical Guide to Style for the 1970's* [38]. But its focus was more on journalistic proofreading than on copyediting. Then there was *Words into Type* [39], the third edition of which appeared in 1974. This all-purpose book provided students with a reference work similar to a style manual, but it has not been revised for a fourth edition and has limited uses now.

An early book that was meant for engineers to learn how to edit their own documents was Bennett's 1970 *Editing for Engineers* [40]. It was, in reality, more of a guide to revising, but did have the unusual (for its time) feature of also focusing on engineering managers who reviewed and edited reports from their team members. It was also one of the earliest to introduce the metaphor of "Coach" and "Judge" to help managers understand their roles better.

Between Bennett's book and Caroline Rude's *Technical Editing*, the first edition [41] appearing in 1991, there were no books for teachers who taught technical editing other than what was to be found in journalism book lists. But in the 1990s, an explosion took place in books for teaching technical editing. For example, Eisenberg's book [42] was followed by Samson's [43]. It in turn was followed by books by Tarutz [44], Mancuso [45], and Coggin and Porter [46]. The books treated technical editing as both a skill and an art. They explained both technical editing and the theories behind it and provided insight into what it meant to be a working technical editor.

Another group of books that teachers could use to assign outside readings focused on the editing outside of technical and journalistic editing. For example, Berg's 1978 book [47] on Max Perkins offers good examples of how to deal with difficult authors.

There were the anthologies published by the Society for Technical Communication [18, 26, 48] and the Association of Teachers of Technical Writing [28], but they were collections of articles from the early society journals, magazines, and conference proceedings rather than texts suitable for classroom instruction because they were mainly personal experiences. Their usefulness in the classroom, however, came in teaching students about what happens on the job with editors. So, they proved to be quite useful supplemental reading.

Things improved somewhat in the 1980s when several books and monographs appeared that were more pedagogically-oriented. Farkas [29] for example, provided guidance to teachers, but this work could also prove useful for students. A more student-oriented work was Clements and Waite's 1983 *Guide for Beginning Technical Editors* [49]. Aimed primarily at editors of scientific papers, the monograph worked well in classrooms because of the descriptions of requirements and duties the editor could expect. The authors trace a manuscript through the process from where the editor receives it until it is published. While not as much is made of the importance of the reader as we will find in later books, nonetheless, the reader hovers in the background of discussion about standards and language skills.

In addition, there were works designed more for the non-technical editor. Examples included Arthur Plotnik's *The Elements of Editing: A Modern Guide for Editors and Journalists* (1982 [50], a companion volume to Strunk and White's *Elements of Style* [51]); Claire Kehrwald Cook's *The MLA's Line by Line: How to Edit Your Own Writing* (1985) [52]; and the first edition of Karen Judd's *Copyediting: A Practical Guide* (1982) [53].

Of course, report writing textbooks included a chapter or section on editing your own work rather than on editing the work of others. But that is more revision than editing, and there is a considerable body of literature on revising your own documents [54]. But little is useful in a technical editing classroom or workshop.

The work of the early 1990s points the way for the appearance in the late 1990s of additional texts that built upon the same principles. Editors were seen as professionals who are highly skilled not only in language but also in communication. Because the books' authors tended to be academics, they brought to the training of technical editors a sense of task analysis and user analysis that they reflected in their classrooms. A fully trained technical editor was seen as an individual who had extensive training in all phases of language and communication. He or she was skillful in helping authors achieve their communication goals. More importantly, the texts and classrooms emphasized the primacy of the reader, the user. However, the debate over the need for technical knowledge has disappeared from the books as the focus of the education programs shift. Oklahoma State's program is typical in that it emphasizes to students that their training will be in how to communicate rather than in how to communicate a specific technical area. Students choose class projects based on their technical interests (which usually come from their undergraduate degree programs) and are responsible for keeping current in that area while studying to be professional technical communicators—writers and editors.

When a practicing technical editor teamed with an academic to produce a technical editing textbook, the flavor of someone who had been there and done that permeated both the practice and theory that the textbook presented. Such a book was the Bush and Campbell text and workbook published in 1995 [55, 56].

THE FUTURE

This legacy of the technical editor as professional and knowledgeable in multiple areas carries into the 21st century. As academic classrooms become the training grounds for technical editors, the emphasis and focus of the research done in technical editing shifts to empirical studies that examine the cognitive processes involved in technical editing (see, for example, David Hutto's investigation of graphics and ethos [57]). Thus, the profession begins to take on even more the status it so richly deserves.

Technical editors continue to grow both professionally and in their understanding of the communication process. As more and more research is done into how our readers read, technical editors gain additional insights into how to make their texts more accessible. New and more complex theories of communication such as those relating to communication and culture found in such authors as Shome and Hegde [58] likewise give the editor insight into the importance of culture in composing and reading texts. The trend toward the editor being the reader's advocate will continue as will the increasing recognition of the importance of the editor's work.

As editors gain understanding of how authors write and readers read, they will realize that these relationships become much more complex. This increase in complexity is not to suggest that editors can ignore the fundamentals; they still must be quite proficient in language and understand their role in communicating information that the user needs. Likewise, they still must have a mastery of the basic reference tools, including style manuals, as well as continue to develop the interpersonal skills that will allow them to query an author's intent.

Resources that technical editors can draw on likewise will continue to play a major part in the profession. Listservs, such as Copyediting-L [59], offer immediate access to a wealth of knowledge and experience not easily found in other sources. This access becomes even more important with the increasing trend of editors to be self-employed. These resources function in much the same way as colleagues function in technical editing departments within large companies. There, editors can ask questions and discuss alternatives with others in their group. With the increase in self-employed editors such discussions are, at best, difficult and listservs can provide needed forums for interactions.

Technology also plays a part in the changing roles of the technical editor, as David Dayton makes clear in his research on the impact of technology on technical communication, especially editing [60-62]. The advances in technology will continue to offer technical editors new and different ways of doing their job. For example, onscreen editing is becoming more and more prevalent as computers become better able to display and manipulate text. But as with other advances in technology, shifting the culture and the expectations of a technical editor requires time and commitment. It requires the editor to approach editing in a way that differs from the way editors used to work when having only hardcopy to mark.

Editors will still be anonymous and continue to work in the background while the author receives the credit. It is rare to find editors mentioned by name. Hildegard's editor, Volmar, is certainly exceptional and is probably remembered for more than editing her manuscripts. 20th-century editors of fiction remain anonymous except for an occasional mention by the author or because of the job done (Perkins, for example). But these are rare exceptions. Since the time of the first editors, accuracy of the text based on the author's manuscript has been more important to publishers. Editors, then, continue to enhance the reputations of both the author and the publisher. We find that same situation in the first decade of the 21st century but with the added editorial responsibility of advocating for the reader. The methods and procedures as well as the definition of editing and the job of an editor may change over time, but the fundamental responsibilities of the editor remain the same: textual accuracy and making the material accessible to the user.

In looking at other future trends, it helps to look back to see where technical editors have come from. Originally, technical editors were experts on the standards used to establish quality. Language was matched against established handbooks of grammar, dictionaries, and style manuals. The format was established by traditional approaches if not for a government assignment, or, if for a government job, appropriate standards such as military standards. After a few years, editors as well as writers became concerned about the readers of the documents as communication became better understood. Both began to realize that their work should be influenced by the people who would use it.

In addition, both authors and editors began to understand how communication happens. Considerable research in composing, for example, found its way into the training of the author and of the editor. Add to that an increasing understanding of how the mind works when composing and editing as well as how the mind operates when someone is reading, and you begin to get a much more detailed picture of how documents can be made more effective. For example, as the studies of how readers read grew in the past, psychologists were showing that reading involves schema—for not only the reader but also the author and the editor. Thus, a new dimension in reader analysis of what could be determined through demographic methods aided both authors and editors in making text more accessible.

Understanding cognitive processes reflects on how the mind works when both composing and reading. The next major step in understanding how readers read, writers write, and editors edit, is at the physiological level. Scientists now understand that the brain works through a combination of electronic and chemical stimuli that are present along the neurons. The electrical part occurs in the neurons' pathway and ends at a synapse. At this point a chemical reaction occurs that bridges that gap, linking the two neurons. This process leads to speculation about how such items as memory and meaning operate. The question for writers and editors to understand is what is the relationship between what they wished to communicate, its method of expression, and the electrochemical reactions that take place in the brain? Also, what is the nature of the signal being sent along the neurons to the chemical synapses? As scientists come to understand more about the electrochemical makeup of the brain, researchers in writing and editing can begin to understand how writers and editors can influence this process through such matters as language, syntax, and context. For editors, understanding what happens when a reader reads can aid in developing text that aids understanding. If the editor understands the schema in play for the reader and its role in generating electrochemical responses, then another step toward making the text accessible will be possible.

To take one instance, consider how understanding meaning has evolved. Originally, meaning was tied exclusively to dictionaries. But as researchers came to understand the communication process better, they realized that meaning in a text was tied to three different structures: language, or semantics, could be understood in both a connotative and a denotative sense; meaning could occur through syntactical placement of elements within a sentence; and meaning could be tied to context in ways that amplified that meaning. All these elements function at the mind level, and now scientists are trying to understand what happens at the neuron level. So the more we can understand how meaning comes about, the better able we are to communicate as authors and editors, producing texts that have reduced levels of ambiguity.

The role of education and academics in this era of understanding how communication works will be to take the physiological research and apply it to the communication process itself. Through articles and conference presentations, academics will make the neurological research available to others. In addition, their training of writers and editors will be modified accordingly so that those writers and editors will have a better understanding of how we communicate. In the future, one can expect to see more emphasis on theories of communication, especially theories that relate to how the mind and brain work when composing and when reading.

The future looks bright, indeed.

REFERENCES

1. E. A. Malone, Learned Collaborators as Technical Editors: Specialization and Collaboration in Early Modern European Printing Houses, *Journal of Business and Technical Communication, 20*, pp. 389-424, 2006.
2. S. Johnson, *A Dictionary of the English Language: In Which the Words are Deduced from Their Originals, and Illustrated in Their Different Significations, by Examples from the Best Writers. To Which are Prefixed, a History of the Language and an English Grammar*. 2 Vols., W. Strahan, London, 1755.
3. R. Lowth, *A Short Introduction to English Grammar*, A. Millar and R. and J. Dodsley, London, 1763.
4. J. B. Howell. *Style Manuals of the English-Speaking World: A Guide*, Oryx, Phoenix, Arizona, 1983.
5. University of Chicago Press, *The Chicago Manual of Style* (15th ed.), University of Chicago Press, Chicago, 2003.
6. American Heritage Dictionaries, *The American Heritage Dictionary of the English Language* (4th ed.), Houghton Mifflin Company, Boston, 2006.
7. *Online Etymology Dictionary*. Available online at: http://www.etymonline.com/index.php?term=edition
8. *Oxford English Dictionary* (2nd ed.), Oxford University Press, New York, 1989.
9. T. Cahill, *Mysteries of the Middle Ages: And the Beginning of the Modern World*, Anchor Books, New York, 2006.
10. W. B. Bezanson, Analytical Editing of Research Papers, *STWE Review, 6*:3, pp. 18-19, 1959.
11. A. Lytel, What Kind of Editor Are You? *STWP Convention Proceedings*, pp. 81-90, 1960.
12. E. Clarke, *A Guide to Technical Literature Production*, TW Publishers, River Forest, Illinois, 1961.
13. H. F. Osborne, Criticism and Creativity, in *Technical Editing: Principles and Practices*, L. M. Zook (ed.), Society for Technical Communication, Washington, D.C., pp. 17-19, 1975.
14. W. E. Britton, What is Technical Writing? *College Composition and Communication, 16*, pp. 113-116, 1965.
15. N. A. Briggs, Publications Management: The Tribalization of Technical Writers: Part I, *Technical Communication, 14*:3, pp. 13-16, 1967.

16. N. A. Briggs, Publications Management: The Tribalization of Technical Writers: Part II, *Technical Communication, 14*:4, pp. 10-13, 1967.
17. T. F. Walton, *Technical Manual Writing and Administration*, McGraw-Hill, New York, 1968.
18. L. M. Zook (ed.), *Technical Editing: Principles and Practices*, Society for Technical Communication, Washington, D.C., 1975.
19. M. F. Buehler, Patterns for Making Editorial Changes, in *Technical Editing: Principles and Practices*, L. M. Zook (ed.), Society for Technical Communication, Washington, D.C., pp. 1-6, 1975.
20. E. P. Dukes, The Art of Editing, in *Technical Editing: Principles and Practices*, L. M. Zook (ed.), Society for Technical Communication, Washington, D.C., pp. 62-66, 1975.
21. A. L. Cox, The Editor as Generalist as Well as Specialist, in *Technical Editing: Principles and Practices*, L. M. Zook (ed.), Society for Technical Communication, Washington, D.C., pp. 7-11, 1975.
22. V. M. Root, Technical Publications Job Patterns and Knowledge Requirements, *Technical Communication, 15*, pp. 5-12, 1968.
23. R. Van Buren and M. F. Buehler, *The Levels of Edit* (2nd ed.), Jet Propulsion Laboratory, Pasadena, California, 1980.
24. L. Zook, Technical Editors Look at Technical Editing, *Technical Communication, 30*, pp. 20-26, 1983.
25. T. L. Warren, Current Research: STC's Research Program, *Proceedings of STC's 40th Annual Conference*, Society for Technical Communication, Arlington, Virginia, pp. 338-341, 1993.
26. C. F. Kemnitz (ed.), *Technical Editing: Basic Theory and Practice*, Society for Technical Communication, Arlington, Virginia, 1994.
27. J. G. Shaw (ed.), *Teaching Technical Writing and Editing—In-House Programs That Work*, Society for Technical Communication, Washington, D.C., 1976.
28. C. D. Rude (ed.), *Teaching Technical Editing*, Association of Teachers of Technical Writing, Lubbock, Texas, 1985.
29. D. K. Farkas, *How to Teach Technical Editing*, Society for Technical Communication, Washington, D.C., 1986.
30. N. A. Briggs, Editing by Dialogue, in *Technical Editing: Principles and Practices*, L. M. Zook (ed.), Society for Technical Communication, Washington, D.C., pp. 56-61, 1975.
31. S. Dragga and G. Gong, *Editing: The Design of Rhetoric*, Baywood, Amityville, New York, 1989.
32. C. E. Shannon and W. Weaver, *The Mathematical Theory of Communication*, University of Illinois Press, Urbana, Illinois, 1949.
33. M. Buber, *I and Thou*, R. G. Smith (trans.), Charles Scribner's Sons, New York, 1958. Briggs also cites Buber's *Between Man and Man*, R. G. Smith (trans.), Kegan Paul, London, 1947.
34. H. Giles, J. Coupland, and N. Coupland, Accommodation Theory: Communication, Context, and Consequences, in *Contexts of Accommodation: Developments in Applied Sociolinguistics*, H. Gilley, J. Coupland, and N. Coupland (eds.), Cambridge University Press, Cambridge, pp. 1-68, 1991.

35. A. M. Nicotera, The Constructivist Theory of Delia, Clark, and Associates, in *Watershed Research Traditions in Human Communication Theory*, D. P. Cushman and B. Kovačlć (eds.), State University of New York Press, Albany, pp. 45-66, 1995.

36. J. R. Hayes and N. A. Chenoweth, Working Memory in an Editing Task, *Written Communication, 24*, pp. 283-294, 2007.

37. J. Bisaillon, Professional Editing Strategies Used by Six Editors, *Written Communication, 24*, pp. 295-322, 2007.

38. H. H. McNaughton, *Proofreading and Copyediting: A Practical Guide to Style for the 1970's*, Hastings House, New York, 1973.

39. *Words into Type*, based on studies by M. E. Skillin, R. M. Gay, and others (3rd ed.), Prentice-Hall, Englewood Cliffs, New Jersey, 1974.

40. J. B. Bennett, *Editing for Engineers*, Wiley-Interscience, New York, 1970.

41. C. D. Rude, *Technical Editing*, Wadsworth, Belmont, California, 1991.

42. A. Eisenberg, *Guide to Technical Editing: Discussion, Dictionary, and Exercises*, Oxford University Press, New York, 1992.

43. D. C. Samson, Jr., *Editing Technical Writing*, Oxford University Press, New York, 1993.

44. J. A. Tarutz, *Technical Editing: The Practical Guide for Editors and Writers*, Addison-Wesley, Reading, MA, 1992.

45. J. C. Mancuso, *Technical Editing*, Prentice Hall, Englewood Cliffs, New Jersey, 1992.

46. W. O. Coggin and L. R. Porter, *Editing for the Technical Professions*, Macmillan, New York, 1993.

47. A. S. Berg, *Max Perkins: Editor of Genius*, Thomas Congdon Books, New York, 1978.

48. H. L. Shimberg, Special Issue on Technical Editing, *Technical Communication, 28*:4, 1981.

49. W. Clements and R. G. Waite, *Guide for Beginning Technical Editors*, Society for Technical Communication, Washington, D.C., 1983.

50. A. Plotnik, *The Elements of Editing: A Modern Guide for Editors and Journalists*, Macmillan, New York, 1982.

51. W. Strunk and E. B. White, *The Elements of Style* (4th ed.), Longman, Boston, 1999.

52. C. K. Cook, *The MLA's Line by Line: How to Edit your Own Writing*, Houghton Mifflin, Boston, 1985.

53. K. Judd, *Copyediting: A Practical Guide*, Kaufmann, Los Altos, California, 1982.

54. B. W. Speck, D. A. Hinnen, and K. Hinnen, *Teaching Revising and Editing: An Annotated Bibliography*, Praeger, Westport, Connecticut, 2003.

55. D. W. Bush and C. P. Campbell, *How to Edit Technical Documents,* Oryx Press, Phoenix, Arizona, 1995.

56. D. W. Bush and C. P. Campbell, *How to Edit Technical Documents Workbook,* Oryx Press, Phoenix, Arizona, 1995.

57. D. Hutto, Graphics and Ethos in Biomedical Journals, *Journal of Technical Writing and Communication, 38*, pp. 111-131, 2008.

58. R. Shome and R. S. Hegde, Postcolonial Approaches to Communication: Charting the Terrain, Engaging the Intersections, *Communication and Theory, 12*, pp. 249-270, 2002.

59. Copyediting-L. Available online at:
https://listserv.indiana.edu/cgi-bin/wa-iub.exe?A0=COPYEDITING-L

60. D. Dayton, Electronic Editing in Technical Communications: A Survey of Practices and Attitudes, *Technical Communication, 50*, pp. 192-205, 2003.

61. D. Dayton, Electronic Editing in Technical Communications: The Compelling Logics of Local Contexts, *Technical Communication, 51*, pp. 86-101, 2004.

62. D. Dayton, Electronic Editing in Technical Communications: A Model of User-Centered Technology Adoption, *Technical Communication, 51*, pp. 207-223, 2004.

CHAPTER 4

The Teaching of Technical Editing

Carolyn D. Rude

When I started teaching technical editing in the early 1980s, few classroom resources were available. Academic programs were just beginning to prepare career professionals for "technical writing," as it was then called. Although several comprehensive textbooks were available for introductory writing courses, faculty invented materials as they taught new courses, such as technical editing and user documentation, in the expanding curriculum.

The Chicago Manual of Style offered a comprehensive resource for making decisions about style and consistency, but it is a reference book, not a textbook. Its emphasis is editing for university presses, and at around 900 pages, it intimidates undergraduates (and even their professors). In its 13th edition (1982), it declared that "substantive editing" (distinguished from copyediting) could be learned only through experience [1, p. 51]. Yet, faculty understood that they would have to help students gain some understanding of substantive editing and not wait for their on-the-job experience. Van Buren and Buehler defined editing by a taxonomy of editorial functions in *The Levels of Edit* [2]. *The Levels of Edit* aimed to help editors manage the process in part by educating authors about the varieties of editorial intervention. Both references showed how much more complex editing is than "proofreading," the definition that beginning students of editing often imagine. However, with their emphasis on accuracy and consistency, primarily at the sentence level, these references offered advice primarily for basic copyediting. The "levels," for example, stop with style. In these references, based on a linear, print model of publication, editing takes place at the end

51

http://dx.doi.org/10.2190/NPOC4

of content development and writing, when there is little chance to influence content and organization.

Beyond these two resources, a number of articles through the 1980s offered advice and guidelines about editing. The most common topic in articles about technical editing up to the mid-1980s was the author-editor relationship [3], a relationship fraught with mistrust and even antagonism. Editors were cast into the role of fixers of errors and often accused of changing the material because they didn't understand it. They worked at the end of a document development process, pressed by publication deadlines on the one hand and high expectations for what they could accomplish in a short time on the other. The solution to author-editor conflict was usually techniques of interpersonal relationships rather than editing itself or the editorial process.

In spite of the frustration apparent in the articles, some editors had concepts of editing that remain pertinent today. For example, Zook [4] distinguished "detail" from the "long view" and offered an expansive definition of what editors could contribute to the information development process. Cheney and Schleicher [5] illustrated the impact of "comprehensive editing" on an abstract of a paper written for a scientific journal and estimated that 80% of the 16 scientific papers they edited required revised titles, abstracts, and introductions along with other substantive revisions. Farkas [6] introduced administrative and policy issues in technical editing.

Today the editing course is well established in the curriculum, and textbooks and other resources are available, but editors now work in a digital world and have had to look up from their pages and even beyond their screens. Technology has changed the procedures of information development and management as well as the role of technical editing and therefore the teaching of technical editing. Other changes have also influenced the way we think about editing. We recognize, in ways the resources of the early 1980s did not explicitly foreground, that effective documents depend not just on good sentences and consistency but also on choices of content and means of distribution that are appropriate for users and on organization of information for comprehension, retrieval, and reuse. Information developers with editorial minds can help with the planning and development of documents, not just ensure consistency and accuracy at the end of the process. The scope of editorial responsibility has expanded to include more features of texts and types of texts as well as new methods of information distribution and use and global audiences. Articles on editing now appropriately focus on editing and the editing process. Editing is less a matter of damage repair than of consultation.

The job title "technical editor" has represented a fairly small number of the members of the Society for Technical Communication (STC). In the 1990 STC Salary Survey, only 7% of respondents in the "writer-editor" category identified themselves as technical editors, though all those surveyed for a study on electronic editing declared some responsibility for editing [7, p. 335]. In 2003,

Dayton described editing as a "de-specialized, distributed function in most technical communication workplaces" and reported that only 4% of the STC members he surveyed "identified themselves as working in jobs dedicated exclusively to editing others" [8, p. 192].

What justifies the continued prominence of an editing course in the curriculum? How has the course adapted to changing times? What does it contribute to the understanding and effectiveness of the information developer?

Changes in the procedures and functions of editing have required adaptations in the classroom. This chapter offers a review of the principles that shape a course in technical editing, a review of course content and pedagogical methods, and an assessment of the value of the editing course in the 21st century. Throughout, I try to link course design and decisions with an analysis of student achievements and needs. The information is based on more than two decades of teaching editing and feedback from students and other teachers using the textbook *Technical Editing* [9].

THE EDITING CLASS:
OPPORTUNITIES AND POSSIBILITIES

The broad goal of an editing course is to prepare students in the best professional practices. It takes them from an entry point and helps them develop an understanding of principles and processes that will let them respond effectively to editorial challenges on the job. In a rapidly changing realm of information development, a course cannot anticipate all the editorial situations that a practitioner might face. But it can offer students fundamental knowledge of the ways in which texts work to satisfy their purposes, increased expertise in the conventions of language use, an appreciation for information design, respect for the users of texts, and procedures for working with texts from the point of conception and planning to review and distribution. These goals have remained constant over time even as the texts that technical editors work with have changed from print to digital; from mostly verbal to variations of verbal, visual, oral, and multimedia; and from comprehensive, bound documents to topics that can be reused and retrieved for multiple purposes. As our understanding of texts expands and the editorial role grows more amorphous, principles and processes take on new significance. Understanding how texts work, competence in applying the principles of editing, and initiative in problem solving are the outcomes of the course. Students who complete the course should also understand, at least conceptually, how texts are tagged and stored in databases for retrieval and reuse. This knowledge affects how they structure texts and their components.

Texts work in a more complex way than style guides and handbooks imply. They work at the sentence level, to be sure, but usable texts also require visual and organizational consistency, support for information retrieval through indexes (print or digital) and other means, a structure that matches the information and the reader's perception of the information, content development with the expectation of adaptation and reuse, and, above all, a match of content and medium to the needs for the text. Comprehensive editing requires imagination as well as the ability to look for conventions of usage in a manual of style.

The editing class develops students' ability to solve problems with texts. The problems are not necessarily errors. They may relate instead to factors outside the text, including budget constraints, the need for frequent updates, or the expectation of translation into multiple languages. They may also relate to the complexity of content or to readers with different backgrounds. Editors know a range of possibilities for texts, from the details of sentences to ways of arranging, displaying, and publishing information. They bring this knowledge to the task of making texts work for users. They add to the quality of the document by applying their specialized knowledge about texts. As Corbin, Moell, and Boyd claim [10], they are part of the quality assurance goals of information development. Their knowledge complements the subject matter knowledge of the author.

In order to solve problems, editors have to think both about the details of sentences and facts and about the broad consequences for users of editorial choices. Although detail and vision may seem superficially disparate, they both serve the goals of meeting the needs of readers and of problem solving. Each choice made by the writer or editor, whether at the sentence level or more comprehensively, influences what a user understands and does. The approach to detail can be visionary if editors see their choices about sentences, like their choices about content, structure, and medium, as enabling readers to understand. Detail and vision are also connected by the importance of structure at the sentence level and the structuring of information for retrieval of specific information and for reuse. Understanding structure is as important for an information architect as for an architect of buildings. That understanding begins at the sentence level and expands to the organization of information in databases. Likewise, a visionary perspective on editing includes recognition that the details of content must be appropriate for the purpose and trustworthy and that the details of grammar and mechanics must enhance understanding and use, not distract readers.

An orientation to users of texts and respect for the full range of textual features has enabled editors to find new ways to contribute to information development. Even as the nature of texts, editing, and the means of production and distribution have changed, the role of the editor has remained consistent in these regards: to think of readers and users of information and to help shape the text according to those needs. What we understand now, as some understood in the 1980s, is that an editor can consult a handbook and guidelines for only a small part of this purpose. Editors need to take advantage of handbook material because the conventions represented there work in the best interest of users. Employers and other partners in information development also expect this expertise in editors. But at some point editors need to rely on their own imaginations and comprehensive knowledge to think of the best ways to make texts work in a specific situation. Editing, as part of information design and development, is like any other design field. Student editors learn to contribute to the design of information by understanding language and various textual choices well and by knowing principles and procedures of editing.

CONTENT AND METHODS IN THE EDITING COURSE

The content and methods of a course are the means to the end of developing editors with the expertise to make good, user-based decisions about texts. A comprehensive editing course can easily take two semesters, but because a one-semester course is typical, faculty members will choose what to emphasize depending on student needs and course goals.

Content may include

- The marking of texts using the established languages of print and digital markup
- Principles of grammar, punctuation, and consistency and the use of editorial resources
- Principles of style, organization, visual design, and illustrations
- Genre conventions (including the genres of digital and multimedia publication)
- Editing for special purposes, including editing for international audiences and editing quantitative and visual material

In addition to studying these topics, students benefit from learning

- A method of analysis for comprehensive editing
- Strategies of communication with authors, including editorial plans, letters of transmittal, queries, and face-to-face discussion
- How texts are tagged and organized in databases for retrieval, repurposing, and reuse
- How to edit online
- The management of information, including planning and development, publication, distribution, and updates
- The ethical bases for editorial choice: what a client prefers may sometimes be naive about safety, intellectual property law, environmental consequences, and human rights

In the editing course, students practice editing online and on paper, using documents with various technical subjects and in various workplace genres.

Course Structure

There is not necessarily one right way to structure the editing course and its contents. A progressive structure, beginning with basic copyediting and progressing toward comprehensive editing, has worked best for my students over the years. It begins at the beginning, without too many assumptions about what students know either about editing or even about writing the kinds of documents that enable users to make decisions or get work done. It can offer an entry into technical communication as a practice for students without courses in the field. The common starting point is language: its conventions and the effect of choices about language on comprehension. As we build understanding of the details of texts, we expand to more comprehensive choices about texts, including content development and organization. The textbook *Technical Editing* [9] is organized this way.

The progressive structure parallels the increasing responsibilities of a career that might begin with limited editing tasks under the supervision of a senior editor but develop into managing projects and the work of other editors. (When the students complete the section on basic copyediting and move to assignments on style and comprehensive editing, I tell them they have earned a promotion.) From the start, students engage with the idea that editors do not look just at the text but through it to the text in use. Through the semester, in addition to working on assignments, we build a vocabulary of editing and a habit of thinking not of one's own preferences in writing and what "sounds good" but rather of the deliberate choices that make a text work well. Knowledge about texts grows as student editors practice these concepts on different types of projects. They increase their capacity for editorial problem solving.

Some faculty use a top-down structure, beginning with the most comprehensive concepts of document development and progressing toward the details of sentences and mechanics. This structure parallels the way editors with comprehensive responsibilities work on the job. They don't bother with basic copyediting if the entire section of the text might be reorganized or even discarded. Conceptually, I like this structure because it reflects practice on the job. In industry, the team as a whole, with the editor in consultation with the writer or the editorial manager, might decide that a text in its infancy needs the big-picture kind of edit. An editor charged with deciding which level of edit to use needs to have command of all editorial tools. However, from a practical perspective, the top-down course structure asks students to make judgments about whole texts before they have concepts and a vocabulary for thinking about texts. It could inadvertently reinforce the problematic editorial perspective that it's OK for an editor to possess the text and claim it as his or her own—to impose what the editor "likes."

Beginning with comprehensive assignments also puts instruction on punctuation, grammar, and style at the end of the course, when students have already had the freedom to think in visionary ways. They could easily become dismissive or even just tired as their editorial interventions seem increasingly limited. The place of the editing course in a curriculum—introducing other courses or concluding a sequence—might influence one's structuring of the course. If students have already been prepared by other courses in technical communication, they may have the knowledge to approach their assignments with a comprehensive perspective from the beginning of the course.

Throughout the course, we have chances to discover and reinforce the importance of editing for usability and comprehensibility, to learn the tools for editing, and to discuss the responsibility of a professional person to know the content, methods, and language of his or her specialization, and the value of respecting writers, clients, and users. These are concepts that should permeate the curriculum rather than being isolated as units of the course in order to teach a way of thinking about editing.

The Question of Grammar and Punctuation

It seems counterintuitive to link the term *question* with grammar and punctuation in a chapter on teaching editing. Expertise in grammar and punctuation is the default editorial skill, something that no one else in information development offers so well as an editor. Why would there be a question?

One reason is that if content, structure, and visual design influence usability and comprehension more than sentences, shouldn't the time in the editing course be devoted to understanding of these features? Shouldn't student editors learn more about ways of organizing information digitally? It's a reasonable question, given how packed the syllabus can be.

A second reason for the question relates to the knowledge that students bring to the course. The education of students in this era has often de-emphasized the formal study of language for the very reasons that I have emphasized the importance of comprehensive editing: a text that's perfect in grammar, punctuation, and mechanics may still be an inept text as judged for its usability or substance. Even if students have studied the structure of language, they probably have not done so for some years. Like many people who are good writers more than editors, students in an editing class use the language well without thinking about how it works. They might be able to edit intuitively up to a point. Editing well requires more. Intuitive editing invites author-editor stress because of inevitable presumption and mistakes. Thus, if students are to exit the editing course with reasonable expertise in grammar and punctuation, they need intensive (time-consuming) review.

A third reason for the question is that students resist what they regard as dry and boring—and teachers resist getting accused of being boring. Students have probably been praised for their ability with words and are comfortable with their knowledge. Students sometimes even speak with a measure of pride about their lack of specific knowledge, confident that they can write and edit well enough without knowing the terms. It's true that most of us do not think explicitly about these details as we write, but editing the writing of others is a different matter. Willed limited knowledge seems a risky position for an editor, and as an instructor, I feel a responsibility to nudge the students toward more respect for their presumed expertise. They really have no claim to the title of "editor" if they are not expert on these basics. That means not just punctuating and using grammar correctly but knowing why.

If editors are to be regarded as specialists and professionals, they should at least know the vocabulary of grammar and punctuation. I like to joke with students who wonder why they should be able to distinguish a dependent clause from an independent clause when they put the commas in the right place anyway that they would not like a surgeon to propose operating on a body part he or she can't name or to say, "trust me, I know what I'm doing." Professionals know their own vocabulary, and the vocabulary of grammar and punctuation is still an expectation of editors. Writing intuitively may be OK in many situations, but editing the work of someone else requires the discipline of information.

I try to teach grammar and punctuation from the perspective of sentence structure that enhances reading, not of error. Who wouldn't resist learning a list of the ways they can make mistakes? But if students understand that choosing strong verbs that do what the grammatical subject says and understand punctuation as a signal to accurate reading, they can see the positive value of conventional choices. Somewhat wickedly, from a student point of view, I require them in editing exercises to state the reasons for editorial choices: "comma before a coordinating conjunction in a compound sentence" and the like. The payoff, whether or not they know it during the course, is that they will base their editorial choices on knowledge, not feelings or guesses, and authors will appreciate what editors can contribute, not get mad because the editors have meddled. The other payoff is that the edited content will make more sense to readers than it might have without the editor's interventions.

Methods of Teaching

Editing classes, like writing and other information development classes, are performance classes. This means that students, like students learning to paint or play a musical instrument, have to practice what they are learning, and they learn while practicing. Workshop and tutorial methods dominate, and lecture is minimal. A typical class day is a workshop targeted on a specific learning objective, such as punctuating sentences, using strong verbs, or structuring illustrations to foreground the essential information. When students work in groups on these assignments, they learn to talk about texts and editing and help each other learn concepts and vocabulary. They also learn about working cooperatively with others.

When the class turns to comprehensive editing and handbooks have limited authority, we practice a procedure for analyzing the text and its purposes and developing an editorial plan. This analysis and planning is part of the process of problem solving. Students prepare for each assignment an analysis of the editing needs and goals. The analysis should precede the editing to give editors a global perspective on what they are trying to accomplish, an alternative to working line by line. I give students a heuristic for analysis and planning in table form that begins with an assessment of audience and purpose and provides a row for each category of text features, such as style and organization.

For example, my classes have sometimes worked with a manual for residents in public housing. Editors can think best about the document and goals for editing if they first define its purposes. If the assignment were a client project, they could interview the client, but in a classroom assignment, they are free to imagine the possibilities. They can imagine that the manual exists so that residents will live harmoniously together according to some rules established by a board of directors or a facilities manager. The residents will need to know how to complete tasks, such as paying the rent or getting the refrigerator repaired. They also need to know expectations on such matters as having guests. They will use the manual for reference, as tasks or issues arise, so it needs to provide easy ways of finding information. Some of the residents are not native speakers of English. Understanding the goals helps students edit with a purpose.

Assessment follows this understanding of the audience and purpose. The sentences are long, and many are in passive voice. The tone is condescending and even hostile, as though the managers expect the residents to misbehave. There are gaps in content (residents are told to do something without being told how). The organization is alphabetical rather than task-based (getting repairs, moving out) or grouped by related tasks or sequences of tasks. There are few visual signals about content. There are no accommodations for readers for whom English may be a second language or who have vision problems.

Editing goals are the means of solving the identified problems. The main problem is that the manual won't accomplish its purpose of enabling residents to understand expectations and follow procedures; the reasons are the long sentences, alphabetical order, and difficulty of finding information on the page. The editing goals focus on the gaps between what the manual could be and what it is now. Goals for style include shortening sentences and using active voice and imperative mood for actions. Organizational goals include grouping related tasks and using a meaningful table of contents. Visual design goals include the use of a table of contents, headings, and a running header. For gaps in content, a goal is to determine what is needed and sometimes to ask an author in specific terms to provide it.

This analysis helps students become purpose-driven, thoughtful editors as it guides comprehensive editorial decisions. The analysis predicts the quality of performance. When students have written a thoughtful analysis and plan, their editing is almost always strong. Gaps in the analysis predict gaps in the editing. As they gain experience on the job, editors may no longer need a formal analysis, at least for short documents, because the pattern of thinking will be established. But the formal analysis could well provide the terms for a work plan for a large project.

With all the focus on readers guiding the editing process, students cannot forget authors and clients. Part of the skill of editing is developing partnerships with the people who have a stake in the project. That means listening to them, being transparent about the plans for editing and progress, being willing to negotiate or to modify plans if the editor has not understood, and working together to the benefit of users. In their assignments, students practice editorial queries, learning to distinguish when to ask and what to find out for themselves. Letters of transmittal express editorial goals and achievements in professional, not evaluative, terms. Modeling their English teachers, students may try to rehearse in correspondence what's good and bad in the document. A teacher may need to explain how teaching and editing differ and to characterize the author-editor relationship as a partnership and the editor's role as problem solving, not as critique. Writing the letter helps to develop and practice a way of communicating productively.

Assignments and Workshops

Assignments and in-class workshops give students practice in editing for various text features, moving, in the progressive course structure, from basic copyediting to editing for content, organization, style, and visual design. In this scaffolding of assignments, an early assignment may require students to mark a text for consistency without worrying about style and organization. Although later assignments are cumulative in requiring student editors to pay attention to marking for consistency or style, the need to edit for organization or visual design would dominate so that students can focus their attention on the text feature they are coming to understand.

In the early assignments, students use style manuals and grammar handbooks to guide their text choices and learn to see the details of the text. Many good students have at least one humiliating experience on a project or workshop assignment in which, confident of their knowledge of language, they hurry through. They may mark typos but fail to see the kinds of details that editors see—consistency in the use of numbers or punctuation marks, especially hyphens, or unfamiliar names assumed to be spelled correctly. Like typical readers they may skip over illustrations, tables, and reference lists and miss problems of various sorts with captions, patterns of arrangement, or numbers. I don't want to catch them doing something wrong, and I warn them that they may need to review the document more than once to see all that an experienced editor sees, but a warning does not always penetrate overconfidence. The safety net for students is multiple projects and grades so that one miscue does not hurt their chances for a good course grade. They almost always work more carefully on the next project.

The editing course is a good place for students to learn about writing for translation and localization. They can review criteria for accessibility of Web sites, perhaps using the resources at the Web Accessibility Initiative Web site (www.w3.org/WAI/). They can use the guidelines in editing and compare their edited document to the criteria.

The final project for my courses is a client project that students locate on their own. I set guidelines on the type of text (genres that they might encounter in a workplace setting—no poems or stories, no academic articles) so that the project represents the type of work they might do on the job and provides a good example for their portfolios. The document must require comprehensive editing. I want the students to work with actual clients, not just texts, so that they can learn to question and listen to clients and negotiate with clients as necessary, sometimes helping the clients see possibilities for the text that they had not previously considered, sometimes learning information and perspectives from clients, often working within constraints such as budgets and naive client preferences.

Whatever the overall structure of the class, positioning the client project at the end of the course gives students the opportunity to develop some expertise so that they have something substantial to offer a client. It is important in their professional development to recognize editing as a specialized process that offers value, something more than proofreading or inappropriately changing a text. To send students to work for clients before they have this knowledge cheats both the client, who may get mediocre work, and the student, who may think that intuition rather than specialized knowledge is good enough for an editor. Expert work for clients also helps clients to perceive the value of editorial work and to recognize it as specialized work. Such recognition counters a common perception among people who work in fields other than information development that anyone who uses language can edit, a perception that contributes to low salaries or other unrealistic expectations for editors.

As assignments grow more complex, the need to manage the process of editing increases, especially for client projects or collaborative projects. Even within the confines of a project, students can learn basic management strategies, setting deadlines, distributing work assignments, and meeting to review progress. If asked to estimate how much time an editing project will take before they do it and then to keep records of their time, students are almost always surprised by how much they have underestimated. That information should improve the accuracy of their future estimates.

Tools and Technology

Since the 1980s, technology has changed information development in three substantial ways that affect the roles of editors. The first (and ongoing) change is in production, including the development and publication of texts. The second change is expansion of the genres with which editors work to include Web sites, help topics, presentations, and multimedia. The third change lies in the concept of texts themselves and even of information. For example, the print manual, taking months to write and publish and updated periodically but not as often as needed, has given way to collections of help topics that are published digitally in databases.

Digital tools enhance and simplify editing and enable the production and distribution of texts. But even though contemporary students have used computers for their entire lives, they are often surprisingly unaware of available tools in word processing, such as page numbering and running headers, let alone styles for formatting. Digital markup and document types are alien concepts for most of them.

What tools and technologies to teach in the editing class depends, in part, on other courses in the curriculum. In the universities where I have taught, students learn page layout and illustration software in a course in document design, and they learn coding in courses on Web design and user documentation. In these universities, the focus in the editing class is on word processing, especially on document styles. Creating styles for different text elements and tagging texts with styles is a tool of visual consistency, and it saves the time of marking or formatting each instance of repeated text elements. Styles also have their parallel features in other software, so the concept of tagging will be reinforced in other classes. Tagging should make it easier for students to learn XML markup in other classes.

Students seem to learn tools, such as styles or XML markup, in short lessons that continue through the term better than in intensive tutorials. They benefit from an initial workshop to learn concepts and test the software. Brief refreshers and new information are useful as assignments require them.

The tagging of documents with styles can lead nicely to a discussion of single sourcing and editing so that documents can easily be used for multiple purposes. This discussion connects as well to increased awareness of document structures and the various parts of a document.

Learning document types and the details of coding may be beyond the scope of a one-semester course. Whether to prioritize this knowledge might depend on whether graduates usually work in large firms with massive information products or are more likely to work in nonprofits or other small organizations. Some of these issues can be resolved at the program level as the faculty coordinate the curriculum. If students learn the concept of single sourcing and see how the code works, they may begin to see the significance for editing and be a step ahead in a course that does teach them the technical specifics. Albers [11] may be good background reading on editing in an environment of document databases and single sourcing.

In workshops and assignments, students may edit digital texts, using comments and tracking changes. They may discuss the effectiveness and reliability of spelling and grammar checkers. They may experiment with various page layout features of word processing software. They can learn alternatives to the typescript layout with double-spaced lines and centered headings. They may consider landscape orientation, columns, or tables for using the space on the page effectively. They may learn about em dashes and the difference between rules and underlining. All of these possibilities increase their visual literacy and complement what they may learn in a course on visual design.

As students edit digital genres, they need some orientation to the genres themselves. What makes a series of help topics fit together as a collection? What consistencies in terminology and structure will make the individual topics cohere? What index terms are users likely to recognize? Students' experience with structures of sentences and whole documents and with consistency will resonate with this new application. They also need to develop genre knowledge about Web sites and use this knowledge in their analyses and editorial plans.

Technology has also affected the way students read and search for information, and that affects teaching in subtle ways. These observations are anecdotal and not based on systematic research, but students, like the rest of us, are able to find specialized information almost instantly from their homes rather than getting to a library and can link quickly to an alternate site if the information they find does not look like the best possible option. They learn in the bullet points of presentation slides and are impatient with nuanced, detailed reading material. In this environment, the pace of class meetings needs to move quickly, and podcasts and Web sites may work with printed textbooks, if not replace them, in providing information. Of course, books are portable, and commuting students may especially appreciate the convenience of a book, but students are living in a period of transition in the way textbook information is made available.

THE VALUE OF AN EDITING COURSE

The editing course plays a critical role in the curriculum that prepares future technical communicators or information architects. Because editors need to understand texts on so many levels, the course can be a microcosm of the entire field of information design and development. Students, like working editors, see the information products from concept to development to use. They use the tools of production as well as expertise in language. They may work with a variety of genres, with visual as well as verbal information, and in digital and print media. They see the range and possibilities of information products. The course also relates to every other course in the curriculum, either introducing or reinforcing goals that may be developed in those courses.

The editing course, more than writing courses, foregrounds the process of information development and use and makes explicit the way texts work. Student editors become conscious of their craft by observing and analyzing the writing of others. This awareness of craft increases their competence in writing and as future practitioners. When knowledge is only intuitive and internal, it is hard to make it grow. With explicit knowledge of language and texts, students gain tools for improving documents. In an environment where editing is distributed and the jobs of writers and editors blur, students will be prepared for a range of information development assignments.

The editing class also offers the opportunity to shape attitudes. Inherent in the definition of editor as problem solver is respect for writers and other members of the information development team as partners with shared interest in creating effective documents. By thinking of editorial interventions as helping to enhance the usability of the text, they also gain respect for users, including users with different strengths for finding and understanding information and users in a variety of cultures using a variety of languages. And fundamental to respecting information development partners and users is the self-respect that comes from developing expertise that they know can contribute to the quality of the information products. The ability to think about the details of the text but also beyond the text and by doing so to make the text work for users is the gift and strength editors bring to information development.

I like the editing class itself for the way it engages students in guided practice, especially as they work in groups and discuss their work. In workshops and assignments, they solve editorial problems and know how they did it. An engaged and even noisy class, with teacher as consultant when students exhaust their options for solving problems, is a class in which students are learning.

REFERENCES

1. University of Chicago Press, *The Chicago Manual of Style* (13th ed.), University of Chicago Press, Chicago, 1982.
2. R. Van Buren and M. F. Buehler, *The Levels of Edit* (2nd ed.), Jet Propulsion Laboratory, Pasadena, California, 1980.
3. C. D. Rude and R. W. Castle, Technical Editing: A Selected, Annotated Bibliography, in *Teaching Technical Editing,* C. D. Rude (ed.), Association of Teachers of Technical Writing, Lubbock, Texas, pp. 173-204, 1985.
4. L. M. Zook, We Start with Questions: Defining the Editing Curriculum, in *Teaching Technical Editing,* C. D. Rude (ed.), Association of Teachers of Technical Writing, Lubbock, Texas, pp. 3-9, 1985.
5. P. Cheney and D. Schleicher, Teaching Comprehensive Editing: A Proposal for University Writing Programs, in *Teaching Technical Editing,* C. D. Rude (ed.), Association of Teachers of Technical Writing, Lubbock, Texas, pp. 10-20, 1985.
6. D. K. Farkas, Teaching the Administrative and Policy Aspects of Editing, in *Teaching Technical Editing,* C. D. Rude (ed.), Association of Teachers of Technical Writing, Lubbock, Texas, pp. 165-169, 1985.
7. C. Rude and E. Smith, Use of Computers in Technical Editing, *Technical Communication, 39,* pp. 334-342, 1992.

8. D. Dayton, Electronic Editing in Technical Communication: A Survey of Practices and Attitudes, *Technical Communication, 50,* pp. 192-205, 2003.
9. C. D. Rude, *Technical Editing* (4th ed.), Pearson Longman, New York, 2006.
10. M. Corbin, P. Moell, and M. Boyd, Technical Editing as Quality Assurance: Adding Value to Content, *Technical Communication, 49,* pp. 286-300, 2002.
11. M. J. Albers, The Technical Editor and Document Databases: What the Future May Hold, *Technical Communication Quarterly, 9,* pp. 191-206, 2000.

CHAPTER 5

The Editor Within
the Modern Organization

Michelle Corbin

In 1988, I took an intern position (or cooperative education position) at IBM, where I learned about the technical communication practices involved in producing software documentation. In 1989, I became a full-time information developer with IBM, responsible for writing online help systems and printed guides, and I had my first experience with a dedicated technical editor who became my mentor and coach and taught me how to improve my writing and communicate better with our users. After seven years as a technical writer, and after some career counseling, I discovered that the editing or revision process was where I excelled. I left IBM for a position as a development editor at a publishing company that produced retail books on computers and the Internet. In that position, I found my passion and focus for my career. Although that company closed its doors only a few short years later, I took that passion for editing and turned writer positions into writer/editor positions or ultimately simply editor positions. In 1999, I returned to IBM, taking a full-time technical editor position. In the past eight years, I have applied my editing skills and passion, taking on the role of information architect (and sometimes team lead), all the time remaining a technical editor at heart. I present this brief summary of my career to provide a backdrop or foundation to the views and explanations that I offer in this chapter about the editor in the modern organization.

INTRODUCTION

Editing is a fundamental part of any publication process. Editors help writers communicate information to readers by revising and correcting the text, graphics,

67

http://dx.doi.org/10.2190/NPOC5

and other media. Regardless of the subject domain—computer products (software or hardware), marketing or promotional materials, or the news media (newspapers, Internet and the blogosphere, and so on)—editors work to improve the communication with their readers. As Zook states, "A good editor can do useful work in virtually any type of subject matter and any kind of communication product" [1, p. 4].

Kamiya, who works in publishing, describes editors as "craftsmen, ghosts, psychiatrists, bullies, sparring partners, experts, enablers, ignoramuses, translators, writers, goalies, friends, foremen, wimps, ditch diggers, mind readers, coaches, bomb throwers, muses and spittoons—sometimes all while working on the same piece" [2]. Despite the flowery language for some of the labels, even in the technical communication field (and especially in the modern organization) most of these labels still apply. Most notably, though, most editors in working to build a positive, collaborative relationship with their writers would agree with one particular label in that list: coach [3-5]. Their expertise in language and in communicating clearly with their audience makes them a critical member of any information development team.

As I reflect on editors and editing in the modern organization, my experiences in software development organizations influence my views, but the broader industries seem to bear out similar views. All organizations (small, medium, or large)—scientific, academic, marketing, or my own world of software development—have management structures, various positions with different roles and tasks to complete, and everyone all working together to achieve their common goal. Editors are part of the information development team, and the information development team is part of the product team, and the product team is part of the division, which all contribute to the company's bottom line.

PERCEPTIONS OF EDITING

Two perceptions of editing exist today, often within the same organization. The first perception is that editing equates to copyediting or mechanical editing [6, 7]; the second perception is that editing is a quality assurance process [3, 8]. Sometimes these perceptions are mismatched, as Weber describes what people think editors do, what they do, and what they should do [7]. In studying the writer's conceptions about editing through a detailed survey, Eaton discovered that writers held both of these perceptions [9], but that many editors themselves perpetrate both perceptions, often because of limited time and resources.

Although Hackos repeatedly extols editing as a quality assurance process and a best practice for managing information development organizations [3, 10], she also reports too many organizations relegate editing to final copyediting. Hackos states, "Only by elevating the role of quality assurance and making it an essential part of the process can we hope to avoid further inroads into editorial standards" [11]. She even goes so far as to suggest that we need to avoid the title of "editor" or the task of "editing" because of the perceptions [11]. (I'm not willing to go that far, though.)

I strongly believe that editing is a quality assurance process, of which copy-editing is just one type of editing in our arsenal. From the outside looking in to the writing process, most people will think only of their scholastic experiences of the teacher correcting their papers and equate editing to the grammar, punctuation, and basic mechanics. However, from inside the writing process looking out to the rest of the organization, writers and editors (and managers) must advocate and change these perceptions and work to show editing as a quality assurance process that ensures that the information that we produce is easy to use and easy to read.

So Many Types of Editing

Editors in the modern organization rely on many different types of editing to ensure the quality of the information. The classic levels of edit system by Van Buren and Buehler defined nine types [12], but editors continue to work to simplify the number of levels and focus on the most important types of editing that editors can perform for a team. Tarutz defined a more informal set [5], and Rude simplified the levels down to just two types of editing: comprehensive editing and copyediting [4]. Nonetheless, editors define or classify their tasks as a means of providing the most value to their teams and organization.

Almost since the classic levels of edit system was published, editors began encouraging organizations to focus more on content-based editing [3, 4, 6, 8, 13-17], acknowledging the impact or added value that these types of edits have on the quality of the information. Because time and resources are most frequently cited as the reason for doing lower-level, mechanical edits, Nadziejka suggests that editors revise these lower levels of editing and turn away from the rules and mere legal issues to focus on the technical accuracy in the limited time that most editors have [17]. Hackos considers development editing one of her key best practices: "If you are serious about ensuring that information coming from the same corporation or organization or department looks, reads, and is structured consistently, then you need development editing" [3, p. 524].

Most modern organizations develop a levels of edit system that contains several types of edits. Some types, such as policy or legal edits and production edits, will focus on the rules, but the majority of the edits do focus on content and delivering quality technical information. For example, in IBM we have one type of edit, the Editing for Quality (EFQ) edit, that includes an in-process measurement that produces a quality rating for the information [18]. Ultimately, modern organizations need structure and classification to define the work of technical editors.

Planning and Prioritizing the Editing Tasks

Organizations define levels of edit systems for many reasons. Tarutz highlights four reasons: to ensure that your team understands exactly what tasks you'll complete, to establish and track costs for the work, to train and evaluate editors, and to manage schedules by estimating, planning, and prioritizing the editing tasks [5]. Nadziejka describes how "most levels systems are set up so that problems of increasing depth and complexity are addressed as more time or money becomes available," [17, p. 278] which is really his biggest criticism and argument for requesting a revision to the lowest levels of editing containing more content-based editing tasks.

One of the most common reasons organizations develop their own levels of edit systems is to help plan and prioritize the workloads of their writers and editors. Tarutz and Bush both discuss a "triage" system that defines a set of decisions that editors make to determine exactly what editing tasks can be done, given the definition of what should be done (as per the levels of edit system) [5, 13]. Many modern organizations define criteria or information character-istics that help their editors plan and prioritize their workload, usually encour-aging editors to perform the most comprehensive type of editing possible, given the time, resources, and information involved.

Justifying Editors and Editing

Having a defined levels of edit system and a defined set of characteristics by which to plan or prioritize your editing tasks is certainly a best practice within an organization. However, without dedicated editors to perform the editing tasks, you are still fighting the perceptions that editing is mere copyediting (which could even be automated or done by the computer) and that editors are not a required member of the writing team.

Most modern organizations report an ebb and flow to having dedicated technical editors on staff. Hackos reported in 2005 that "there are fewer editors working in departments than there were 5 or 10 years ago" [11]. Later, in 2007, she reiterated that organizations are just not keeping editors on their teams, and instead are making do with peers and others trying to fit in the quality assurance tasks that she highlights as best practices [3]. Establishing corporate standards and processes around technical editing helps in maintaining editing positions within the modern organization.

The ideal ratio of editors to writers seems to be about 1 editor for every 10 to 12 writers. Weber reports her personal experience to be that 1 editor can support 9 full-time writers [19], which does support Hackos's estimate that editing take approximately 15% of the writing time [10, pp. 555-558]. These ratios depend on many aspects of the information development process, such as the type of information (all new information versus lots of legacy information), the number of different products involved, and the types of writers (new writers, experienced writers, or English as a second language [ESL] writers).

Often, teams feel it is a luxury to have a technical editor as part of their team, and they must justify (often repeatedly) the need for technical editors. My response to a request from one of my managers to justify the value of technical editing was to research and write a journal article comparing technical editing to software quality assurance processes; the basic thesis of this article is that software companies do not distribute their product without proper software testing, so why should they distribute their documentation without proper editing [8]. It has proven to be a very powerful argument indeed.

ORGANIZATIONAL SCENARIOS

These perceptions of editing seem to permeate the modern organization, regardless of how technical editors are organized in that organization. Beck believes that we should consider the publishing world (newspapers, journals, retail books, or even novels) and follow the "common principle: *every writer needs an editor*" [20, p. 335]. In most product development environments, where the information or documentation is just one aspect of that product development, it is just not economically feasible that *every* writer have an editor, even though everyone agrees that every writer benefits from having an editor.

To gain a better perspective on how editors are organized in the modern organization, I interviewed a few managers within IBM and a few managers outside of IBM. Although I can speak to my own perspective of working in different organizational scenarios, I think the management perspectives are most interesting. Three organizational scenarios emerge for editors in the modern organization:

- Working across a division
- Working within an information development department
- Working within a department of editors

Working Across a Division

In this organizational scenario, editors focus on writing in general. One editor is responsible for editing all types of content for all types of writers—executives, marketing professionals, product developers, or possibly even technical communicators. These editors support large numbers of writers, covering as much content on as many different products as they possibly can.

This organization is more likely in smaller organizations, where the technical writing function is also a smaller task, but where they still value producing high-quality content for all aspects of their product—from product Web pages, to their marketing messages, to their support organization, to their product documentation. Editors might advertise an "editing boutique," letting people bring whatever type of information needs quality checking. Hiring managers and technical communication professors are encouraging those editors starting out in their careers to evaluate and determine what other roles they might enjoy growing into or adding to their repertoire [21]. The editor might report to the same manager as the technical writers, but the editor might also report to the test department or a different product management department. Unfortunately, because the editor is spread so thin across the division, the editor can likely do mostly copyediting and less substantive or technical editing. Also, peer reviewing or peer editing is much more likely.

Working Within an Information Development Department

In this organizational scenario, editors focus on the quality assurance of the product documentation. Throughout most of my career, I have worked in this organizational scenario the most: I was the editor for a department of technical writers, with all of us reporting to the same manager. The ratio of 1 editor for every 10 to 12 writers is most likely to occur in this scenario, because of the added organizational principle of the average size of most departments in a product development area. Rude describes this organization scenario in her introduction to technical editing [4]. Hackos also speaks to this organizational scenario in discussing mature information development organizations [3].

Because the editor focuses on a few products and one type of information, the editor can complete the most appropriate type of editing for the information, usually completing more developmental edits and technical edits. Additionally, this close alignment of the editor with the technical writers allows the editor to gain subject matter expertise and be a stronger, more valuable technical editor that provides that quality assurance focus for the team [22]. To ensure this deeper knowledge of the product and ensure quality assurance of the information, teams might have more part-time editors who complete other tasks so that quality does not suffer in light of resource constraints [23]. Often, technical editors focus on adding the most value, and lower-level edits are handled by trained peer reviewers, based on a set of standards and checklists developed by the technical editors.

Working in a Group of Editors: Focused on the Discipline of Technical Editing

In this organizational scenario, editors focus on the discipline of editing. This organizational scenario in some cases resembles that found in the publishing industry, although it does not seem to bring teams closer to the principle of every writer getting an editor. Depending on where this discipline-focused or specialization-focused department reports into the overall product development structure, the impact and effectiveness of the editors vary. If the department of editors reports into a centralized information development organization, it likely functions most similarly to working within an information development department; however, if it reports into a different part of the organization, it might function more like the publishing industry, with specialized types of editors (copyeditors, developmental editors, and so on) or more levels of editors available in the career track [24], or it might function more like an editor working across a division.

Because this organizational scenario puts a strong focus on the discipline of editing, editors are less likely to be asked to take on non-editing tasks. Editors more naturally collaborate more closely, often sitting physically together, working together to solve common problems across the product development teams that they are assigned to. Most often, to keep a close connection with the products, they are assigned to specific focus areas or a portfolio of products, to keep their technical product knowledge high. Consistency and communication also seem to happen more naturally, because of the specialization-based organization [24, 25].

CAREER TRACK FOR EDITORS

Probably few technical editors started out as technical editors or set out to be technical editors when applying for or attending college. Most technical editors discover the field, or in my case their passion for the field, after studying or working in another career, often a technical writing or other writing position. I certainly discovered the field after burning myself out as a technical writer, discovering that I loathed the blank page and much preferred the revision process.

Most researchers and most managers seem to agree that a technical editing position is a senior position that requires good writing skills [5, 7, 10, 22]. Zook states this rather definitively:

> I want to be explicit on one point: To be a good editor, one must be a good *writer*, with strong, versatile, and flexible language skills. Someone whose writing is only (shall-we-say) "adequate" may learn to handle routine copy editing duties but will not be able to provide solid help to an author or to do substantive editing when that is appropriate [1, p. 2].

But being a good technical editor is more than just being a good writer—both hard skills and soft skills are necessary. Certain skill sets can lead you to become an editor, and ultimately can lead you to become an excellent technical editor, but as Tarutz describes, editing is "a mind set, not just a skill set" [5, p. 31]. As you continue to climb the technical career path, the editor role can lead you to other roles and responsibilities.

Skills Required to Be a Successful Editor

To be a successful, effective technical editor in the modern organization, you must acquire both a core set of hard skills and a broad set of soft skills. Hard (core) skills include the aforementioned writing skills and superb sensitivity to language and communication. Other hard skills or core skills that most modern organizations are likely to require include information design skills, graphic arts skills, project management skills, and time management skills [5-7]. Hayhoe discusses just how important these core skills will be going forward with all the new ways of producing technical information [26]. In addition, editors often learn skills that are specific to an environment. For example, editors in an enterprise software development environment must learn a certain amount of programming skills, science and medical editors must ensure manuscripts adhere to the scientific method and the scientific insistence on provable truth, and editors who work for government agencies might have to juggle conflicting meanings of "the public good."

No list of skills stops with these hard skills. Everyone always includes soft skills or other skills they feel are critical to success. These include analytical and problem-solving skills, negotiating skills, diplomacy and tact, an ability to learn quickly, an ability to coach and teach, patience, attention to detail, and the list goes on [5-7, 27]. Tarutz goes so far as to suggest a set of soft skills that lead to an editor's mindset that differentiates an editor; these skills include empathy, restraint, good judgment, adaptability, flexibility, persuasion, and decisiveness [5]. Editors will not succeed if they cannot negotiate critical changes, mandate change respectfully, communicate both up and down the chain of command, or adapt and persevere. Perhaps these soft skills are needed across the teams and organization, but editors require them even more than ever.

On Becoming an Editor

In the modern organization, few technical editors start out as technical editors but instead mature into that role as they progress through their career. Unless the editor is doing just copyediting (that pesky perception most organizations are continually fighting against), the technical editor role is seen as a senior-level position that one attains later in their career. (Degrees are offered in technical communication, offering many different courses in technical writing but only a few in technical editing.) Ultimately, editors must gather not just the core and soft skills to be a good editor, but also technical expertise and an authority.

Many (some might say most) transition from being a writer to being an editor, but you might see teachers or Webmasters or others with strong language skills transition into a technical editing career. In 2006, I initiated a discussion on the STC Technical Editing SIG discussion list to try to discover how technical editors learn how to edit, and I summarized the results of that discussion in a newsletter article in 2007; our members most frequently stated college courses, community courses, and conference sessions in editing but also in writing, because "understanding the writer's perspective was critical to being a good editor" [28, p. 7].

In researching how one becomes an editor, I discovered a discussion thread in the STC Forum where someone asked about the career path for a technical editor. Ann Wiley responded, recounting a story from a fellow technical editor that the best way "to advance is to simply progress, from one great publication to another" [29]. If you truly want to be an editor and focus only on the technical editing discipline, then this seems to be sage advice.

Although a publishing house might offer a more traditional career track of moving from copyeditor, to development editor, to acquisitions editor, this is not a typical career track for an editor in the modern organization. Technical editors certainly advance in a technical career path (performing a variety of types of edits) from one level to the next, but modern organizations might have fewer junior or entry-level editor positions, or the higher-level positions might require that editors take on additional roles, such as information architecture or overall leadership development [30].

"Editor-Slash" Roles

In the modern organization, as you move higher in the technical career track, you are more likely to take on additional roles and responsibilities, expanding or applying the editing skills or editing mindset in broader and more strategic ways. I refer to these new, senior roles as "editor-slash" roles, or roles that incorporate two roles in one: editor/writer, editor/ information architect, editor/project manager, editor/manager, and so on. I guess I'm not willing to give up the role of editor as I progress in my career, so instead I tack on a second one after a slash.

Although I see these editor-slash roles as a natural progression of an editing career, especially editor/architect, Dayton's survey on online editing techniques reported some interesting statistics on editor-slash roles: 33% reported that they were writers/editors, 26% reported that they were writers who routinely did peer editing (I'd call them writers/editors), and 10% reported that they were editors/managers [31, p. 198]. Even back in 1992, Tarutz reported that many organizations combine the writing and editing functions into one role [5, p. 364]. This same ebb that Hackos [3, 11] reported is reflected in the self-reporting of roles in Dayton's survey.

Smaller organizations or smaller teams within organizations might offer the editor/manager role for senior technical editors. Hackos [10] certainly refers to this possible role (more as a project manager than a people manager), as does Farkas [32]. If editors aspire to go into management instead of remain in the technical career track, it might be possible to maintain editing responsibilities and the editor/manager role (or perhaps it'd be the manager/editor role, with the editing responsibilities being secondary to the management responsibilities). However, this dual role responsibility has "inherent friction" built in, as writers worry more about their performance review when their manager is also their editor [21].

The most obvious or natural editor-slash role is the editor/information architect role. Because of the popularity and ubiquitousness of the Internet and the Web, the role of information architect has evolved as a common role for technical communicators [33, 34], who naturally work with the structure, organization, retrievability, classification, and usability of technical information. If nothing else, editors must work closely with the information architects to ensure that the architecture is implemented and delivered [35]. Many similarities exist between the different types of editing (developmental editing, usability editing, technical editing, and so on) and many of the information architecture tasks for organizing, structuring, and classifying technical information. Even more so than technical writers, technical editors flow naturally into the role of information architect, because they must fully understand users and often are the only ones who review the complete set of information.

EDITORS AND EDITING IN THE FUTURE

Many technical editors have taken the time to ponder the future of technical editors and editing. In 1992, Tarutz included a chapter in her book on technical editing titled "Is Editing Becoming Obsolete?" and pondered whether software might replace editors; she reiterated, "to survive as an editor, you need to add value, acquire new skills, and educate your managers" [5, p. 366]. (Once again, we fight the perception that technical editing is no more than copyediting.) In 1995, Bush discussed the notion of sequential collaboration versus simultaneous collaboration, and how more and more people will participate in the editing tasks [13, pp. 6-7]. In 2007, Hayhoe pondered the future of technical writing and technical editing, given the new delivery of information on the Web, in multimedia, and from single-sourcing, and ultimately concluded, "I am more convinced than ever of the centrality of these skills" [26, p. 282].

So what do I see when I look into the future? What challenges and opportunities await technical editors in the modern organization? Today, I see technical editors wrestling with these environments:

- A fluidity of how information is delivered, including modular or single-sourcing writing environments
- A fluidity of how frequently our information is published, adopting and adapting to iterative and agile development processes
- Collaborative writing environments, where information is influenced by the latest Web technologies, allowing users themselves to add and edit information in knowledge bases, wikis, and blogs.

Modular or Single-Sourced Writing Environments

More than ever, the technologies that writers use to generate information are influencing and impacting the tasks of technical editors. Most notably, XML technologies enable writers to create modular documentation and single-sourced information. "Topic-based writing, and the technologies that support it, provide the promise of reuse and many other panacea for producing high-quality product information more quickly, more cheaply, and more easily" [36].

Hayhoe said it best, in considering how writing and editing for single-sourcing is changing how we work:

> In the new world of strategically managed content and single sourcing, much of what we think we know about writing and editing must be relearned. One set of instructions may be assembled from text modules authored by multiple writers over a significant span of time. The context that we take for granted, especially in writing for print, cannot be assumed. And the principles of editing are likewise significantly altered [26, p. 282].

Rockley modifies the role of editor in a "unified content strategy" environment, stating that editors must "not just look at the words, but look at how the information is used to ensure it is written effectively for reuse" [37, p. 417] and that they must expand their skill set to understand content strategies, information models, writing for multiple media and multiple audiences, as well as standard structured writing techniques that XML technologies provide. This focus on content strategies and information models definitely brings the tasks of the information architect into the editor's domain, thus supporting that editor/architect role.

Hackos [11] suggests that modular documentation might help increase the quality of our information overall because the subject matter experts are more likely to review and test our information. She also emphasizes that because modular documentation is often written by multiple writers, editors play an even more important role in ensuring the quality and usability of that modular or single-sourced information. Corbin and Jenkins echo this thought [36].

In the STC Technical Editing SIG newsletter, Baker analyzes how XML changes the different types of edits that most editors perform, showing how XML allows editors to focus on content and language and less on layout and formatting [38]. Alternatively, Carey, Corbin, and Rouiller suggest that editors must actually learn the XML technology in order to communicate effectively with the writers but also to help the writers deliver the best content possible [39].

One way the role of technical editors has changed for me in IBM is in how I edit topics written in DITA XML (DITA stands for Darwin Information Typing Architecture). DITA provides strong types and specific templates for creating topic-based information (modular documentation). As writers are learning this DITA XML technology, editors often insert their comments directly into the

XML files, recommending or showing the proper structure and tagging, some-times even completing "code reviews" of the DITA XML tagging. This focus on the XML technology is an added task that while might be perceived as focusing on lower-level details really focuses on producing highly structured, highly consumable, and highly reusable information.

Agile or Iterative Development Environments

Related to this single-sourcing or modular writing environment is the agile or iterative development environment, in which writers and editors are working today. O'Connor describes agile development like this: "Each iteration is a miniature software project, including all the tasks necessary to release new functionality in small increments" [40, p. 17]. Agile development is intent on delivering products that are extremely valuable to the users [41]. Gentle suggests that topic-based writing, as well as minimalist writing, is more readily supported in these agile environments [42].

Kuhnen developed an "agile content development manifesto," in the spirit of the agile software development manifesto, that includes these tenets: "individuals and interactions over processes and tools," "examples and illustrations over definitions and prose," "customer collaboration over controlled authorship," and "responding to change over following a plan" [41].

Agile development processes recommend automated testing and test-driven development. Although spell-checking processes, some grammar-checking processes (depending on the quality of your tooling and the rigor of your processes), and now some controlled-language processes (such as acrolinx's automated acrolinx IQ tool, described by Kohl [43]) could be automated, the majority of the types of technical editing cannot be automated. Steinmetz suggests that herein lies the disconnect that technical editors are working to address as we participate more fully on agile development teams [44].

As teams start to apply agile development methodologies, information development teams must adapt to new ways of producing our information. Writers and editors are both getting involved much earlier [45]. Hackos states, "lean and agile approaches to product development place quality assurance at the top rather than the bottom of the list of critical project components" [11]. Editors are performing more developmental edits as a result of this earlier involvement.

Also, editors are realizing now more than ever that not everything must be edited, that some writing (and therefore editing) is "thrown away" as a natural part of iterative development, and that editing schedules are much more fluid. Because of the dynamic and hectic nature of agile development environments, having editors work on multiple projects at once is proving to be more difficult, possibly leading to more writer/editor roles.

Collaborative or Social Writing Environments

One step beyond the agile or iterative development environments is the collaborative or social writing environments brought about by the latest trends in Web and Internet technologies. In discussing the impact of Web 2.0 technologies on technical communication, Hoffman says, "The evolution of the Internet from a static collection of Web pages to a living, breathing, social network is changing the way people write, edit, and interact with content" [46, p. 7].

The very nature of blogs, wikis, and other collaborative writing environments invites anyone to be a writer, editor, and publisher. In discussing his agile content development manifesto, Kuhnen includes customer collaboration as one of the tenets, stating "The proliferation of customer-written wikis and blogs are evidence of customers' willingness to contribute to the body of content about virtually any subject or product" [41]. Gentle presents some ideas about what type of product documentation might benefit from being presented in a wiki, such as reference information, knowledge-base (support) information, and possibly some task information [47, p. 18]. She suggests that we "call on those with a vested interest in maintaining the quality of the content—for example, customer support personnel, developers, and marketing staff. Build your own gang of editors among users who love the content and help keep it fresh" [47, p. 19].

Writing within the traditional publishing industry, Kamiya suggests, "In the brave new world of self-publishing, editors are an endangered species" [2]. However, he goes on to say:

> Editors and editing will be more important than ever as the Internet age rockets forward. The online world is not just about millions of newborn writers exulting in their powers. It's also about millions of readers who need to sort through this endless universe and figure out which writers are worth reading. Who is going to sort out the exceptional ones? Editors, of some type [2].

Talking about the implications for product development environments, Brown definitely sees a shift in the roles of writers and editors—there is a "shift in our jobs from content creation toward developing the framework to support content creation," including these collaborative or social writing environments [48]. The editor-slash role of editor/architect seems to be one that is critical in this collaborative and social writing environment.

Clearly, writers are taking on new roles in this collaborative and social writing environment, so what does this mean for the traditional technical editor? Will more writers simply become editors such that we'll have more editors? Will the competition for editor positions be fierce because of this transition of the writer's role? Will the role of the editor become an even more senior position, overseeing all new editors in this collaborative and social environment? To be honest, I think only time will tell, as we more fully integrate these types of writing environments into the more traditional product documentation environments that exist in the modern organization.

THE EVER-CHANGING AND EVER-EVOLVING ROLE OF THE TECHNICAL EDITOR

The role of the technical editor in the modern organization is evolving. As a matter of necessity, the role is growing and changing with the technologies, the fast-paced processes, and the new growing and social writing environments. As much as the role changes, though, it remains grounded in its traditional publishing roots. Ludwig describes journalism editors as guardians, historians, questioners, coaches, teachers, leaders, gatekeepers, thinkers, advocates, writers, artists, managers, ethicists, and democrats [49]. I believe that as we participate in the whirlwind evolution, we must remember where we came from.

Kamiya in his praise of editors says:

> The art of editing is running against the cultural tide. We are in an age of volume; editing is about refinement. It's about getting deeper into a piece, its ideas, its structure, its language. It's a handmade art, a craft. You don't learn it overnight. Editing aims at making a piece more like a Stradivarius and less like a microchip. And as the media universe becomes larger and more filled with microchips, we need the violin makers [2].

To be these violin makers, we must embrace our role as technical editor. We must live our passion for quality in every mark or comment that we make. Let us work together to put the perception that editors are mere copyeditors to rest once and for all and allow the perception that technical editors are quality assurance professionals to shine. And, finally, we must focus on developing the soft skills and the editor's mindset. These skills will allow us to grow into editor-slash roles, such as editor/architect, so that we can more fully participate in the brave new worlds of modular, iterative, and social writing environments. But, again, we must keep the heart of a technical editor.

REFERENCES

1. L. M. Zook, The Defining Effort: An Introduction, in *Technical Editing: Basic Theory and Practice*, C. F. Kemnitz (ed.), Society for Technical Communication, Washington, D.C., pp. 1-5, 1994.
2. G. Kamiya, Let Us Now Praise Editors, *Salon.com*, July 24, 2007. Available online at: http://www.salon.com/opinion/kamiya/2007/07/24/editing/print.html
3. J. T. Hackos, *Information Development: Managing Your Documentation Projects, Portfolio, and People*, Wiley Publishing, Inc., Indianapolis, Indiana, 2007.

4. C. D. Rude, *Technical Editing* (4th ed.), Pearson Longman, New York, 2006.
5. J. A. Tarutz, *Technical Editing: The Practical Guide for Writers and Editors*, Addison-Wesley, Reading, Massachusetts, 1992.
6. L. K. Grove, When the Basics Aren't Enough: Finding a Comprehensive Editor, *IEEE Transactions on Professional Communication, 37*, pp. 171-174, 1994.
7. J. H. Weber, The Role of the Editor in the Technical Writing Team, *Technical Editors' Eyrie*, 2002. Available online at: http://jeanweber.com/newsite/?page_id=25
8. M. Corbin, P. Moell, and M. Boyd, Technical Editing as Quality Assurance: Adding Value to Content. *Technical Communication, 49*, pp. 286-300, 2002.
9. A. Eaton, P. E. Brewer, T. C. Portewig, and C. R. Davidson, Examining Editing in the Workplace from the Author's Point of View: Results of an Online Survey, *Technical Communication, 55*, pp. 111-139, 2008.
10. J. T. Hackos, *Managing your Documentation Projects*, John Wiley & Sons, New York, 1994.
11. J. T. Hackos, Quality is Essential, *CIDM Information Management News*, June 2005. Available online at:
http://www.infomanagementcenter.com/enewsletter/200506/feature.htm
12. R. Van Buren and M. F. Buehler, *The Levels of Edit* (2nd ed.), Jet Propulsion Laboratory, Pasadena, California, 1980.
13. D. W. Bush and C. P. Campbell, *How to Edit Technical Documents*, Oryx Press, Phoenix, Arizona, 1995.
14. D. Bush, A Course in Content Editing, *Intercom, 47*:10, pp. 36-37, 2000.
15. D. Bush, The Other Kind of Editing, *Intercom, 47*:6, pp. 40-41, 2000.
16. D. Bush, Still Another Rule? *Intercom, 47*:8, pp. 36-37, 2000.
17. D. E. Nadziejka, Needed: A Revision of the Levels of Editing, *Technical Communication, 42*, pp. 278-283, 1995.
18. E. Wilde, M. Corbin, J. Jenkins, and S. Rouiller, Defining a Quality System: Nine Characteristics of Quality and the Editing for Quality Process, *Technical Communication, 53*, pp. 439-446, 2006.
19. J. H. Weber, Question Time: Ratio of Writers to Editors, *Technical Editors' Eyrie, 6*, 1999. Available online at: http://www.jeanweber.com/news/tenews6.htm#q6
20. C. E. Beck, Every Writer needs an Editor: A Paradigm for Writing in Business, Industry, and Education, *Technical Communication, 42*, pp. 335-339, 1995.
21. G. Romaine, Personal communication, May 2, 2008.
22. L. Fisher, Personal communication, February 27, 2008.
23. F. Eldredge, Personal communication, February 29, 2008.
24. P. Moell, Personal communication, March 4, 2008.
25. D. Sutarno, Personal communication, February 29, 2008.
26. G. F. Hayhoe, The Future of Technical Writing and Editing, *Technical Communication, 54*, pp. 281-282, 2007.
27. C. E. Putnam, Myths about Editing, in *Technical Editing: Basic Theory and Practice*, C. F. Kemnitz (ed.), Society for Technical Communication, Washington, D.C., pp. 7-10, 1994.
28. M. Corbin, Learning How to Edit, *Corrigo, 7*:1, p. 7, Mar. 2007. Available online at: http://www.stc-techedit.org/

29. A. Wiley, Career Path of a Technical Editor, Mar. 29, 2007. Message posted to http://stcforum.org/viewtopic.php?pid=2960
30. S. Benham, Personal communication, April 3, 2008.
31. D. Dayton, Electronic Editing in Technical Communication: A Survey of Practices and Attitudes, *Technical Communication, 50*, pp. 192-205, 2003.
32. D. K. Farkas, Professional and Informal Editing in Complex Organizations, in *Communications: A Means of Exchange, Record of the Proceedings of the 1984 Canadian Regional Business and Technical Communication Conference*, R. C. Scott (ed.), pp. 3-10, 1984.
33. A. L. Ames and M. Corbin, Information Architecture: Contributing Strategically to the Success of Our Customers and our Businesses, *Technical Communication, 54*, pp. 11-15, 2007.
34. M. G. Haynes, Information Architecture: You Do It, You Just Don't Know It, *Intercom, 50*:4, pp. 4-7, 2003.
35. L. Kowalski, A. Ames, M. Corbin, and D. McCaleb, Integrating Information Architecture into Your Information Development Processes, *Proceedings of STC's Annual Conference*, Society for Technical Communication, Arlington, Virginia, pp. 328-333, 2004.
36. M. Corbin and J. Jenkins, Topic-based Authoring: It's Not All About the Technology: Why Content Is King and Technical Editors Are Critical to Topic-based Authoring, *Information Management News: A Monthly e-Newsletter from the Center for Information-Development Management, 5*:6, June 2005. Available online at: http://www.infomanagementcenter.com/enewsletter/200506/second.htm.
37. A. Rockley, *Managing Enterprise Content: A Unified Content Strategy*, New Riders, Indianapolis, Indiana, 2003.
38. J. Baker, The Impact of XML on Technical Editing, *Corrigo, 8*:1, pp. 1-3, 2008. Available online at:
http://www.stc-techedit.org/
39. M. Carey, M. Corbin, and S. Rouiller, Editing DITA Topics: The Changing Role of the Technical Editor in the Age of DITA and Topic-based Authoring, *Best Practices: A Publication of The Center for Information-Development Management, 9*:6, pp. 129, 133-135, December 2007.
40. V. O'Connor, Agile Development: Challenges and Opportunities, *Intercom, 54*:2, pp. 16-18, February 2007.
41. E. Kuhnen, Excellent and Consistent Content Development Through Agile and Scrum, *The Content Wrangler*, 2008. Available online at:
http://www.thecontentwrangler.com/article/excellent_and_consistent_content_development_through_agile_and_scrum/
42. A. Gentle, Writing End-user Documentation in an Agile Development Environment, 2007. Available online at:
http://justwriteclick.com/2007/07/02/writing-end-user-documentation-in-an-agile-development-environment/
43. J. Kohl, Case Study in Controlling Documentation Quality with Acrocheck: Assisted Writing and Editing at SAS, *The Content Wrangler*, 2008. Available online at:
http://www.thecontentwrangler.com/article/case_study_in_controlling_documentation_quality_with_acrocheck_assisted_wri/
44. D. Steinmetz, Personal communication, February 29, 2008.

45. C. Frakes, Documentation Development in an Agile World, *IEEE Professional Communication Society Newsletter, 52*:4, April 2008. Available online at: http://ewh.ieee.org/soc/pcs/newsletter/archive/2008/pcsnews_apr2008.pdf
46. K. M. Hoffman, Writing and Web 2.0, *Intercom, 54*:1, pp. 4-7, January 2007.
47. A. Gentle, The "Quick Web" for Technical Documentation, *Intercom, 54*:8, pp. 16-19, September/October 2007.
48. K. Brown, Implications of Web 2.0, *IEEE Professional Communication Society Newsletter, 52*:2, February 2008. Available online at: http://ewh.ieee.org/soc/pcs/newsletter/archive/2008/pcsnews_feb2008.pdf
49. M. D. Ludwig, And Now, a Word (or 14) about Editors: They're More Than Just the Hacks in the Corner, *Poytner online*, 2005. Available online at: http://www.poynter.org/content/content_view.asp?id=89723

CHAPTER 6

Copyediting and Beyond

Jean Hollis Weber

What technical copyeditors do and how they do it is changing rapidly and dramatically with the emergence of online methods of both production (writing and editing) and delivery of technical materials.

Definitions of *copyediting* generally focus on "correcting" written material and preparing it for publication. This emphasis obscures a range of other contributions that copyeditors can—and should—make to the development and publication of documents.

This chapter looks at past and present roles of technical copyeditors and the tools we use and speculates on our future.

WHAT IS COPYEDITING?

Copyediting is the process of reviewing information to improve organization, content, accuracy, completeness, correctness, coherence, methods of presentation, literary and pictorial quality, consistency, retrievability, ease of use, and suitability for the audience.

This definition expands upon the traditional description of *copyedit*: "To correct and prepare (a manuscript, for example) for typesetting and printing" [1].

The Traditional View of Copyediting

A typical approach to technical editing is that taken by Carolyn Rude, who divides editorial tasks into two main categories: *copyediting* and *comprehensive editing* [2]. Although this is a convenient and useful way to organize the teaching of a range of tasks and skills, in practice many aspects of comprehensive (or substantive) editing overlap in important—often essential—ways with copyediting,

85

http://dx.doi.org/10.2190/NPOC6

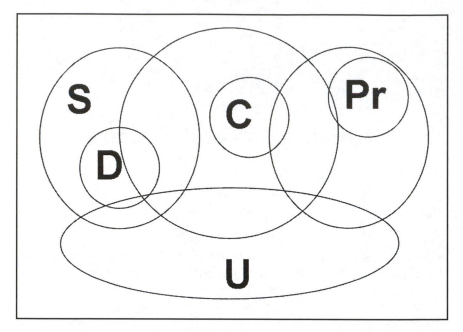

Figure 1. Relationships among various categories of editing. S = Substantive editing, D = Developmental editing, C = Copyediting, P = Production editing, Pr = Proofreading, U = Usability editing.

not least because many employers, managers, and clients think that a narrower definition of *copyediting* is synonymous with *editing*.

Rude says, "The copyeditor adds value to the content by making the text correct, consistent, accurate, and complete. The copyeditor also marks the text for page design" [2, p. 107]. However, she also notes that a document may achieve the four criteria and yet not meet the needs of its audience. Editors must also "consider a document's concept and content, organization, design, and style" [2, p. 231].

Relationship with Other Categories of Editing

Copyediting overlaps with other categories of editing, as shown in Figure 1.

Substantive Editing

Substantive editing (also known as *comprehensive editing*) focuses on the document's logic and structure and includes its concept and intended use, content, organization, design, and style. The purpose is to make the document functional for its readers, not just to make it correct and consistent. Does it all fit together into a coherent whole? Is the order of presentation logical from the target audience's point of view? Is all the necessary information included and unnecessary information deleted? Substantive editing may involve restructuring or rewriting part or all of a document, particularly when the original author is no longer available (as is common on software documentation projects, for example).

Developmental editing, a subset of substantive editing, occurs during the planning and development of the document.

Language editing overlaps both substantive editing and copyediting. It is concerned with how ideas are expressed: for example, sentence complexity and use of active or passive verbs; conciseness; clear, logical development of ideas; and the use of jargon or technical terms.

Production Editing

Production editing focuses on formatting issues and the appearance of the document. With online publications in particular, it may include components of usability editing. The production editor ensures that the book follows the formatting guidelines, using the specified template and applying the correct styles (headings, paragraphs, lists, and so forth); checks page elements, such as headers, footers, and page numbers; verifies that the index and table of contents include correct page numbers and wording and cross-references refer to the correct heading, figure, or table; and looks for poor page breaks, typesetting errors, and a variety of other problems that can occur when a manuscript is converted from a word-processing program to a page-layout or Web-layout program. Copyeditors are often called upon to do this work, especially when layout is done simultaneously with writing, as is common for user guides produced by software vendors.

Proofreading

Proofreading, traditionally the practice of reading a proof (typeset) copy of a document in order to detect and correct any typographic or formatting errors in transcription from the manuscript, is a subset of production editing. The term is often used as a synonym for *copyediting*. The two are separate but overlapping activities, but in modern practice they are often combined; the combined role may be called "editorial proofreading."

Usability Editing

Usability editing overlaps the other classifications, as it is concerned with the suitability of a document to meet its readers' needs in terms of organization, presentation, word use, and other factors. Usability issues include terminology, icons, design of the table of contents, design of the internal navigation scheme (if online), design of the index, page design, writing style, and the use and presentation of lists, tables, and diagrams to supplement or replace prose.

Usability testing is a familiar term in Web site design, but less so for printed materials, even though many documents—particularly those, such as user guides and repair manuals, that provide instructions—would benefit greatly from such testing.

Although usability testing is ideally planned and conducted by trained testers, in reality editors are often the only people available to do the job. Editors also often act as de facto usability testers, as they find ambiguous statements, query missing information, and otherwise attempt to make sense of written material.

Michelle Corbin and others discuss aspects of usability editing and its importance in quality assurance, with emphasis on retrievability and accessibility of information [3]. Steve Krug describes how to conduct tests on Web sites [4, Chapter 9]; his principles apply equally to printed materials. I provide some details on planning, timing, and conducting tests which can be readily adapted to an editing environment [5, Chapter 11].

THE COPYEDITOR'S ROLE

The copyeditor's role varies depending on the industry. Traditional book and magazine publishers generally have a well-defined hierarchy of editors (including such roles as acquisitions editor, managing editor, and proofreader; see the Bay Area Editors' Forum for one set of descriptions), but most technical writing and editing is done outside the traditional publishing circles [6]. In my experience, software and hardware companies often expect authors to cover all steps of writing, editing, layout, and production of user guides or online help; or they have only one person who handles a range of editing jobs, with varying degrees of authority.

Not only is the editor's role defined differently in different organizations, but too often that role is poorly defined, not always explained to the people the editor will be working with, not seen as needing serious management support, and not seen as requiring authority appropriate to the responsibility level. In short, copyediting is often viewed as an optional extra or as a mainly clerical task that can be assigned to an untrained junior employee.

Types, Levels, and Degrees of Edit

A classic definition of technical editing tasks is given in Van Buren and Buehler's 1980 pamphlet "The Levels of Edit," which divides technical editing into nine types and five levels [7]. The classifications they described became a de facto standard for technical editors and are still very useful for describing the range of duties. However, many people found the nine types either too detailed or encouraging the wrong emphasis. For example, a substantive edit is included only in a Level 1 edit (the most thorough), thus reinforcing the idea that quality objectives can be achieved without it.

Other people have simplified Van Buren and Buehler's list of copyediting tasks into *degrees* of edit: *light* (the editor reads the document quickly, correcting obvious errors in spelling, grammar, punctuation, consistency, and completeness), *medium* (the editor and the client agree on what level of edit, in addition to a light edit, will be done), and *heavy* (the editor covers all the levels of edit, including substantive). The Bay Area Editors' Forum elaborates on the levels in this classification scheme; their pages are valuable reference material for editors negotiating exactly what they are expected to do.

Many editors have noted that all of these classifications put little or no apparent emphasis on the content itself: its accuracy and its suitability for the target audience. In 1999, David E. Nadziejka proposed a different system, dividing the levels of edit into rush, standard, and revision, with at least some attention to technical content at each level [8].

Rarely is enough time available to polish a document to perfection, so editorial changes should be prioritized by their importance. Priority 1 (Essential) changes must be made because content is factually incorrect, unclear, or ambiguous and may lead to serious misunderstanding. Priority 2 (Important) changes improve the writing or presentation but are not essential to understanding. Priority 3 (Nice to have) changes are ones that the vast majority of the audience won't care about or may not even notice. Many consistency issues are in this category.

Rules-based and Analysis-based Editing

Editing can also be divided into *rules-based* and *analysis-based* edits. This scheme overlaps the others by providing a clear way to determine which editorial decisions are negotiable with the writer and which are not negotiable.

Rules-based editing covers ways to make a document correct, consistent, accurate, and complete, using standards and guidelines specified by the company. Examples include spelling, grammar, punctuation, capitalization, and hyphenation; adherence to legal requirements (copyright, trademarks, and so forth); internal consistency, typically having to do with design (typography, layout, and illustrations); and the form of bibliographic references and citations. Rules-based editing is usually not negotiable: the editor enforces the rules.

Analysis-based editing covers the process of evaluating a document for concept, content, organization, form, and style, to make it more functional and appropriate for its readers. Much analysis-based editing should be negotiable: the editor should suggest improvements rather than make corrections. Editing for logic and structure is almost entirely analysis-based, whether at the document level or at the paragraph, sentence, or word level. This type of editing includes language and substantive edits.

COPYEDITING AS QUALITY ASSURANCE

Copyediting includes many quality-assurance aspects, as do other forms of technical editing. Several books and papers address such issues as: What constitutes quality in writing? Can quality be measured, and if so, what metrics (numbers) are useful? How can editors contribute to quality?

Gretchen Hargis and others provide a thorough and practical discussion of factors contributing to quality technical information, with examples and checklists [9]. Elizabeth Wilde and others, building upon Hargis' nine characteristics of quality information, describe a standard editing process that produces a measurement of information quality [10].

Defining and measuring quality can be valuable, but the process often places too much emphasis on easily measured items (such as grammar, word lists, sentence length, consistency of presentation, and parallelism) while avoiding less easily measured items such as usability.

Standards, Guidelines, and Templates

Some reasons to use standards, guidelines, and templates include to ensure documents conform to corporate image and policy, including legal requirements; to inform new writers and editors of how things are done in the organization; to define what's negotiable; to improve consistency within and among documents, especially when more than one writer is involved; and to remove the necessity to "reinvent the wheel" for every new project.

Editors often use style guides such as Chicago or APA or publications from Sun or Microsoft [11-14]. Many organizations develop their own corporate style guides.

Standards are usually nonnegotiable and enforced by the editor, while *guidelines* may be either rules (nonnegotiable) or suggestions and examples (negotiable between the writer and the editor). However, usually rules and suggestions are mixed up in the same document (often called a "guide" or "guideline"), and it's not always easy to determine what is negotiable and what is not. Which items should be rules and which should be suggestions is a matter of opinion and corporate policy.

Templates are an effective means of assisting writers and editors in applying specific layout choices, particularly page and paragraph styles, and providing guidance on the sequence and structure of required information. This latter use is particularly important when numerous authors are contributing to a database of information from which Web pages or user guides will be compiled.

Style Guides and Style Sheets

Mark Bright describes a process for creating, implementing, and maintaining corporate style guides. His article "provides recommendations for gaining management support, determining content, encouraging employee buy-in, and maintaining" the style guide [15, p. 42].

Corporate style guides may contain both *design* information and *style* information.

Design decisions may be made at a corporate level, with writers and editors required to follow those decisions; or page layout and typesetting may be done by some other staff in the company. This way of working is typical of the publishing industry and of Web site production, but may be unfamiliar to many people who work in the computer software industry. However, even software documentation is changing; information content is increasingly being stored in databases for reuse in a variety of situations and media.

When layout and design are done by people other than the writer and editor, the most an editor might need to know is which style name to use for which purpose. However, if editors are responsible for the final layout of the document they are working on, they need to be familiar with (and follow) the design guide in detail.

Style guides should contain topics such as these:

- The version of English (American? international?) and any variations
- The system of measurement (American? metric?) and whether conversions should be included in parentheses
- The capitalization style for headings, vertical lists, figure and table captions, and other situations.
- The punctuation style for running lists and vertical lists
- What wording to use for cross-references within the document and to other documents
- Whether and when illustrations and tables need captions and whether they must always be referenced in the text
- When to use bold or italics type
- When to spell out numbers, when to use numerals, the use of commas or spaces in numbers over 999
- Word use (for example, company-specific or product-specific terms, acronyms and abbreviations, and words to be avoided)
- Whether the singular "they" is acceptable
- Glossaries, bibliographies, and footnotes—what style, and when to use
- How to indicate and acknowledge trademarks

Style sheets supplement the style guide, if there is one. Editors use them to record decisions made for a particular product or publication, especially those details not covered by the style guide, both for their own reference and for the writer or another editor.

AVOIDING THE GRAMMAR TRAP

Too many copyeditors focus on the details and don't pay enough attention to the bigger picture. Some reasons for an editorial focus on details have to do with editors themselves; other reasons arise from the perceptions and priorities of managers and writers.

From my observations, many copyeditors know how and want to contribute substantively, but they don't have time—or aren't allowed—to do so. Some are more comfortable enforcing rules than making critical suggestions and then dealing with writers and others who may not appreciate those suggestions. Still others don't believe they can contribute substantively because they haven't been trained in substantive editing or they aren't sufficiently familiar with the subject matter they are editing.

Many managers, writers, and other clients believe one or more of the following statements: "Editors are obsessed with nitpicky details; that's what editing is all about." "A copyeditor's job does not include substantially revising a writer's work or commenting on the technical content or usability of that work." "Substantive, technical, and usability editing take too long and cost too much." "Editing is done after the manuscript is written, leaving insufficient time to change anything major that an editor might find—so why spend the time and money finding the problems?"

As I describe elsewhere, much of the value that copyeditors can provide is largely ignored or challenged by those managers, writers, and editors who disagree with the idea that there might be something "more important" than getting the grammar correct [16]. Several well-known and respected editorial voices, for example Don Bush, have said much the same: in technical communication, content (and comprehensibility) is more important than formal grammar [17, 18].

How much attention should technical communicators pay to formal rules of grammar, punctuation, and usage? Does informal grammar, punctuation, or usage detract from the value and usability of publications? Does the audience care, or even notice, if formal rules are broken?

Distinguish between Essential, Nonessential, and Fake Rules

Rules of grammar, punctuation, and usage can be essential or nonessential—or even fake. *Essential rules* are those that are necessary for clear, unambiguous communication. *Nonessential rules* are those that are not required for clarity and unambiguity. *Fake rules* may actually be matters of word choice, style, or conventional usage, not rules of grammar; or they may be things many of us were taught were wrong, but which are in fact acceptable variations in usage.

Copyeditors need to pay attention to the essential rules, but can spend less time on nonessential rules—particularly in the face of tight deadlines—and they can ignore the fake rules or choose one variation and apply it consistently.

Examples of Essential Grammar and Punctuation Rules

Use of commas when errors can cause ambiguity or misunderstanding. However, note that not all comma errors lead to ambiguity, and some comma usage varies between U.S. and U.K. English.

Use of apostrophes in possessives and contractions, but not plurals. Incorrect placement of apostrophes changes meaning (often causing confusion or ambiguity) or is completely wrong.

Subject-verb agreement (but see notes on "data" and "they," below). When the subject and verb are separated by many other words, this agreement may be difficult to sort out. Often the best solution is to rewrite the sentence.

Avoiding dangling modifiers, unclear antecedents, and other constructions that can create ambiguity, even when most readers will eventually figure out what's meant.

Examples of Nonessential Grammar and Punctuation Rules

The distinction between "different from," "different than," and "different to."

The use of old forms of English: Use of the subjunctive, the pronoun "whom" as the objective form of "who," and several other somewhat old-fashioned (though correct) forms of English.

Many (but not all) rules about the use of commas: for example, whether to use a comma after an introductory word or (short) phrase or clause; and whether to use a comma before "and" in a run-in list.

The distinction between "which" and "that" in some clauses. Although technically there is a significant difference, in most cases readers will not misinterpret the meaning of the sentence, and conventional usage varies between U.S. English and U.K. English.

Some apostrophe use. For example, does the use of "user's guide," "users' guide," or even "users guide" or "user guide" lead to any confusion or ambiguity? I think not. (But do pick one variation and use it consistently.)

Some rules, such as those about dangling participles and not ending sentences with prepositions, are nonessential because readers can figure out the meaning; but they are still important rules to follow in those cases where following the rule would make the writing easier to understand. For example, split infinitives are acceptable in English ("to boldly go"), but if you replace the adverb ("boldly") with a long adverbial phrase, the meaning becomes more difficult to decipher.

Examples of Fake Grammar and Punctuation Rules

Fake rules include issues such as not using split infinitives or ending a sentence with a preposition. Others are actually matters of style that have been turned into "the way we do things here" rules. These may be important to improve consistency in a company's publications, especially when several writers contribute to a single document, but editors and writers need to recognize them as style choices, not rules of English grammar.

Examples include punctuation order (whether commas and periods go inside or outside a quotation mark, with conventions varying between U.S. English and U.K. English), punctuation and capitalization rules for vertical lists, whether "data" is a singular or plural noun (in computing, "data" is typically collective and singular; in mathematics, it is usually the plural of "datum"), and the rule against using "they/them/their" as a singular indefinite pronoun (in fact, the singular "they" has a long history as being acceptable and is becoming increasingly common).

Focus on Clear Communication

Realize that grammar is important, but policing it is only part of a copyeditor's job. In addition to expunging the usual collection of wordy phrases from documents, copyeditors commonly attempt to tighten up writing to make it more direct, clear, and concise.

John Brogan provides an excellent set of exercises to help writers and editors learn how to tighten up writing effectively; his categories include removing redundancies and ponderous writing, using powerful verbs, and stressing what is important [19]. Another excellent resource is Campbell [20].

COPYEDITING ONLINE CONTENT

Documents intended for online publication have some requirements in common with those published on paper and some requirements that are different.

Differences between Online and Printed Publications

Online and printed publications differ in significant ways that affect the role of the editor.

- The main difference is *hypertext*: text linked together in a complex, non-sequential web of associations in which the user can move through related topics. Online publications may have an easily determined sequence of subject matter, but links within the text or the site navigation allow readers to move through the text in unpredictable ways.

- Online publications may include multimedia components (audio, video, and animated graphics such as Flash) as well as text and static graphics.
- Reading online is generally more difficult than reading printed publications, so people are likely to skim online material looking for what they want.
- Web pages are more likely to be read (or at least visited) by people from a wide variety of cultures, with a range of ability to understand English.
- Web pages can be customized for individual readers or groups of readers by pulling information out of a database as the page is assembled and downloaded, for example in response to a reader's request on a previous page.
- Web pages can be updated more easily and more often, so readers expect them to be up to date.

How People Read Online

Research in the 1980s found that reading from a computer monitor is 25% slower than reading from a printed page [21]. Although this difference has probably changed since then, most people find large blocks and long lines of text more difficult to read onscreen than in print, so they are likely to skim material and jump quickly from one topic to another, looking at headings to decide whether to read the text.

Eyetracking studies have shown how people orient themselves on a page and focus quickly on the part that interests them. "Users typically looked first in the center, then to the left, then to the right" [22]. More recent research on eyetracking shows that users often read Web pages in an F-shaped pattern: two horizontal stripes followed by a vertical stripe [23]. This research shows that users don't read text thoroughly; the first two paragraphs must state the most important information; and subheads, paragraphs, and bullet points need to be started with information-carrying words that users will notice when scanning down the left side of the content.

What Does All This Mean for Copyeditors?

Copyeditors need to do more structural editing; for example, restructuring for skimming: looking at chunking, headings, links, placement of page elements (keeping eyetracking studies in mind), and expanded use of "international" English.

Redish describes four basic types of Web pages: the home page (identifies the site and gives readers an overview of what they can find there), "scan, select, and move on" pages (menu pages below the home page), "scan and get information pages" (where the real content is), and forms pages (to give or verify information) [24].

Redish's third type of page may provide instructional, reference, or procedural information: essays, research reports, news, and other articles. Technical copy-editors are most likely to be responsible for editing these topics.

Often, the copyeditor's only job is to edit the content, not the presentation. Just as in print publishing, editing is often done on material before it goes to the people responsible for layout, or the layout is determined by someone else. Editors might be able to influence some elements of presentation, such as the length of pages or the use of lists, and they might proofread or do production editing on the final version before publication.

The principles of editing for effectiveness apply to online publications as much as to printed publications. A few points are particularly important online, where readers are even more likely to skim, scan, and skip information: organize information into short, logical chunks; use lots of meaningful headings; break up long paragraphs into shorter ones, or turn paragraphs into lists; and rewrite in newspaper style, putting the most important information first, summarizing the main points, and linking to details.

Editing for Online Readability

Guidelines provided by Nielsen, Redish, Hackos and Stevens, Price and Price, and many others suggest that writing for the Web is different from writing for print, but Gregory points out that good practices for writing for print publications apply equally to writing Web pages [21, 24-27]. Gregory suggests that editors should cut out unnecessary words, as long as they don't sacrifice meaning; use short paragraphs and short sentences, to assist scanning; use strong verbs and direct writing; and use alternatives to paragraphs (for example, lists).

Editing Links

Links can be text, graphics, or part of a graphic or image map. Some common linking problems that editors must look out for include poor choice of words, links too close together and thus difficult to tell apart, links too long (more than a few words) or too small (only a few characters), links not easily distinguished from other text, and the use of too many colors to distinguish types of link (for example, links to other Web sites, within the same Web site, and to pop-up definitions).

Some Web pages contain mainly links to other pages; "contents pages" for major subdivisions of a Web site may be of this type. In such situations, editors should ensure that the link text is as informative as possible within the limitation of a few words. Links with descriptions (often presented in a "definition list" format) are recommended for Web pages but can be useful in many other situations as well. Compare the following types of link, each useful in a different situation.

A link without a description, useful in a narrative where the content is clear from the context:

See also Chapter 6.

A link with a bit more information, when the context does not provide it:

See also Chapter 6, "Producing the Table of Contents and Index."

A link with a longer description presented in definition-list form; very good for readers skimming lists of links:

Chapter 6, "Producing the Table of Contents and Index"

Diagnosing problems, what to look for, how to fix problems, and examples of good and bad tables of contents and indexes.

Editing for Layout and Presentation

Some things that an editor should check must be done on the finished product, just as you would check the page proofs for a book. Checking for layout and presentation problems is best done onscreen, not on paper, although you could record your suggested changes on a printout.

At the production editing stage, copyeditors should not be looking for problems with the words. Their focus should be on problems with layout and presentation, such as headings at the wrong level, images in the wrong place, misaligned columns in tables, bad indentation or spacing of numbered or bulleted lists, unreadable color combinations, and links that are difficult to distinguish from other text.

SOME TOOLS OF
THE COPYEDITOR'S TRADE

Until as recently as the early 1990s, copyeditors made marks on paper; these marks were then transferred by the writer or another person (a typist, for example) to the document itself. Since the arrival of word processors, editing has been evolving to a greater use of onscreen editing, with or without change tracking. Geoff Hart's chapter in this book covers this topic in detail.

This section looks briefly at tools in addition to templates, style guides, and style sheets, which were discussed earlier in this chapter.

Checklists are very useful, especially if the list of tasks is in the order of priority for the work to be done. Hargis includes an extensive collection of editorial checklists [9].

Numerous books, articles, and Web sites describe the traditional *proofreaders' marks* used in copyediting and proofreading to indicate changes and markup information (heading levels, for example). These marks are used today only in limited situations. Change tracking and use of styles in word processor files have made handwritten marks largely obsolete; and when handwritten marks are used, in most cases the authors are unfamiliar with the traditional ones, so communication is improved by using a less formal system.

Commonly-used *word processing* software includes a change-tracking feature, and copyeditors can use styles for indicating heading levels and other typographic features. If the document will be loaded into another program for final layout and publication, using the same style names in both programs can assist in the production process.

PDF (Portable Document Format) files are often used for editing and proofing graphics, online help, and Web sites, as well as proofreading final layout for print documents. Recent versions of Adobe Acrobat (particularly the Professional edition) contain tools to assist editors in electronically marking up PDFs with insertions, deletions, and notes or queries. The online help for these tools is extensive. While they may seem unfamiliar and cumbersome at first, most editors soon become accustomed to them. Adobe Acrobat also provides tools to directly edit the text in a PDF. It's generally preferable to edit the source document and then regenerate the PDF, but time constraints sometimes mean that minor changes must be made to the PDF itself.

Some copyeditors may need to be familiar with *graphics tools*. They may need to make changes to graphics, for example to correct a spelling error in a callout or label. Ideally, a graphic artist will incorporate these changes; but again, time constraints or staff shortages sometimes mean the copyeditor must do the job. If at all possible, corrections should be made to the source document (using the same program that created it) and the graphic regenerated in whatever format is required.

The choice of *tools for working with Web sites* depends on a variety of factors, including the available technology, the stage of development of the Web site, the location of the writers and editors, the skill levels of the writers and editors (both in using the tool and in writing or editing), the working environment and its pecking order, and the requirements of auditors.

When content is edited before layout time, the text may be in a word processing program's format, so it can be edited as for print publication, using the word processor's change-tracking feature. If content is created, maintained, or updated from a database, spreadsheet, or other files, those files can be edited using the appropriate software. That software may or, more often, may not have a change-tracking feature. If editors do not have (or know how to use) the necessary software, they may need to use techniques similar to those described below.

- **RTF, DOC, ODT, or other editable files.** The online document can be exported to RTF, DOC (Microsoft Word), ODT (OpenDocument), or another format that a word processor can read and write. The copyeditor inserts changes and comments into the file using change tracking. Someone else then transfers the changes to the online document itself. A variation is to copy text from the online document and paste it into a word processor file for editing.

- **HTML files with text editor.** The copyeditor uses a text editor or word processor to edit a copy of the pages, code and all.
- **PDFs.** The copyeditor uses Adobe Acrobat or a similar program to capture the page as a PDF and then uses Acrobat's tools to electronically annotate it.
- **Screen captures**. The copyeditor uses a screen-capture program or simply presses the Print Screen key on the keyboard to take a picture of problems that show onscreen but not in a PDF or printout of the Web page. Then a graphics program is used to mark changes on the graphic, and the file is sent to the writer or layout person.
- **Web-based collaborative writing and editing tools.** The copyeditor imports or copies the text into the tool (for example, Google Docs), edits, and gives the writer access to the edited document.

WORKING WITH WRITERS

Most articles about the personal aspects of the editor-writer relationship assume that the writer will be the acknowledged author of the work, or that the writer has the final say in accepting or rejecting editorial changes. In many cases this is true, but the importance of preserving the "author's voice" very much depends on industry and context. Many technical books and articles carry their authors' names, but many others do not. Or they are compiled from the contributions of numerous writers and must be massaged into "one voice" by the copyeditor before publication. For example, Rockley summarizes the situation for single-sourcing projects: "The traditional concept of ownership changes in a collaborative authoring environment. While in the past, an author may have been responsible for a product document . . . an author may now be responsible for creating content for a set of common features that appear across multiple products. . . . content that is reused in multiple information products (for example, user guide, help, training)" [28, p. 352]. In some circumstances—such as database delivery of chunks of information—the author's voice becomes increasingly irrelevant and the editor's role more essential.

When copyeditors do need to deal with authors, they should start from a genuine spirit of "let's work together to make this document the best it can be" rather than "I'm correcting your mistakes." Negotiation and collaboration skills are important, as is a constant awareness that authors are—or should be—the technical experts, even if they can't express themselves well in English. These issues become even more critical when dealing with outsourced documentation production, especially when the writers are in another country: whether their native language is English or some other language, their cultural practices and expectations may be quite different. If the outsourced documentation is being written for an audience in the writers' country, the writers may in fact have a much better idea of culturally-appropriate writing styles, word usage, and punctuation than the copyeditor has—and communicating questions, answers, and directions needs to take cultural differences into account.

Numerous articles discuss these relationships and offer suggestions [for example, 29-33]. This section summarizes a few practical aspects of working with writers.

Some typical sequencing scenarios for copyeditors and writers are as follows:

- **The editor marks corrections on a printout of the document, and the writer inserts the changes into the file.** This is the classic situation, which is becoming less common as editors and writers learn that it's far more efficient for everyone to work electronically.
- **The editor types in changes and questions (using the revision feature, so changes are marked), and the file goes to the writer to accept or reject the changes or to request clarification if required.** This method is useful when the writers are experienced or will have their names on the resulting document, or when the writers are inexperienced and markup will assist in their education; it is equivalent to markup on paper.
- **The editor types in questions and changes (without using the revision feature), and the amended file (or a printout or PDF) is returned to the writer to check and answer questions.** This method is useful when the editor is dealing with writers who prefer to see only the revised version or when the software (such as a wiki) does not support easy revision marking.
- **The editor types in changes and questions and discusses the markup with the writer.** This method is useful when training inexperienced writers or those new to the company style, or if the editor has many comments or questions that are best resolved through discussion.
- **The editor provides comments in a separate file or e-mail message and the writer or layout person makes changes to the document.** This method is especially useful for more general comments or things that need to be discussed with the writer, rather than detailed copyediting. It is also used when the editor does not have the appropriate software to edit the file directly.
- **The editor types in changes, and the result goes directly to layout and production.** This method is best when the writer is not available or very fast turnaround is required (for example, with news). It may be used in any situation where the editor has the final say, including in multiple-authoring environments and database storage of information. The writer may proofread a printout of the final layout.

Following are some typical scenarios regarding timing:

- **First-pass copyediting is done before technical reviews.** This method is best when dealing with inexperienced writers or those unfamiliar with the company style, so that the review copy is free of grammatical, spelling, word use, and other errors that might distract the subject matter experts from focusing on the accuracy of the information.
- **Technical reviews are conducted before copyediting.** This method is best when a complex document is likely to be changed substantially by subject matter experts during their review, so that the document is reasonably stable and accurate before it reaches the copyeditor.
- **Copyediting is done on parts of a document rather than the entire document.** Time constraints often mean that the copyeditor must edit pieces of a document separately (often interspersed with other work), rather than receiving the entire document to edit at one time. In this situation, the editor needs a detailed style sheet and must take extra precautions to spot inconsistencies. This method is also common when dealing with documents assembled from chunks of information in a database.

THE FUTURE OF COPYEDITING

Editors and employers need to distinguish between the *means of production* and the *medium of publication*. Much material destined for publication on paper is already being edited electronically; this trend will increase, and the tools used will diversify. At the same time, material destined for online publication may go through some stages of being edited on paper: for example, paper prototypes of online help systems may be developed before any coding is done [5, p. 63].

Web sites, wikis, online help, and interactive tutorials are typical of today's electronic materials. Copyeditors who learn to work with these new publishing forms should find plenty of work; those who don't may find their opportunities more limited.

Another consequence of online publication and multimedia use is the need for more usability editing of the material. Editors who specialize in this field will find an increasing need for their services—though whether employers will recognize the need and be willing for pay for it is another matter.

More Electronic Publication and Multimedia

Books, reports, and other printed technical documents are unlikely to go away, but they are increasingly being provided in electronic form (such as PDF) or supplemented by online documents—primarily help systems delivered with, or embedded in, software—and Web pages in a variety of forms for just about everything.

Web publishing formats include wikis using MediaWiki (http://www.media wiki.org/) and similar software, content management systems such as Plone (http://plone.org/) and Drupal (http://drupal.org/), and blogging software such as WordPress (http://wordpress.org/). These systems store documents in various ways. Copyeditors may need to use a system's Web interface to edit documents stored in the system, or they may edit the documents in more traditional ways before storing them online.

Wikis enable documents to be written and edited in a simple markup language using a Web browser. Although most well-known wikis (such as http://wikipedia.org/) can be edited by anyone, wikis can be password-protected to restrict access to writers and editors.

Because electronic documents can contain audio and video components as well as static text and graphics, editors often need to work with them as well, at least to the extent of determining whether accessibility or other guidelines are met.

More Electronic Editing, Including Web-based

In 2005, Web-based collaborative writing and editing tools—other than wikis and content management systems like Plone and Drupal—were rare. By early 2007, several tools were available, but rudimentary. At the time of writing (early 2009), they are rapidly acquiring such features as change tracking that may make them serious alternatives to word-processing programs—even as those programs are moving online in various guises.

Examples of Web-based "office suite" applications include Google Docs (http://docs.google.com/), Zoho (http://www.zoho.com/), and Thinkfree Online (http://product.thinkfree.com/online). With Google Docs, writers can upload a variety of document types (including HTML, DOC, ODT, and RTF), several people can edit the files within their Web browsers, and the files can be exported to the same range of formats.

More Single Sourcing and Database Storage of Information

Many Web pages are produced "on the fly" by combining chunks of information stored in a database. This trend includes documentation, for example to match a particular set of features or modules (hardware or software) that a customer has purchased. Copyeditors must cope with topics, paragraphs, or even sentences that can be combined in a variety of ways. Challenges include ensuring the chunks are consistent in tone, word usage, and other characteristics, even if they have been written by different people; and ensuring that the chunks make sense in whatever context they may be read.

Database storage is one form of single sourcing, the practice of producing several documents (or the same document in several forms) from one source—a document, series of documents, or database—instead of copying the material into several places and attempting to maintain and update the same information in all those places. The principle of "write once, use often" is becoming increasingly common. Who will ensure all is consistent and fits together into a coherent whole? Editors, of course, including copyeditors. Albers notes, "To maximize the information content, future technical editors require tighter control over information consistency and content" [33, p. 191].

More Editing for International Audiences

As more materials are being produced for the Web, more attention needs to be paid to editing for international audiences, recognizing that the vast majority of the world's speakers of English, including native speakers, often use different conventions from "standard" American English. In addition to minor differences in punctuation and spelling, these differences include measurements (most of the world uses the metric system), date formats (day-month-year or year-month-day instead of month-day-year), telephone numbers (the country code is needed as well as the area code, and many "free call" numbers do not work when calling from a different country), seasons and holidays, sports metaphors, and references to current events or "well-known" people.

Just as important is sensitivity to the vast differences in levels of English comprehension in people whose first language is something else. Many of these people learned English at a very early age and so are quite bilingual. Some people whose first language is not English actually have a much better grasp of English grammar than many native speakers. English as a second language (ESL) does not equate to "poor skills in English." However, idiom, colloquialisms, and slang are often big problems for ESL readers. Copyeditors will need to be even more aware of these issues than they are today.

Finally, cultural awareness is valuable: for example, readers' preferred level of conceptual or instructional detail and the preferred use of illustrations or words varies greatly across cultures [34, 35]. Although editing at this level is more properly the job of a developmental or substantive editor, copyeditors may well be the ones who bring anomalies and inconsistencies to the attention of writers and others.

REFERENCES

1. American Heritage Dictionaries, *The American Heritage Dictionary of the English Language* (4th ed.), Houghton Mifflin, Boston, 2000.
2. C. D. Rude, *Technical Editing* (4th ed.), Pearson Longman, New York, 2006.
3. M. Corbin, P. Moell, and M. Boyd, Technical Editing as Quality Assurance: Adding Value to Content, *Technical Communication, 49*, pp. 286-300, 2002.
4. S. Krug, *Don't Make Me Think* (2nd ed.), New Riders, Berkeley, California, 2006.
5. J. H. Weber, *Is the Help Helpful? How to Create Online Help That Meets Your Users' Needs,* Hentzenwerke Publishing, Whitefish Bay, Wisconsin, 2004.
6. Bay Area Editors' Forum, Definitions of Editorial Services. Available online at: http://www.editorsforum.org/what_do_sub_pages/definitions.php

7. R. Van Buren and M. F. Buehler, *The Levels of Edit* (2nd ed.), Jet Propulsion Laboratory, Pasadena, California, 1980.

8. D. E. Nadziejka, *Levels of Technical Editing*, Council of Biology Editors, Reston, Virginia, 1999.

9. G. Hargis, *Developing Quality Technical Information: A Handbook for Writers and Editors* (2nd ed.), Prentice Hall, Upper Saddle River, New Jersey, 2004.

10. E. Wilde, M. Corbin, J. Jenkins, and S. Rouiller, Defining a Quality System: Nine Characteristics of Quality and the Editing for Quality Process, *Technical Communication, 53*, pp. 439-446, 2006.

11. University of Chicago Press, *The Chicago Manual of Style* (15th ed.), University of Chicago Press, Chicago, 2003.

12. American Psychological Association, *Publication Manual of the American Psychological Association* (6th ed.), American Psychological Association, Washington, D.C., 2010.

13. Sun Technical Publications, *Read Me First! A Style Guide for the Computer Industry* (2nd ed.), Prentice Hall, Upper Saddle River, New Jersey, 2003.

14. Microsoft Corporation, *The Microsoft Manual of Style for Technical Publications* (3rd ed.), Microsoft Press, Redmond, Washington, 2003.

15. M. R. Bright, Creating, Implementing, and Maintaining Corporate Style Guides in an Age of Technology, *Technical Communication, 52*, pp. 42-51, 2005.

16. J. H. Weber, Escape from the Grammar Trap, 2003. Available online at: http://www.jeanweber.com/newsite/?page_id=23

17. D. W. Bush, The Friendly Editor, a column that has run for many years in *Intercom*.

18. D. W. Bush and C. P. Campbell, *How to Edit Technical Documents*, Oryx, Phoenix, Arizona, 1995.

19. J. A. Brogan, *Clear Technical Writing*, McGraw-Hill, New York, 1973.

20. C. P. Campbell, Using Transformational Grammar as an Editing Tool (a paper given at IPCC 95, Savannah, Georgia, on September 29, 1995). Available online at: http://infohost.nmt.edu/~cpc/trangram.html

21. J. Nielsen, *Designing Web Usability: The Practice of Simplicity*, New Riders, Indianapolis, Indiana, 2000.

22. W. Schroeder, Testing Web Sites with Eye-Tracking, September 1, 1998. Available online at: http://www.uie.com/articles/eye_tracking/

23. J. Nielsen and K. Pernice, Eyetracking Research. Available online at: http://www.useit.com/eyetracking/

24. J. Redish, *Letting Go of the Words: Writing Web Content that Works*, Morgan Kaufmann, San Francisco, California, 2007.

25. J. T. Hackos and D. M. Stevens, *Standards for Online Communication*, Wiley Computer Publishing, New York, 1997.

26. J. Price and L. Price, *Hot Text: Web Writing That Works*, New Riders, Indianapolis, Indiana, 2002.

27. J. Gregory, Writing for the Web versus Writing for Print: Are They Really So Different? *Technical Communication, 51*, pp. 276-285, 2004.

28. A. Rockley, Single Sourcing: It's About People, Not Just Technology, *Technical Communication, 50*, pp. 350-354, 2003.

29. J. Mackiewicz and K. Riley, The Technical Editor as Diplomat: Linguistic Strategies for Balancing Clarity and Politeness, *Technical Communication, 50*, pp. 83-94, 2003.
30. I. Leki, The Technical Editor and the Non-native Speaker of English, *Technical Communication, 37*, pp. 148-152, 1990.
31. H. L. Shimberg, Editing Authors' Style—A Few Guidelines, *Technical Communication, 28*, pp. 31-35, 1981.
32. C. R. Lanier, The Implications of Outsourcing for Technical Editing, in *Outsourcing Technical Communication: Issues, Policies, and Practices*, B. Thatcher and C. Evia (eds.), Baywood, Amityville, New York, pp. 147-161, 2008.
33. M. J. Albers, The Technical Editor and Document Databases: What the Future May Hold, *Technical Communication Quarterly, 9*, pp. 191-206, 2000.
34. W. Fukuoka, Y. Kojima, and J. H. Spyridakis, Illustrations in User Manuals: Preference and Effectiveness with Japanese and American Readers, *Technical Communication, 46*, pp. 167-176, 1999.
35. P. Honold, Learning How to Use a Cellular Phone: Comparison Between German and Chinese Users, *Technical Communication, 46*, pp. 196-205, 1999.

CHAPTER 7

The Editor and the Electronic Word: Onscreen Editing as a Tool for Efficiency and Communication with Authors

Geoffrey J. S. Hart

Editing has existed as long as there have been writers. Whether the editor was a spouse staring over one's shoulder ("did you *really* mean to say that?") or the publisher's weary gatekeeper ("it looks interesting, if only we knew what you were trying to say"), some form of reality check has always been necessary. The problem originates in our blindness to the assumptions that shape our own words. As writers, we're intimately familiar with the world within our own head, and it's not always clear how to communicate that world to someone who isn't living in the same head. The medium used to bridge two minds doesn't help: even when the words themselves are clear and follow their dictionary meanings, the manner of their assembly may need work, there may be significant gaps in the content, and understanding the resulting sentences may require knowledge of a great many authorial assumptions not shared by the audience. Also, most words have multiple meanings that vary among audiences and among cultures, making precision difficult. This aspect of human psychology seems unlikely to change. Anyone who's been in a long-term relationship can confirm that even after many years of learning a partner's idiosyncrasies, we fail to communicate dismayingly often. How much harder, then, must it be to communicate with complete strangers?

Although the value of an editor's assistance is clear, the author–editor relationship is often a troubled marriage, and many challenges emerge. These begin with the need for clear communication, since editors (author opinions

http://dx.doi.org/10.2190/NPOC7

notwithstanding) are every bit as human as authors and suffer from the same communication difficulties. The egos of authors and editors add another layer of complexity to the communication. Where the relationship between authors and editors exists within a hierarchical structure, issues of authority and agency further complicate the dialogue [1], and when authors and editors have nearly equal power, consensus must more often be negotiated than imposed. Last, and never to be neglected, there is the difficulty of balancing the author's need to communicate with the reader's need to understand and the editor's responsibility to meet their own need to perform work they'd be proud of.

Editors perform a range of types of editing to help authors communicate. For the surprisingly many authors who have difficulty ordering their thoughts, developmental editing helps them to assemble a clear, effective blueprint and musters the wood and carpenter's tools in one place. Next, after the writing has begun, substantive editing ensures that the pieces fit together, and helps the author position those parts until they can be fixed in place. Copyediting buffs off any rough edges that remain, and prepares the product for its final coat of varnish. Proofreading provides that final polish.

The rapid technological evolution that characterizes modern times seems unlikely to change these basic aspects of who we are and what writers and editors do. Whether we write in cuneiform on damp clay tablets or dictate our thoughts to speech-recognition software on a fast new computer, the same need for a reality check remains, and editors are the professionals who provide that sober second look.

Complicating this task is the information age's demand for ever-increasing efficiency: as the pace of modern life accelerates, deadlines seem ever tighter and the urgency to finish work *now* seems greater than ever before. As a result, heroic efforts are often made to reduce cycle times (for example, [2, p. 196]). Accompanying this context is an ever-increasing trend toward assembly-line writing, most familiarly in the move toward single-source publishing [3-5]. In such an environment, the kind of fine-tuning of text that used to be accepted as standard practice may be eliminated because of time constraints. Indeed, high-pressure workplaces—including some newspapers and many computer and software documentation departments—have dispensed entirely with the time-consuming editorial stage and rely solely on peer review to catch and fix any problems.

Because most words are now being created on the computer, and the *raison d'être* of computers is efficiency, it seems illogical to move words from computer to paper solely to permit editing. As a result, onscreen editing has become increasingly important. (In this chapter, I define *onscreen editing* as any form of editing that uses a computer, rather than pen and paper, to review and revise the text. It doesn't matter whether the text will eventually appear on paper or a computer screen.) The good news is that the many efficiencies of onscreen editing make it easier to give existing editors more time to do their work or even allow managers to restore an editorial stage in workflows that lack one. The bad news is that we've got a long way to go before onscreen editing fulfills its full promise.

To understand where technological evolution has led us, it helps to start by understanding whence we came.

A BRIEF HISTORY OF TEXT PROCESSING

At least as far back as the first Mesopotamian and Egyptian scribes, and more familiarly the stereotypical teams of medieval Christian monks who laboriously copied manuscripts before the invention of the printing press, the creation of documents has been the domain of workers trained specially for this task. By the early 20th century, increasing literacy meant that most educated individuals could write, often many tens of words per minute, but text transcription remained inefficient, and the faster the writing, the less legible the result. The invention of the typewriter improved upon these results, allowing even a moderately skilled typist to produce twice as many legible words per minute as was possible with handwriting, and the beloved image of cowled monks evolved into one of secretarial typing pools, rooms filled with female typists. Because typing paradoxically required considerable skill, while being an activity with little perceived value (now that anyone could do it), creators of information such as managers and engineers and scientists rarely performed this activity. Instead, they scribbled their thoughts on paper and handed them to the typing pool or a personal secretary to clean up. (Many of these early typists eventually became editors because of their hard-won skill at imposing order on authorial chaos.)

In the last half of the 20th century, computers began displacing typewriters, but the social context that had given rise to the typing pool left such pools and their data-entry equivalents a familiar corporate fixture. But early in the computer revolution, the computers used for writing were large and expensive and were thus centralized resources used only by experts. This, combined with organizational inertia, perpetuated the typing pool model. Even once video terminals connected to mainframe computers became widely available (by the early 1980s), making the possibility of modern word processing available to most corporate employees, a large proportion of documents originated on paper and passed through the hands of a roomful of secretaries who spent the day shackled to their typewriters and word processors. By 1971, an estimated one-third of all working women in the United States were working as secretaries [6]. Review and revision were conducted entirely on paper printouts, with the changed text laboriously recopied into the word processor files in a process even the earliest scribes would have instantly recognized. Authors and editors then reviewed the printouts to ensure that their changes had been correctly implemented, marked any errors on the printout, and then returned the corrected typescripts to the typists, repeating the process *ad nauseam* until the manuscript was perfect.

As computer technology became increasingly powerful and inexpensive, complex early word processors such as the early AES and Wang systems were gradually replaced by more author-friendly software such as WPS for VAX computers. Nonetheless, most professionals who were not primarily authors continued to work on paper, handing their manually annotated printouts to the word processing staff. By the time personal computers had become more than a toy for electronics hobbyists, early word processors such as WordStar and AtariWriter became increasingly available and easy to use. Simultaneously, a sea change in which companies struggled to become more efficient by "trimming the fat" led many to gradually eliminate their typing pools and make authors responsible for their own writing. No longer were professionals deemed sufficiently rare and irreplaceable that they could afford to have someone else do their typing, although word processing specialists remained available to help authors too important (or insufficiently competent) to embrace the new technology—managers, for instance. This workplace evolution continued, with responsibility for typing and revising manuscripts increasingly shifting to even manager-authors, and with word processors such as Microsoft Word and WordPerfect virtually eliminating the older software. This evolution continues today, with open-source word processors such as OpenOffice Writer (http://www.openoffice.org/) posing an increasingly credible challenge to the established giants.

With the growing internationalization of business, Web-based programs have emerged to offer online writing and collaboration. These range from expensive proprietary systems such as XMetal Reviewer (http://na.justsystems.com/content.php?page=xmetal-reviewer) to free suites such as GoogleDocs (http://docs.google.com/). At the same time, the Web and maturing online help technology have created enormous demand to move information online, as has the increasing cost of printing and shipping printed materials. (Indeed, large printed manuals for computer software and hardware seem to be an endangered species.) Moreover, modern documents evolve freely between print and Web versions. Added to this is the challenge of nonlinearity: readers can enter online information through many portals, not only in the linear order an author may have originally intended, and information may be assembled on the fly from chunks of text drawn from databases. Accompanying these changes, the traditional single-building workplace, with authors working next door to editors, is no longer the only option; in the modern workplace, authors and editors may be distributed around a city, country, or continent, and sometimes even around the world. From a single monolithic corporate culture, we have moved to the full global diversity of cultures, adding cultural differences to the list of challenges editors face [7]. All these changes pose both challenges and opportunities [8].

Modern editors have had to learn new skills to handle the increasingly fluid and multicultural identity of modern texts. These include the skill of onscreen editing, as we'll see later in this chapter. By 1999, when the tools available to support onscreen editing were finally becoming truly efficient, an estimated 38% of editors and writer–editors used onscreen editing "often or very frequently," and an additional 32% used this approach at least occasionally [9]. Dayton [10] notes that many people still find working on paper easier and more flexible, particularly with respect to the affordances provided by paper and the ability to see the overall structure of a document, but also emphasizes the importance of individual perception in determining the acceptance of onscreen editing. In my own experience as a teacher of onscreen editing skills, I've seen radical improvements in the attitude toward onscreen editing once editors learned how to customize the tools to fit their work style and learned how to use the tools efficiently.

It's worth noting that because Dayton's study [9] included a relatively small proportion of respondents who worked primarily as editors (only 4% of the sample), the true proportion of editors who were using onscreen editing as a key part of their toolbox would have been much higher than he reported. This is supported by anecdotal evidence from the Copyediting-L discussion group (http://www.copyediting-L.info/). In addition, there is clearly a generational change occurring, in which the younger generation is embracing onscreen reading far more readily than the older generation that forms the majority of people who are currently working as editors. Speaking at the 2008 WritersUA conference in Portland, Oregon, Cheryl Lockett Zubak emphasized the importance of this change for the authors of user assistance ("online help").

WHERE WE STAND TODAY

Modern editors work in a wide range of contexts. These include in-house employment by traditional publishers such as magazine and book publishers, where much of the writing is done by authors from outside the organization and an in-house editor works with the text they submit. With more integrated publishers, such as newspapers and computer hardware and software companies that employ professional authors (technical writers) to produce their information, the authors and editors work for the same employer and often in the same building, and are part of the same workflow. Finally, freelance editors may work with a wide range of authors either directly or through a contract agency. These differing contexts lead to differences in how well editors can communicate with authors to discuss their work. Although you'd expect integrated publishers to provide the greatest opportunities for communication and collaboration, such companies often "protect" authors from editors because they do not want the author's work to be interrupted. Thus, in different examples of each context, editors may work directly with the author, work with the author only through a human intermediary, or work with the author only through the medium of the edited manuscript. Dayton [11] has clearly demonstrated how differing workplace contexts such as these affect both the perception of and opportunities for onscreen editing.

Nonetheless, the nature of the work remains more similar than different, particularly with respect to the flow of that work. Writing always begins with an idea and an author, but the process diverges greatly from that point onwards into a variety of archetypal paths. Authors who publish their own information may review and revise their own writing, then immediately publish it; formal editing occurs only belatedly if readers complain about the quality. Workplace publishing processes tend to be more demanding and include at least one review and revision phase, though many more phases and types of review may occur [12]. In a mature process adopted by an organization that understands the importance of quality control, the publishing process can be truly rigorous. Writing still begins with a carefully crafted outline that serves as the blueprint for the final document [13], but that outline may be intensively critiqued by the author's manager, an editor, and others before writing begins. Some enlightened organizations even involve all stakeholders who have authority to approve or reject the final text (possibly even a senior manager) to avoid any unpleasant surprises late in the publishing cycle. Only once the outline is approved can writing begin.

Between the outline stage and final publication, manuscripts may be reviewed by many stakeholders, each with different responsibilities. Manuscripts often undergo an expert or peer review that focuses on the technical details of the content. Where manuscripts are being written for a client, whether someone inside the organization who pays for the services through some form of charge-back or a client working for a different organization, client reviews may also occur. In hierarchical organizations, there is usually some form of management review in which a senior manager approves the manuscript for publication. Editorial review often starts with a developmental edit, then proceeds through substantive editing and copyediting to a final proofreading, though these phases often overlap. Editorial review may occur only after a manuscript has survived all the other forms of review, may precede these reviews, or may occur both before and after these reviews. In my experience, the latter approach is more effective, because a carefully edited manuscript lets reviewers focus on the content instead of being distracted by typos, unclear wording, flawed logic, and a range of errors of omission and commission that are obvious to anyone but the author. At the same time, a final edit after these reviews offers a chance to catch any errors or infelicities introduced during the review process. Depending on the length and complexity of the overall document, editors may work on small chunks of information as each chunk is completed, or may only begin their work once the entire manuscript is complete.

Whether editors have the luxury of working on a single manuscript for a single author at a time or must juggle many different manuscripts and authors simultaneously, task management is clearly important: it's impossible to meet deadlines and remember all details without some way of tracking deadlines and which tasks remain to be completed. This work has traditionally been done manually, and you'll still see wall charts (or whiteboards, their modern equivalent), even in high-tech companies. But software is increasingly used to support this process. For editors with relatively few manuscripts and deadlines, task management may be no more sophisticated than a to-do list typed up in a word processor file, possibly combined with calendar software. More demanding workloads require more sophisticated tools such as the scheduling and task-management features built into Microsoft Outlook. Large publishers often use full-blown project-management tools such as Microsoft Project to handle the complexity of their work.

Routing of manuscripts between stakeholders can be similarly variable. I've worked for employers who handled this manually, using nothing more sophisticated than e-mail software, and for employers who used automated "dispatch" systems that automatically moved manuscripts to the next person within a defined workflow as soon as each person completed their step in the process. More sophisticated publishers such as newspapers and magazines may develop highly integrated systems in which writers, editors, and publication designers all work on a publication simultaneously, with each person "checking out" a given document (so that it is unavailable to the others) while they work on it, and the document automatically becoming available to others when it is "checked back in" into the system. Adobe's InCopy software (http://www.adobe.com/products/incopy/) is a modern example of mass-market software, but high-volume publishers such as Cadmus Communications (http://www.cenveo.com/cadmus.asp) often develop their own proprietary systems for collaborative writing and editing.

Because multiple reviewers may need to work on a manuscript, and because it is often necessary to retain older versions of a manuscript (for example, to create "paper" or "audit" trails), some form of version control may be necessary. Again, this can range from simple manual archiving of files with a creation date and reviewer name appended to the file name to sophisticated version-control software such as Microsoft's Visual SourceSafe (http://msdn2.microsoft.com/en-us/virtuallabs/aa740435.aspx).

THE BASIC TOOLS

The intellectual tools that editors use to edit don't change when moving from on-paper to onscreen editing, although a certain facility with computers is required to support the use of those tools. The biggest challenge onscreen editors face is learning to think clearly about how computers change the rules of the game. A first step in making this adjustment requires us to clearly understand what humans and computers do best. We humans understand the nuances of language and audience and can identify the assumptions authors make and the gaps in content and deficiencies in approach that these assumptions create;

machines wholly lack this understanding, which is hardly surprising given that even experienced editors don't always understand these skills well enough to teach them to their editing students. Computers, on the other hand, are unmatched at doing mindless, repetitive tasks such as finding or replacing a word everywhere in a long document. Clearly, then, effective onscreen editing is a process in which we use the computer's strengths to supplement our weaknesses, and vice versa. In this sense, learning onscreen editing does not involve creating a new paradigm, but rather learning how to make the old paradigm work more efficiently. Surprisingly, there seem to have been few efforts to teach these skills. Though its author now considers the book to be outdated, Weber [14] appears to have been the first book to specifically deal with the topic of onscreen editing. My own book [15] seems to be the first comprehensive successor to that earlier book, though a shorter primer appeared nearly simultaneously [16].

Editors use several broad categories of software for onscreen editing. First, and most obviously, there are word processors, the primary modern tools for creation of text. Microsoft Word remains the most widely used software because of its enormous power, general ease of use, and ubiquity (it is bundled with a large proportion of new computers). Corel's WordPerfect, a longtime Word competitor, remains popular in the home computer market, as well as in government and law offices. Despite the dominance of these programs, many less-known word processors, such as Nisus Writer for the Macintosh and IBM Lotus Word Pro for Windows, have their own dedicated cadres of users. An interesting recent change is the emergence of powerful free tools such as OpenOffice Writer and GoogleDocs that are available for the Windows, Macintosh, and Linux operating systems and that are posing an increasingly credible challenge to older word processors. Special-purpose text editors include the exceptionally powerful and broadly popular Emacs group of applications (http://en.wikipedia.org/wiki/Emacs), which have remained popular for decades in professions such as computer programming and are sometimes used in Web development.

Publishing tools form the next largest group, with Quark Express remaining popular, Adobe's Pagemaker now replaced by the increasingly popular InDesign, and Corel's Ventura Publisher no longer supported but clinging to its own niche along with more obscure programs such as RagTime. FrameMaker occupies a unique niche in the technical communication field because of its strengths in creating large documents. But here, there has been a sea change. Traditional desktop publishing (DTP) tools are still widely used, as the number and variety of printed publications continues to increase, but a rapidly increasing proportion of text is being created as online information published for use on the Web or on your computer (for example, PDF files and online help). The Internet's growth over the past two decades has led to an explosion of specialized "authoring" tools, such as Adobe's Dreamweaver and Microsoft's FrontPage and specialized online help–authoring tools such as Adobe's RoboHelp and MadCap's Flare. Then there are the myriad programs for creating wikis (http://en.wikipedia.org/wiki/Wiki) and Web logs, better known as "blogs" (http://en.wikipedia.org/wiki/Blog); blogs are particularly interesting because they bring publishing to even the least talented computer user, leading to what may be the single most rapid explosion of new published information in history. Online authoring tools share many of the text-creation tools used by word processors, though the tools are often less mature because their designers often emphasize flash over substance, or managing collections of online documents. A new category of tool, the "structured document processor," has been developed to solve two significant information-creation problems: imposing structure on large bodies of information and efficiently publishing this information using two or more media ("single-sourcing"). Typical programs in this category include FrameMaker+SGML, Arbortext, and WebWorks ePublisher Pro.

In addition, computers permit the creation and manipulation of many other categories of information. Database software such as FileMaker and Microsoft Access, a wide range of tools based on the SQL database query language, plus many others are designed to store information so that it can be searched efficiently and so that subsets of the information can be rapidly extracted. Spreadsheet software such as Lotus 1-2-3, Quattro Pro, and Microsoft Excel serve a similar function for numbers, but with the addition of powerful calculation and graphing tools. In addition, graphics software such as CorelDraw and Adobe Illustrator now let even amateurs create credible graphics, or at least facsimiles that professionals can refine.

Modern editors may have to cope with any or all of these different programs at some point in their career.

Basic Requirements for Onscreen Editing

Although it's possible to print copies of all computer information and revise it on paper, this is patently inefficient, and most high-volume producers of information recognize the need to edit the information on the computer screen to take advantage of the potential efficiencies [17]. Regardless of the technology used by the author and editor, the heart of editing is communication between editor and author. This communication may take place in real time, whether in person, by telephone, or using instant-messaging (chat) software; or with a delay, whether by postal mail, e-mail, or transfer of annotated files between computers. Whatever the medium, onscreen editors must clearly communicate three essential types of revision to authors:

- Inserted (new) text
- Deleted (old) text
- Comments, including suggestions, questions, requests for clarification, and explanations where an insertion or deletion would not be self-explanatory

Just as copyediting and proofreading marks became standardized to permit efficient communication between authors and editors, so too are best practices emerging for how to communicate these edits in the onscreen medium. Although all changes to text that authors have leeway to accept or reject are implicitly suggestions, editing is an inherently adversarial activity that communicates the concept "your writing sucks and as editor, I'm a better writer." Thus, the third category of revision is particularly important because comments give editors an opportunity to initiate a dialogue about the revisions, converting an author's natural resistance to being edited into an opportunity for collaboration [18].

When implemented effectively, onscreen editing can be a remarkable tool for supporting the communication between author and editor and greatly improving the efficiency of editing and revising text. That's particularly true once editors learn to customize their software and use its features. Needless to say, things aren't that simple.

Problems and Challenges

In an ideal situation, such as when the editor and author are using the same version of the same word processor on the same operating system (and for the same language family), that software's revision tracking features can be used to clearly identify all three types of revisions. This makes it easy for authors to see and understand what the editor has done. Moreover, better revision tracking tools such as those provided by Microsoft Word efficiently guide authors through the process of finding, reviewing, and implementing or rejecting each suggested revision, thereby minimizing the risk that any edits will be missed.

Unfortunately, the reality is seldom ideal. "Computer standard" is a pernicious modern oxymoron, and the truth of this statement is abundantly clear to anyone who has ever tried to move text between nominally compatible programs. Incompatibilities abound even between versions of the same word processor, forcing editors to keep an alert eye open for problems. Although it would be sensible to edit in the creator application to avoid these problems, few editors can afford to purchase copies of every application version used to create information, and even fewer have time to master this many tools. The problem is worse and the solutions more demanding when, as is the case with almost all software other than word processors, the software lacks mature revision tracking tools or any such tools, forcing editors to develop a range of variously elegant or kludgy solutions to solve the communication problem.

Moreover, despite nearly 25 years of progress since the first mass-market personal computers became available, computers remain extremely difficult and frustrating to use. Editors must learn how to customize their word processor so that it works comfortably (a process similar to breaking in a new pair of shoes), and how to use the tools efficiently—information that is generally lacking in the documentation produced by the software's developers because editors are not seen as an important target audience for these developers. Indeed, my own book [15] appears to be one of only two books currently in print (the other being [16]) that focus exclusively on teaching these skills.

The diversity and recalcitrance of modern software is bad enough, but the single biggest challenge we face is the accessibility of software to an increasingly large pool of users. Whether there are more amateur creators of information than there used to be is debatable, but it's unquestionable that computer tools empower even amateurs to produce more information faster than was ever previously possible. Whereas traditional information creators typically follow a traditional write–edit–design production cycle—what I have frequently called the "design thrice, publish once" approach—many newer publishers and authors are unaware of this paradigm. The need for a rigorous design and revision cycle is thus not part of the mental model of most nonprofessional and many professional publishers of information. As a result, information is often published with an emphasis on speed and little or no effort at quality control. It can be challenging, and sometimes impossible, to communicate the importance of editing to many of these authors, and teaching them how to work effectively with an editor becomes an onerous task for many modern editors.

The increasingly international modern workplace adds another layer of complexity to the task of communication. Even within a language family such as English, the wide range of dialects that exist leads to widespread variations in connotations, posing many traps for the unwary. The problem grows worse when author and editor speak closely related languages, such as English and French, and choose to communicate in only one language, typically English. Many words look the same, but their use and meaning have changed dramatically (these false cognates are known as *faux amis* in French). The problem can become insurmountable when the author and editor speak languages from entirely different linguistic families, such as English and Chinese, and when formidable cultural differences are added on top of the linguistic differences. Editors who work with multilingual, multicultural audiences must quickly learn to rigorously examine their own words and to explain themselves simply and carefully [7].

ADDITIONAL TOOLS

The most obvious tools that onscreen editors use are their word processors. But many other computer tools can improve the effectiveness of editing.

Research Tools

One of the larger editorial responsibilities involves fact checking, whether the facts are as mundane as the date and page range of a publication or as abstruse as the meaning of genre-specific jargon. Traditionally, such checks required a well-stocked shelf of reference books, an address book full of the phone numbers of experts willing to be consulted to resolve thorny issues of fact, and a well-stocked research library populated by friendly and skilled librarians. Such tools remain valuable assets to any editor, but the last two decades have seen the development of a new resource: the Internet, and particularly the Web. The unprecedented interconnectedness between computers, combined with the improved ability to create large quantities of information quickly and publish it at little or no cost, has provided a stunning array of research tools editors can use to enhance their research.

Most obvious are information search tools. These fall into three broad categories. The first comprises general-purpose search tools that give editors a previously unimaginable ability to sift through a cornucopia of information. Google (http://www.google.com/) is probably the best-known of these tools. In addition to its primary text search tool, Google offers many specialized variants such as its image search (http://images.google.com/), geographical search (http://maps.google.com/), scholarly article search (http://scholar.google.com/), and book search (http://books.google.com/). These tools let editors quickly find and verify both general information and information in a specific category such as images.

The second category comprises research portals, in which the tool's creators compile human-organized directories of information published by others. Yahoo (http://www.yahoo.com/) is one of the best-known in this category, as their staff have devoted considerable effort to categorizing and linking to a wide array of resources such as discussion groups (http://groups.yahoo.com/), financial information (http://finance.yahoo.com/), and technology (http://tech.yahoo.com/). Many merchants also belong to this category. Booksellers such as Amazon (http://www.amazon.com/) are the best known example in this group, but similar Web-based merchants exist for almost any category you care to name. Using these tools is analogous to onscreen editing because it combines what humans do best (creating and organizing information) with what computers do best (storing and providing access to information).

The third category provides access to information published by its creators. Familiar examples include the U.S. Library of Congress (http://www.loc.gov/) and Worldcat (http://www.worldcat.org/) library catalogs. Other examples include journal publishers (such as http://www.springerlink.com/, http://www.elsevier.com/, http://www.blackwellpublishing.com/), governments (for example, http://www.usa.gov/, http://www.canada.gc.ca/, http://europa.eu/), government agencies such as the U.S. National Institutes of Health (http://www.nih.gov/), organizations such as the World Trade Organization (http://www.wto.org/), and professional societies such as the Society for Technical Communication (http://www.stc.org/) and the IEEE Professional Communication Society (http://ewh.ieee.org/soc/pcs/).

Editors quickly learn to use these tools in a variety of innovative ways. For example, it's often possible to use a general-purpose search tool such as Google to find a directory category offered by Yahoo that leads you to a specialized purveyor of information such as an antiquarian bookseller.

Communication Tools

Whereas the abovementioned search tools provide access to "static" information, which is published and sometimes forgotten until someone remembers to update it, the many discussion groups that have arisen on the Internet provide a significantly different and uniquely powerful tool: they provide "dynamic" information that is generated continuously by a host of minds, with communication occurring and bodies of information being updated and growing around the clock. The ability to solve problems by taking advantage of the assembled expertise of thousands of professional colleagues is just one example of how this technology greatly empowers editors. For example, Copyediting-L (http://www.copyediting-L.info/), founded in 1992 by Carol Roberts, brings together nearly 1,600 professional editors; and TECHWR-L (http://www.techwr-l.com/), founded in 1993 by Eric and Deb Ray, brings together more than 3,000 technical communicators. Both include subscribers from at least 25 countries on most continents, so someone is generally available to answer thorny questions at pretty much any time of day. (The actual number of countries is undoubtedly far larger, since the nationality of subscribers with Hotmail, Google, and Yahoo e-mail addresses, among others, is not obvious.)

Groups of non-editors are also an enormous resource. Special-interest groups composed of both amateurs and experts have sprung up to discuss pretty much any topic you can imagine, and these groups provide something never previously available to editors: a guaranteed ability to observe and interact with their audience. Although some forward-thinking publishers have always allowed their technical writers and editors direct access to users of the publisher's information, a surprising number militantly resist this contact, possibly from fear of annoying their audience or learning some unpleasant truths. But the Internet provides easy access to most such audiences by allowing us to participate in their online communities. This allows us to better understand and advocate for our audiences, both of which are important if we are go beyond our responsibility to the author and effectively meet our responsibility to their audience.

The Internet also facilitates communication with our authors in real time, even when they live on a different continent and are people we'll never meet in person. The ability to talk to our authors using "chat" (instant messaging), perhaps combined with real-time editing and updating of Web pages, allows real-time collaboration on a manuscript and other forms of information. Wikis (http://en.wikipedia.org/wiki/Wiki) and blogs (http://en.wikipedia.org/wiki/Blog) offer a particularly good example of this approach because they are explicitly designed to facilitate the creation and publishing of information. When authors and editors cannot meet in person to cross pens over a printed manuscript, this approaches the holy grail of the author–editor relationship: dialog, negotiation, and consensus in real time.

File-Transfer Tools

Of course, the Internet also facilitates some of the mundane tasks editors face. Most importantly for authors and editors who don't work in the same physical location, we can exchange files quickly and for essentially no cost. Most familiarly, we can exchange files via e-mail. When our service providers limit file sizes to 5 or 10 megabytes, as is common, various services (for example, http://www.yousendit.com/) let us exchange much larger files by uploading the files to a server, where the author can then access and download them directly. Where security is important, many corporations and some individuals offer their own secured file transfer (FTP) sites for clients and colleagues. Of course, in a pinch, we can and still do exchange files with our authors on CDs shipped by courier or postal mail.

SPECIAL CHALLENGES

In addition to the traditional challenges I've already discussed, the modern editor faces some new and not-yet-solved problems.

One of the more interesting challenges involves the emerging philosophy of communal creation of knowledge. In a wiki, for example, all members of the community can add and modify content, leading to a continuously evolving body of information. This leads to the development of what has been referred to as a "community of knowledge," in which information is developed and maintained collectively, potentially undergoing review and critique by all members of the community. One advantage of this approach is that many individuals will be consulted while creating the knowledge base, thereby reducing the risks that important information will be omitted or that errors will remain undetected. This can also create a more egalitarian system in which many voices are heard, not just that of the publisher [1]. The Wikipedia (http://www.wikipedia.org/) provides one of the best examples of this, as well as an illustration of its biggest drawback. In a recent study by the journal *Nature*, investigators found that the Wikipedia's content was, on the whole, as accurate as that in the famed *Encyclopædia Britannica* [19]. But one significant problem is that without taking special precautions, the information is vulnerable to vandalism, such as changes intended to be humorous or made to promote political agendas. There are two simple solutions: first, protect the content so that only trusted members of the community can modify it; second, use a two-phase approach in which modifications can be proposed by anyone, but must be reviewed and approved by qualified experts. Another problem is that without an editorial review process, the content quality may be low; Giles notes that many Wikipedia entries "need a good editor" and are "poorly structured and confused" [19].

Another challenge relates to the perception of editors as word specialists. Unfortunately, much of the information currently being published is "non-words." These include a wide range of graphics (including static images, animations, and video), sound (including podcasts [http://en.wikipedia.org/wiki/Podcast]), data-bases of numerical information, and spreadsheets. Two challenges arise: first, the word specialist's potential lack of familiarity with these alternative media, and second, the fact that most of the tools used to create these media lack any form of revision tracking tools. There are workarounds, but these are stopgap measures. The real solution lies in teaching creators of this information to adopt a quality-control process such as the one I described previously ("Where We Stand Today") and persuading the developers of the authoring tools to incorporate revision tracking functionality. It's also important to note that editors love words, and this leads us to assume that others share this love; in fact, for most of the information we will edit, excluding fiction, readers want to get the information they're seeking with as little effort as possible. This will force us to learn how to "let go of the words" [20] and focus instead on efficient, concise communication, using a combination of as few words as possible, com-plemented by appropriate use of other media.

Online information poses another special challenge. In a printed book, the physical structure tends to impose a fixed, linear sequence on the information. Even when we use the book only as reference material and enter its pages at some arbitrary point (for example, by following an index entry), we still see at a glance where information fits within the overall structure of the book, and we know from experience that if we don't understand what we've found, the explanation is likely to lie earlier in the sequence of pages. Hypertexts such as the Web and online help files pose a very different challenge. Because much of the structure of a body of information is invisible, we cannot rely on these familiar tools. Instead, we must strive to ensure that each chunk of information is self-contained and that either it can be understood without leaving that chunk in search of new information, or the chunk provides clear links (cross-references) to important related information that may be required to understand the current information. This means that for online information, developmental editing cannot be skipped if we are to ensure that all the necessary information is either immediately present or easy to find. And just as we proofread printed text to ensure that cross-references point to the correct pages, we must proofread online information to confirm that all links take us to the correct chunk of information.

The latter challenge also arises in single sourcing. The holy grail of single sourcing is to create information only once and then reuse it without any manual modifications everywhere else it is needed. But this raises the question of whether it is truly possible to produce context-free information that can be reused, unmodified, many times in other contexts. On the face of it, the answer is a clear no: all information is highly contextual, and without understanding that context, it's impossible to communicate effectively. But that's clearly a *reductio ad absurdum* analysis. In reality, careful consideration of the known contexts in which information will be reused, combined with a careful analysis of each chunk of information to identify any dependencies and related information, should make single sourcing possible. Whether this happens in practice is less clear. Developmental editing is one way to bring the practice closer to the theory, but publishers will also require subsequent substantive editing to ensure that the information is comprehensible in each context and proofreading to ensure that links to related information are correct, ensuring that the resulting information works as well in practice as it is expected to in theory.

SPECIAL HINTS AND TRICKS OF THE TRADE

The skills that all editors should learn [21] fall into three general categories:

Software Skills

All professionals must master certain tools, and in our case, those tools are the computer software that lets us perform onscreen editing. To attain this mastery, we must monitor how we work to identify inefficiencies that could benefit from the automation permitted by software. We must spend time exploring the capabilities of our software and learning new features and tricks for how to use those features efficiently. We must learn how to reuse information, whether through the creation of templates and online style sheets or through single-sourcing tools. We must also spend time identifying why a tool feels uncomfortable. Some discomfort vanishes with time and practice, but other problems require a search for how to customize the tool so it better fits how we prefer to work.

Soft Skills

Communication with authors is essential, and learning to communicate clearly and in a way that helps us be seen as allies, not obstacles to publishing, is crucial for our success. Communication begins with the dialogue that introduces us to the authors, and helps us learn their needs, their problems, and their fears. Armed with that knowledge, we can spend time finding ways to make each author's job easier by accounting for their needs, solving their problems, and allaying their fears. All of this becomes easier when we learn to empathize with authors and communicate with them tactfully.

Survival Skills

One of the hardest lessons for any editor to learn relates to where we fit within the publishing process. We must learn both our role and how the larger organizational context within which publishing occurs will affect our work. Most organizations have annual and other cycles (such as the product development cycle) that affect our workload, the availability of time to learn and practice new skills, and access to authors when we have questions. But we have our own rhythms and cycles, too. Some of us are morning people, and some emphatically are not, and scheduling the most difficult work for times when our mental resources are at their peak lets us do that work efficiently and well; for those other times when our mental resources are at their lowest ebb, we can do the more mechanical, rote work.

THE FUTURE: SPECIAL CONCERNS

The need for editing has not changed and seems unlikely to ever change in the absence of some fundamental and unanticipated improvement in how humans communicate. The difficulty of bridging the gap between minds using such primitive tools as words and images makes it essential to subject all information that will be published to a reality check by professionals skilled in understanding the problems that bedevil communication. These difficulties are exacerbated by the challenges of multilingual and cross-cultural teamwork with an increasingly global team of cooperators [7].

The tools available to support our editing are powerful and support tremendous efficiencies, but they remain *in silico* implementations of how we formerly worked on paper. There have been few breakthroughs in which software designers carefully monitored how editors work and developed solutions that specifically support that work. Tools such as revision tracking are impressive alternatives to their paper equivalents, but have not yet shaken off their origins in paper to fully embrace the new paradigm of working on a computer. Real-time collaboration by combining chat software with rapid updating of a Web page to show the results of that collaboration, as is possible through such means as Google Docs, is in its early stages.

Unfortunately, market pressures lead software developers to release unstable software before it is ready for use in a production environment, with features designed based on marketing specifications rather than real needs. Untrained and unskilled authors make things worse by using the tools badly and don't yet understand the need for editing and the possibilities for improvement made possible by working with a professional. A particularly intractable problem is the perception that speed is more important than quality, an attitude that makes editing an annoying last step that delays publication rather than an integral part of quality control. This creates problems such as choosing editors based on the lowest cost and fastest turnaround time rather than on quality. The resulting outsourcing of work to countries with lower costs of living frightens many editors in developed nations; though many of these competitors have inadequate English skills, others are every bit as good as we are. Though this isn't a trivial concern, there seems to be far more editing work that needs doing than there are competent editors available to do the work. In addition, some authors (for example, [8]) see outsourcing and offshoring as a potential source of new opportunities, with offshore technical writers becoming a new clientele for onshore editors, particularly since we have knowledge of the local audience that few offshore writers ever attain. The challenge is how to demonstrate the value of what we do. For every combination of cost and quality, there's a client willing to pay that price.

Some editors fear we might someday be replaced by technology. Not any time soon. Apart from the ongoing failure of software developers to produce reliable software, semantic analysis that goes beyond the most basic copyediting (for example, subject–verb accord) is an intractable problem. Substantive editing requires an enormous knowledge of facts and of the unwritten human rules that tie these facts together. We gain this information over decades of life experience, and training software in these rules would require a similarly capacious education. Editing goes far beyond a mechanistic–stochastic assessment of the probabilities that a word represents different parts of speech. Despite many breakthroughs, science still doesn't really understand language processing by the brain well enough to encapsulate that knowledge in software. But tools such as spellcheckers and grammar checkers will undoubtedly improve from their current primitive state—forcing us to stay on our toes. The fates of the legendary Paul Bunyan and John Henry, replaced by tireless and more efficient machines, won't be shared by editors any time soon, but as it becomes possible to incorporate ever more of our editorial tasks in software, this will highlight the need for the insights that only humans can provide and will free us to concentrate on that aspect of our work.

Despite these concerns, there are many pleasures and opportunities. The work itself remains fascinating. The pleasure of working with the insights of others and solving the challenge of how to communicate those insights makes editing a satisfying and intellectually challenging career, and one with a long future. In a very real sense, editors are usability experts for communication. Our skill lies in translating between the creator's mind and the reader's mind, and recognizing when it's necessary to create new kinds of information, for example, moving from linear, author-directed learning to nonlinear, reader-directed learning or replacing text with graphics and interactions. That skill is highly portable across types of information—with a little training. I once defined editing as "professional idiocy": working as a professional whose primary skill combines the ability to misunderstand anything (that is, to be an idiot) with the ability to determine why that misunderstanding occurred and prevent it from afflicting anyone else. This ability to empathize with an audience's lack of knowledge should be applicable in any other form of communication, including nonverbal media such as graphics and sound, and even media we can scarcely imagine right now, such as haptics (http://en.wikipedia.org/wiki/Haptics).

Though computers, their software, and extensions of both such as the Web are clearly non-human, they are nonetheless devices for enabling communication, and that's something skilled editors do well. This suggests that in an increasingly electronic world, there is considerable potential for empowering editors and elevating our status by facilitating and increasing our dialog with authors. When we are seen as equals or near-equals in the process of creating information, we can no longer be dismissed as glorified spellcheckers and grammar mavens.

REFERENCES

1. G. J. S. Hart, Bridging the Gap Between Cultural Studies Theory and the World of the Working Practitioner, *KnowGenesis, 2*:3, pp. 14–31, 2007. Available online at: http://www.geoff.hart.com/articles/2007/cultural-studies.htm

2. D. Rosenquist, Information Development Organizations Evolving to Keep Pace with Change: A Collaborative Conversation of Information Development Managers, *Technical Communication, 48*, pp. 194-199, 2001.

3. L. Carter, The Implications of Single Sourcing for Writers and Writing, *Technical Communication, 50*, pp. 317-320, 2003.

4. A. Rockley, Single Sourcing: It's About People, Not Just Technology, *Technical Communication, 50*, pp. 350-354, 2003.

5. J. D. Williams, The Implications of Single Sourcing for Technical Communicators, *Technical Communication, 50*, pp. 321-327, 2003.

6. G. Dullea, Is It a Boon for Secretaries—Or Just an Automated Ghetto? *New York Times*, p. 32, February 5, 1974.

7. G. J. S. Hart, Successful Cross-Cultural Communication Requires Us to Test Our Assumptions, *The Write Stuff* (newsletter of the European Medical Writers' Association), *16*, pp. 111-113, December 2007.

8. C. R. Lanier, The Implications of Outsourcing for Technical Editing, in *Outsourcing Technical Communication: Issues, Policies, and Practices*, B. Thatcher and C. Evia (eds.), Baywood, Amityville, New York, pp. 147-161, 2008.

9. D. Dayton, Electronic Editing in Technical Communication: A Survey of Practices and Attitudes, *Technical Communication, 50*, pp. 192-205, 2003.

10. D. Dayton, Electronic Editing in Technical Communication: A Model of User-Centered Technology Adoption, *Technical Communication, 51*, pp. 207-223, 2004.

11. D. Dayton, Electronic Editing in Technical Communication: The Compelling Logics of Local Contexts, *Technical Communication, 51*, pp. 86-101, 2004.

12. G. J. S. Hart, Designing an Effective Review Process, *Intercom, 53*:7, pp. 18–21, July-August 2006.

13. G. J. S. Hart, Effective Outlining: Designing Workable Blueprints for Writing, *Intercom, 53*:8, pp. 18–19, September-October 2006.

14. J. H. Weber, *Electronic Editing: Editing in the Computer Age*, WeberWoman's Wrevenge, 1999. Available online at: http://www.jeanweber.com/newsite/?page_id=97

15. G. J. S. Hart, *Effective Onscreen Editing*, Diaskeuasis Publishing, Pointe-Claire, Quebec, 2007. Available online at: http://www.geoff-hart.com/books/eoe/onscreen-book.htm.

16. H. Powers, *Making Word Work for You: An Editor's Intro to the Tool of the Trade*, Editorial Freelancers Association, New York, 2007.

17. G. J. S. Hart, Why Edit on Screen? *Intercom, 47*:8, pp. 34–35, September-October 2000.

18. G. J. S. Hart, Substantive Editing: Break It to Them Gently, *Intercom, 49*:6, pp. 34–35, June 2002.
19. J. Giles, Internet Encyclopaedias Go Head to Head, *Nature, 438*, pp. 900-901, 2005.
20. J. Redish, *Letting Go of the Words: Writing Web Content That Works*, Morgan Kaufmann, New York, 2007.
21. G. J. S. Hart, Improving Your Editing Efficiency: Software Skills, Soft Skills, and Survival Skills, *STC's 52nd Annual Conference Proceedings*, Society for Technical Communication, Arlington, Virginia, pp. 364-369, 2005.

CHAPTER 8

Editing Within the Pure Sciences

Barbara Gastel

Editing in the pure sciences (referred to hereafter as "science editing") can encompass a wide range of activities, call on a wide variety of skills, and relate to a wide variety of issues. This chapter presents an overview of this diverse field. It begins by describing the scope of science editing and discussing the relationship to other technical editing. Then come sections on stylebooks and standards in the sciences, ethical issues in scientific publication, interactions of science editors with others, international aspects of science editing, organizations for science editors, education and credentialing in science editing, and economics of science editing. The chapter ends with a brief look ahead.

For purposes of this chapter, "pure sciences" is defined broadly to include not only the natural sciences but also the social sciences and health sciences. Indeed, a large proportion of science editors are employed in medical editing, and much of the science-editing literature focuses on that realm.

SCOPE OF SCIENCE EDITING

Niches within science editing can be categorized in at least three ways. One is by the scientific discipline (for example, biology or physics) in which the editing is done. Another is by the type of document edited, such as journal, book, or grant proposal. A third is by editorial role, such as editor-in-chief, managing editor, or manuscript editor.

Science editors edit materials written and read within the scientific community, materials about science for popular audiences, and other items. Among the scientist-to-scientist writings are journals and journal articles, grant proposals, books, conference proceedings, oral presentations, and poster presentations.

127

http://dx.doi.org/10.2190/NPOC8

Items for the public that science editors edit include magazines and magazine articles, newspaper articles, books, radio stories [1], television documentaries [2], online-only materials, and captions and catalogs for science exhibits at museums. Other items in the sciences that are professionally edited include textbooks, standardized examinations [3], trade magazines, university research magazines [4], government reports, and conference programs [5].

Journal Editing

Several editorial roles exist at journals. *Scientific editors* are responsible mainly for scientific content. When scientific papers—which typically are unsolicited—arrive at journals, scientific editors assign them to peer reviewers (experts in the area of the research) for evaluation. Once the peer reviews are received, scientific editors decide the fate of the papers: either accept as is (a rare decision), accept once requested revisions are made, reconsider after requested revisions are made (for example, if information needed to evaluate the research was missing), or reject (in which case the author may submit the paper to another journal). In reaching their decisions, scientific editors consider the peer reviews received, their own assessments of the papers, the amount of space available in the journal, and sometimes other factors, such as the balance of content in the journal. If a paper is to be revised, a scientific editor informs the authors of the revisions requested and checks the revisions once the paper has been resubmitted.

Large, frequently published journals sometimes have one or more full-time scientific editors, including an editor-in-chief and others, such as deputy editors, associate editors, and assistant editors. At most journals, however, the scientific editor(s) occupy the role only part-time. Typically, the appointment as a scientific editor is concurrent with a primary appointment as a scientist in academia, government, or industry. Most scientific editors are prominent researchers who have shown their editorial ability and interest through excellent service as peer reviewers.

A typical journal staff also includes a *managing editor*. This largely administrative role, which varies from journal to journal [6], can include such duties as creating and managing production schedules, ensuring that peer reviewers submit reports promptly, managing budgets, handling personnel matters, and negotiating with printers and other service providers (such as those posting the journal online). Managing editors can come from any of a variety of backgrounds.

After acceptance, papers are refined by individuals commonly called *manuscript editors* or *copyeditors*. (Cheryl Iverson, of the American Medical Association *Archives* journals, has published a thoughtful exploration of terms used for the role [7].) The intensity of manuscript editing varies among journals. Some journals provide only light copyediting, such as correcting errors in spelling, grammar, and usage and ensuring that references and other items comply with the journal's style. Other journals edit somewhat more deeply, for instance for conciseness and readability. And some journals provide major substantive editing, including reorganization, for those papers that seem to need it.

At some journals, all papers are copyedited by manuscript editors who are part of the journal staff. Other journals outsource the manuscript editing to individual freelance editors, editorial groups, or the companies printing the journals. Yet other journals use a combination of in-house editing and outsourcing. Editors of manuscripts for scientific journals come from a variety of academic backgrounds, including English, journalism, and the sciences.

Additional editorial roles exist at some journals. One such role is that of *Web editor*, or *online editor*, in charge of online content. Another is that of *book review editor* (or more broadly, *media review editor*), responsible for obtaining such reviews. Some journals include news sections and so have *news editors*. Journals that publish images on their covers sometimes have *covers editors*. In addition, some journals have *production editors*, who "shepherd manuscripts from submission through publication" [3, p. 19].

Other editorially related roles at some journals include that of statistical consultant, responsible for evaluating the study design and analysis of research being considered for publication. Some journals have an ombudsman [8, 9], who mediates authors' complaints about editorial administration at the journal. Also, some journals have a commercial editor, who works with the business department of the journal to develop content opportunities for advertisers [10].

Book Editing

Analogous roles exist in book editing in the sciences. *Acquisitions editors* are in charge of acquiring book manuscripts. Often trained as scientists themselves, they not only oversee the evaluation of book proposals and manuscripts that arrive unsolicited, but also keep informed about research and researchers in their fields—for example by reading scientific journals and attending scientific conferences—and then solicit book proposals and manuscripts accordingly. Once a book manuscript is accepted, a *production editor* or *project editor* coordinates various aspects of producing the book: manuscript editing, book design, proofreading, indexing, printing, and more. Commonly, a freelance *copyeditor* edits the book manuscript.

Corporate, Government, and Other Editing

Science editors also work for a variety of other institutions, both as manuscript editors and in other roles, such as that of editorial project manager [11]. Some science editors do so as employees, some on an individual freelance basis, and some as members of consulting firms. Corporations employing science editors include science-based companies such as those producing pharmaceuticals, medical devices, and biotechnology products. They also include companies specializing in the production of continuing-medical-education materials.

Likewise, editors work for science-related government agencies, such as the National Institutes of Health and the U.S. Geological Survey, and for major government laboratories, such as the Fermi National Accelerator Laboratory and the Argonne National Laboratory. Science editors are employed by the U.S. National Academies (encompassing the National Academy of Sciences and related entities), a publisher of many lengthy reports. Some editors edit items for science museums. Some even edit examinations for entities such as the American Board of Internal Medicine, which certifies physicians practicing internal medicine [3].

Author's Editing

Some science editors are employed directly by authors or their institutions to help refine writing before submission. In some cases, these editors, known as *author's editors,* also help make revisions that are requested by the journal or other recipient of the piece. It appears that although such editing existed previously, the role of author's editor first became explicitly known in the late 1960s and the 1970s [12]. Writings by author's editor Martha Tacker in 1976 [13] and 1980 [14] nicely delineated responsibilities and roles of author's editors in the sciences.

Some author's editors work as freelancers, either full time or in addition to holding a job in editing, the sciences, or another realm. Others work for editing services from which authors can purchase manuscript editing [15]. And others work for institutions. In particular, some large, research-oriented medical institutions employ one or more such editors. Among institutions with sizeable, well-established editing offices are the Mayo Clinic [16] and the M. D. Anderson Cancer Center.

Commonly, author's editors in the sciences largely edit scientific papers to be submitted to journals. Among other items edited by such author's editors are books and book chapters, grant proposals [17], oral presentations, and poster presentations [18]. Lang [19, 20] quantified and otherwise characterized the writings that the editorial office at the Cleveland Clinic received for editing during 1991 through 1995, and he calculated time needed to edit various types of submissions.

Teaching by Science Editors

Author's editors at some institutions give courses or sessions on scientific communication. (See, for example, the accounts by Ancker and Moore [21] and by Griner [22].) Indeed, the science editing profession, including journal editors, has long been involved in teaching scientific writing. For example, in the 1960s the Council of Biology Editors (now the Council of Science Editors) prepared a manual for teachers of scientific writing [23]; it was published in 1968 as *Scientific Writing for Graduate Students: A Manual on the Teaching of*

Scientific Writing [24]. This widely used book went through four reprintings, and in 1999 a rewritten, updated version was published under the title *How to Teach Scientific Communication* [25].

For many years, native-English-speaking editors have taught scientific communication domestically and overseas. Those especially active internationally have included Elliott Churchill [26], who during her long career at the Centers for Disease Control and Prevention taught in more than 90 countries. Editors also have provided instruction on writing and publishing through sessions sponsored by researchers' professional associations, such as the American Psychological Association [27]. Regardless of whether their work includes formal teaching, many author's editors view their role as not only improving the current manuscript but also educating authors so they can be more successful in the future.

Freelance Science Editing

As noted, science editing sometimes is done on a freelance basis. Some science editors do only freelance work; others freelance in addition to holding a full- or part-time job. Some freelancers specialize in particular types of documents, such as journal articles, book manuscripts, or grant proposals; editorial roles, such as manuscript editing or project management; scientific disciplines in which the editing is done; or other respects. In addition to editing per se, some freelance science editors offer training in scientific writing. Many freelance editors formerly held editorial jobs; sometimes their clients include their former employers.

For many freelance editors, advantages include flexibility about where and when to work, the lack of a commute, and the opportunity to work independently, interact with a variety of clients, and do a variety of work. Disadvantages include the need to pay for one's own health insurance in the United States; the lack of a steady, predictable income; and, for some, the paucity of social contact. An article in *Science Editor* [28] explores considerations to keep in mind when deciding whether to pursue a freelance editing career.

From an employer's perspective, benefits of using freelancers can include paying editors only when their services are being used; being able to call on editors with various specialties; and not needing to pay employee benefits, provide office space, and pay overhead. Downsides from the employer's perspective can include less control over freelancers than over employees—including lack of a guarantee that a desired editor will be available when wanted.

RELATIONSHIP TO OTHER TECHNICAL EDITING

Science editing has much in common with other technical editing (for example, in engineering or computer science). Of course, both science editing and other technical editing entail working with specialized subject matter and adhering to distinctive stylistic conventions. Other commonalities include the use of basic principles of copyediting, the employment of much of the same editorial technology, and the editing of tables and figures in addition to text.

However, science editing has some distinctive aspects. For example, peer review tends to receive particular emphasis in scientific publication. (See, for instance, [29-32].) Editors in the sciences must deal with the specialized nomenclature and stylistic conventions of the disciplines in which they edit; specialized style manuals in the sciences aid in this regard. In some fields of science, material to be edited contains specialized statistical content; resources for biomedical editors working with statistical material include a book [33] and series of articles [34-40] by editor Tom Lang. In addition, some distinctive ethical issues can arise, both regarding the work of science editors themselves and relating to science editors' uncovering of possible scientific misconduct.

Some of these aspects are addressed in subsequent parts of this chapter. Also, the occasional series "Editing Across the Sciences" [41-47], which appeared in *Science Editor* from 2004 to 2006, summarizes editorial practices and norms in several scientific fields.

STYLEBOOKS AND STANDARDS IN THE SCIENCES

A variety of style manuals provide guidance for editing in the sciences as a whole or within specific scientific disciplines. Science editors sometimes also use more general style manuals, such as *The Chicago Manual of Style* [48], especially when questions arise that stylebooks in the sciences do not address. In addition, some documents present standards for reporting research, and thus for editing, in medical science.

Scientific Style Manuals

Scientific Style and Format: The CSE Manual for Authors, Editors, and Publishers [49] is intended for use throughout the sciences. Prepared by the Council of Science Editors, this manual evolved from the more narrowly focused style manuals published beginning in 1960 by this organization's predecessors, the Conference of Biological Editors and then the Council of Biology Editors [49, pp. ix-x]. As well as sections on general style conventions and on aspects of publishing, the manual includes a section, running nearly 250 pages, on conventions (for instance regarding nomenclature) in particular areas of science. Among the lengthier of the 12 chapters in this section are those on chemical formulas and names; genes, chromosomes, and related molecules; taxonomy and nomenclature; and the Earth.

Many medical editors, including those at many medical journals, use primarily the *AMA Manual of Style* [50], which is prepared by a committee of editors at the American Medical Association. Evolved from a 68-page manual issued in

1962 for in-house use at the AMA [51], the current edition of the AMA manual exceeds 1,000 pages. One part specific to medicine is the extensive chapter on nomenclature, which includes guidance on terminology in a variety of clinical and basic-medical-science disciplines. Other features of the manual include lengthy chapters on ethical and legal considerations in medical publication, on study design and statistics, and on abbreviations. The chapters on style—for example, those on grammar, punctuation, and usage—contain medical examples.

Revised and expanded repeatedly since originating in 1929 as a seven-page article, the *Publication Manual of the American Psychological Association* [52] is widely used in the behavioral and social sciences. The current edition includes material on such topics as tables, figures, and statistical and mathematical copy, in addition to content on general aspects of style. Other features of this manual include guidance on reducing bias in language, advice on preparing supplemental materials for the World Wide Web, sample papers illustrating applications of American Psychological Association style, and a checklist for manuscript submission.

Some style manuals in the physical and other sciences seem to be largely internal documents. One manual, however, that is widely available is *The ACS Style Guide* [53], from the American Chemical Society. Chapters presenting material specific to chemistry include those on names and numbers for chemical compounds, conventions in chemistry, and chemical structures. The current edition of this guide, like those of other style manuals in the sciences, has been updated to include material relating to the use of electronic technology in scientific publication. Indeed, it includes a chapter titled "Electronic Submission of Manuscripts Using Web-Based Systems."

Standards for Some Medical Manuscripts

Documents other than style manuals also provide editorial guidance in some sciences. In medicine, one such document is the Uniform Requirements for Manuscripts Submitted to Biomedical Journals [54]. The idea for these requirements arose when the secretary to an eminent medical researcher "grew tired of retyping his papers to change the format of references when a paper was rejected by one journal and needed to be submitted to a journal with different requirements" [55, p. 17]. The result was a standardized set of bibliographic and other requirements, issued in 1979 by a group of editors of prominent medical journals and updated periodically by this group, known as the International Committee of Medical Journal Editors. By 1997, editors of more than 500 journals had informed the committee that "they adhered to the URM in some form" [55, p. 20]; the committee no longer keeps track of the number. With time, the Uniform Requirements have increasingly included information on ethics in scientific publication, in addition to instructions for manuscript preparation.

In medicine, standards also have been issued regarding content for reports of some types of studies [56]. Perhaps best known is the Consolidated Standards of Reporting Trials, or CONSORT, statement [57], which regards randomized controlled trials. Links to some of these statements and to the Uniform Requirements exist at the Web site "Instructions to Authors in the Health Sciences" [58], which offers access to Web sites providing instructions to authors for more than 3,500 journals.

ETHICAL ISSUES IN SCIENTIFIC PUBLICATION

As reflected in the evolution of the Uniform Requirements for Manuscripts Submitted to Biomedical Journals, ethical issues in scientific publication have received increasing attention in recent years. Many resources now provide guidance about such issues. One such resource is *CSE's White Paper on Promoting Integrity in Scientific Journal Publications* [59]. Another is the Web site of the Committee on Publication Ethics (better known as COPE). This Web site includes flow charts for dealing with a variety of ethical problems, as well as guidelines, cases, and other items [60].

In addition, resources on scientific-publication ethics can be accessed at Web sites such as those of the Council of Science Editors [61] and the World Association of Medical Editors [62]. Other readily accessible sources of guidance on publication ethics include the style manuals such as the *AMA Manual of Style* [50], *The ACS Style Guide* [53], and the *Publication Manual of the American Psychological Association* [52]. In addition, professional-conduct guidelines from some scientific associations, such as the American Physical Society [63], address scientific publication. The book *Ethics and Policy in Scientific Publication* [64], published in 1990, remains a valuable resource as well, in part because it contains many cases. Other sources of publication-related cases for discussion include *On Being a Scientist: A Guide to Responsible Conduct in Research* [65], intended primarily for graduate students and beginning scientists.

Ethical issues faced by science editors include those regarding the conduct of authors, of themselves, and of other parties. Brief overviews of these sets of issues appear below.

Ethics of Authors

Much of the literature on publication ethics focuses on authors' conduct. Perhaps this emphasis exists largely because scientist-authors produce the scientific literature. In addition, editors may tend to be more concerned about others' conduct than their own. Deviations from acceptable conduct on the part of authors range from clear wrongdoing to failure to observe the etiquette of scientific publication, whether through laziness, disregard, or obliviousness. Accordingly, in discussing lapses in the behavior of researcher-authors, the distinction has been drawn between "jerks" and "crooks" [66].

Definite research misconduct includes falsification and fabrication of data, piracy and plagiarism, and mistreatment of research subjects [59, p. 36]. Other examples of failure to meet accepted standards include submitting a manuscript simultaneously to more than one journal, listing as authors some individuals who did not contribute sufficiently to warrant authorship, failing to list all individuals who qualify for authorship, not documenting information sources sufficiently, and not disclosing conflicts of interest when required. Authors sometimes have faced ethical quandaries when commercial or other funders of their research have tried to influence the content of their scientific papers.

As they encounter authors' work, science editors—including journal editors and author's editors—sometimes perceive clues that authors' conduct might not meet accepted standards. In some cases, discussion with an author indicates that no problem actually exists or leads the author to correct the problem. In other cases, however, evidence remains that an ethical lapse does exist and that the author refuses to correct it. In such cases, an editor may be obligated to contact the author's institution or a regulatory body. One source of guidance for editors confronting possible misconduct is the CSE White Paper [59], which devotes many pages to "Identification of Research Misconduct and Guidelines for Action." Another resource is the set of COPE flow charts [67] on steps editors should take after suspecting such problems as redundant (duplicate) publication, plagiarism, or fabrication.

Every researcher should know that, for example, it is wrong to falsify data. However, many researchers are poorly acquainted with international publication norms, such as authorship criteria, documentation requirements, and requirements to disclose conflicts of interest. Authors who are just starting their careers or who come from cultures with different expectations may be especially unaware. In such circumstances, editors can play a useful educational role, whether by specifying ethical expectations in their instructions to authors, providing ethical guidance when working individually with authors, giving workshops, or informing authors by other means.

Ethics of Editors, Peer Reviewers, and Publishers

Science editors too have ethical obligations, and they sometimes face ethical issues regarding their own behavior. These obligations and issues differ somewhat according to the category of editor. For example, the editors-in-chief of journals have some different obligations than do manuscript editors.

The CSE White Paper notes that "[e]ditors of scientific journals have responsibilities toward the authors who provide the content of the journals, the peer reviewers who comment on the suitability of manuscripts for publication, the journal's readers and the scientific community, the owners/publishers of the journals, and the public as a whole" [59, p. 2]. Among obligations to authors are treating all authors fairly, politely, objectively, and honestly; protecting confidentiality of authors' work; and arranging for timely review and publication.

Obligations to reviewers include allowing reviewers sufficient time, not over-taxing individual reviewers by requesting reviews too often, and finding ways to recognize reviewers' contributions. Among obligations to readers are ensuring that each published paper contains adequate evidence to evaluate the conclusions; maintaining the journal's internal integrity, for example, by correcting errors; and providing a mechanism, such as letters to the editor, to discuss scientific merits of published papers. Among obligations to journal owners are operating the journal responsibly from a fiscal standpoint and adhering to the agreed-on mission of the journal [59, pp. 2-6]. Acquisitions editors at book publishers seem to have many of the same ethical obligations as do journal editors.

Editors of journals can face a variety of conflicts of interest. For example, such conflicts can arise when a submitted paper is by a colleague, friend, or former student. They can arise when a paper being considered regards an entity in which the editor has a financial interest. And they can arise when the editor wishes to publish in his or her journal a paper about his or her own research. An option in such circumstances is to delegate to an associate editor or other member of the editorial staff the handling of the paper.

Editors choosing science content for publications other than journals also can experience ethical quandaries. For example, editors of trade magazines in the sciences sometimes feel pressure from advertisers to cover those advertisers' products. Favoring advertisers when deciding on content runs counter to editorial integrity, but loss of revenue from key advertisers may threaten the survival of the magazine. Science editors in the popular media sometimes face pressure to run stories that will increase magazine or newspaper sales or boost broadcast ratings, regardless of whether other stories would serve the public better. In particular, such pressures can lead medical editors in the popular media to focus on what have been half-jokingly called "the only two types of health news stories—New Hope and No Hope" [68, p. 6], rather than providing more balanced, if less dramatic, coverage.

Manuscript editors have ethical obligations and can face ethical dilemmas. Ethical obligations of manuscript editors in the sciences [69] include reporting apparent ethical lapses by authors; discouraging listing of authors who do not qualify; treating communications with authors as confidential; recommending deletion of conclusions apparently not supported by the data; disclosing their own conflicts of interest; strengthening their skills through continuing education; avoiding bias or favoritism among authors; maintaining the author's style; noting editorial changes that could alter meaning; and teaching authors about ethical publication. One situation in which ethical dilemmas can arise is when editors are asked to copyedit materials, such as application essays, that may be used in part to judge writing proficiency.

Other parties involved in scientific publication also have ethical responsibilities. Peer reviewers [59, pp. 25-29] must provide timely, unbiased, constructive feedback; maintain confidentiality; and disclose their own conflicts of interest. Obligations of the publishers, sponsoring societies, and owners of journals include respecting the autonomy of the editor [59, pp. 34-35].

INTERACTIONS OF SCIENCE EDITORS WITH OTHERS

Editing has been stereotyped as a pursuit for the reclusive or socially inept. Some envision it as a solitary occupation. Others view editors as invariably condescending and derogatory. However, as may be apparent from previous material in this chapter, success in science-editorial roles often requires good interpersonal skills, including considerable tact. Advice is available to science editors on interacting with authors [70-72], peer reviewers [73, 74], scientific illustrators [75], indexers [76], and others, including fellow members of the editorial team [77].

The following are some suggestions for interacting with authors. Although most could aid editors in nearly any field, some appear especially pertinent to editing in the sciences.

- Put yourself in the author's shoes. In fact, keep doing some writing, to remind yourself of how challenging writing can be and what interacting with editors can be like.
- When assigning articles, such as reports on scientific conferences [78], make expectations clear.
- Remember to compliment the good, not just criticize the bad. In both written and oral feedback, begin and end positively. Remember that many in the sciences are insecure about their writing skills. Realize that they may accept suggestions more readily if they feel that their writing is valued and respected.
- Remember that the writing is the author's. If something is acceptable, don't change it just because it isn't the way you would have done it.
- Consider asking questions rather than making criticisms or corrections. Doing so can help authors make improvements in their own way. Also, especially in the sciences, doing so often helps draw out information that might be helpful to include.
- Especially if you will continue to work with the author, try to be a teacher or coach. Initially, doing so may be more difficult and time-consuming than simply making corrections. However, in the long run it can save effort and time.
- When commissioning writing from scientists, build extra time into the schedule. Successful scientists often are very busy, and the writing might therefore arrive later than requested.
- If you are angry with an author, cool down before contacting him or her. Authors in the sciences, like other people, sometimes do exasperating things.

However, an emotional confrontation is unlikely to be constructive. Take some time to let your anger dissipate, and then approach the author coolly and rationally.

- Try to match authors (and scientific illustrators, photographers, and others) with types of assignments they enjoy. In addition to gaining loyalty, you are likely to obtain a higher-quality product.
- If commissioning for-pay assignments, see that those producing them are paid promptly.
- Be ready to be a good listener. An understanding and helpful editor often becomes a confidante. If a scientist-author wishes to discuss issues beyond the manuscript at hand, in general take it as a compliment. Realize, though, that your time is limited and that some types of issues might not be appropriate to discuss.
- Let the author take the credit. If your efforts transformed an incoherent piece into a publishable scientific paper, making a snide remark may be difficult to resist when the author's writing is praised. However, let the author take the credit. Such is the editor's role. The author may well acknowledge your contributions. But doing so should be at the author's initiative.

The most adept science editors edit with a light touch. They try to make the least obtrusive changes needed to promote readability and meet the publication's requirements, thus minimizing chances of introducing new problems or antagonizing the author. Such editing often is more difficult than making changes that are more extensive. However, in science editing as in science, elegant simplicity is often the mark of the master.

INTERNATIONAL ASPECTS OF SCIENCE EDITING

Increasingly, effective interaction between science editor and author also entails bridging languages or cultures. In recent years, science editing has become more and more international, at least from a U.S. viewpoint. With English now the international language of science, researchers from many countries seek the visibility of publishing in English-language journals. Indeed, in some countries, employers of scientists provide financial or other incentives for English-language publication.

In addition, the Internet has facilitated international interaction in science editing. Thanks to e-mail, online journal management systems, and electronic availability of publications, authors can submit their manuscripts more easily to journals in other countries, editors can communicate more easily with authors throughout the world, manuscript editing can more readily be outsourced to editors abroad, and the readership of English-language materials in science has broadened.

Given these trends, native-English-speaking science editors in countries such as the United States are increasingly recognizing the need to work with authors from other linguistic and cultural backgrounds. They also are recognizing the importance of editing English-language materials in ways that facilitate understanding by readers with varied such backgrounds. These trends also have engendered more involvement of U.S. and other editors in programs to train and educate science editors and scientist-authors in various countries.

Aiding International Authors

Interaction of U.S. and other science editors with authors from abroad has been receiving considerable attention at conferences and in publications for science editors. For example, in a conference paper and then an article, Cheryl Iverson has explored U.S. medical editors' attitudes toward submissions from other countries. Noting steps journals have taken to increase international submissions and to help international authors, she concludes, "[I]t seems that although there were reasons for at least the *perception* of bias, the reality is becoming not only a lack of bias but a bias *for* rather than *against* manuscripts from outside the United States" [79, p. 77].

Writing on how science editors can work productively with authors for whom English is a not a native language, Carrie Cameron notes, "The process of composing text goes beyond using grammar, word choice, and sentence structure to making complex decisions about organization, rhetorical style, relationship to the audience, and establishment of author credibility" [80, p. 43]. She then identifies, and suggests ways to overcome, some common but often unrecognized sources of difficulty for non-native-English-speaking authors. Among these sources of difficulty are the requirement of a linear style and explicit conclusions, the distinction between patchwriting (for example, the borrowing of stock phrases) and plagiarism, and the use of transitional words and phrases.

Countering the usual idea that material by non-native speakers of English is best edited by native English speakers, Hua He and Ke-Jian Gan [81], of the *Chinese Journal of Cancer*, argue that at least the initial editing of such work by Chinese authors can best be done by editors who are English-fluent native Chinese speakers. Such editors, they note, can understand better the logic of the Chinese language (and thus better infer what the author intended), can communicate better with the authors, and can provide editing less expensively.

In the paragraph above, should the authors indeed be listed as Hua He and Ke-Jian Gan? Or should the surname (He or Gan) go first, in conventional Chinese fashion? Should the surname appear in all capital letters to aid in identification? In references, should the latter author's initial(s) be listed K. J. or only K.? As science editors deal increasingly with authors of varied national origins, such questions are arising more and more. To guide editors and others, *Science Editor* has been publishing articles about formats for names of various national origins [82-86]. These articles can be accessed at http://www.councilscienceeditors.org/publications/names.cfm.

Aiding International Readers, Editors, and Others

English-language science editors also face the challenge and responsibility of making scientific writing readily understandable by international readers, including those with only a rudimentary knowledge of English. Among resources that may be useful in this regard are the book *The Elements of International English Style* [87] and the chapter "Writing Clearly Across Cultures and Media" in *How to Write and Publish a Scientific Paper* [88].

A call has been made for the Council of Science Editors to collaborate more with teachers of English as a foreign language in teaching scientific reporting [89]. Under other auspices, science editors seem to be increasingly involved in educating scientist-authors in various countries; among approaches used are short courses and provision of online resources, for example through the initiative known as AuthorAID [90]. Science editors also are involved in efforts to educate their science-editorial peers from a variety of countries. Such efforts have included a program that pairs editors of African journals with editors of journals in the Northern Hemisphere [91] and a scholarship program through which editors from developing countries attend the Council of Science Editors annual meeting [92].

ORGANIZATIONS FOR SCIENCE EDITORS

Science editors generally work with few, if any, peers: Many scientific journals have small, part-time staffs. The rare academic science departments with author's editors very rarely have more than one. And freelance science editors commonly work as solo practitioners. Even at large journals or in large editorial departments, only one person might occupy a specific editorial role, such as that of managing editor. A way that science editors have overcome this isolation is through science editors' organizations, which traditionally have offered the exchange of information and ideas largely through conferences and periodicals. More recently, e-mail lists of some of these organizations have fostered frequent communication among editors around the world.

The main U.S.-based organization for science editors in general is the Council of Science Editors (http://www.CouncilScienceEditors.org). This organization originated in 1957 as the Conference of Biology Editors, was incorporated in 1965 as the Council of Biology Editors, and assumed its current identity in 2000 [93]. Activities of this organization include holding an annual meeting and associated short courses, publishing the periodical *Science Editor*, and preparing the style manual now known as *Scientific Style and Format* [49]. General science-editorial organizations based elsewhere include the European

Association of Science Editors (http://www.ease.org.uk/), which publishes the periodical *European Science Editing* and holds a major conference every three years.

Organizations also exist for editors in specific fields of science. One well-established such organization is the Association of Earth Science Editors (http://www.aese.org). Also, the Board of Editors in the Life Sciences (http://www.bels.org/), though concerned primarily with credentialing, serves as a professional network for those who have passed its examination. The World Association of Medical Editors (http://www.wame.org/)—better known as WAME (pronounced *whammy*)—is almost solely a virtual organization, functioning largely through its e-mail discussion list and its Web site [94].

Organizations in related fields also offer content of interest and use to science editors. Among such organizations are the American Medical Writers Association (http://www.amwa.org), Mediterranean Editors and Translators (http://www.metmeetings.org), the National Association of Science Writers (http://www.nasw.org), the Society for Scholarly Publishing (http://www.sspnet.org/), and the Society for Technical Communication (http://www.stc.org/). In addition, membership in scientific organizations, such as the American Association for the Advancement of Science (http://www.aaas.org) and societies in individual scientific disciplines, can help editors keep up with science and with science-editorial issues.

EDUCATION AND CREDENTIALING IN SCIENCE EDITING

"Many of us who call ourselves biology or scientific editors began our careers with little, if any, academic training in editing," wrote science editor David L. Armbruster in 1988. "Even today, you cannot major (or even minor) in scientific editing, and few schools offer an editing course beyond basic copyediting" [95, p. 99]. Today, the situation remains largely the same. Whereas well-established academic programs exist in technical communication [96], science journalism [97], and scholarly publishing [98], relatively little seems to exist in the way of formal academic training in science editing. Two decades after the Armbruster article, a recent medical-school graduate has summarized the training opportunities available for prospective physician-editors and called for a more formal approach [99].

Suggested Nature and Nurture of Science Editors

Visions vary as to what, if anything, such formal training should consist of and who is well suited to receive it. "No scientist has identified an editorial gene, and we have no documented reports of the muse Redactia visiting babies in their bassinets. Yet some people do seem better suited to editorial work than others," writes Amy Einsohn [100, p. 99], author of *The Copyeditor's Handbook*

[101]. Einsohn characterizes the "teachable novice" as having several skills and aptitudes, including a strong command of English, a sharp eye, a well-tuned ear, a good sense of logic, and a gift for intuiting "what a writer is trying to say and what the readers are likely to infer." She also identifies as desirable the following traits: a mix of perfectionism and realism, a willingness to work behind the scenes, stamina, "a dash of courage," and "a slightly toughened hide." For prospective editors in the sciences, additional items that seem desirable include an interest in science and an aptitude for understanding scientific content. Possible indicators that a scientist may be well suited for a science-editing career include an enjoyment of working with words, a preference to work broadly in science rather than focusing on a narrow research area, and a tendency to do much of the writing or editing of items produced by research teams on which they serve.

Discussion has long existed (for example, [102]) as to whether formal training in English or in science is preferable for a manuscript editor in the sciences. Perhaps the best answer is "some of each." Excellent science editors have come from each of these backgrounds—and from others. Many, it seems, of those who have most rapidly become proficient have had some education in each realm. Perhaps more important than the specifics of one's educational background is the motivation and ability to learn whatever basics one still must acquire to function competently as a science editor and then to keep learning, as new types of tasks arise and as science and editing continue to change.

In the late 1990s, two well-established biomedical editors presented their vision of appropriate curricula for those entering the field. First, Susan Eastwood [103] proposed an educational program encompassing both undergraduate and graduate work. Undergraduate courses were to be taken in basic science; bibliographic retrieval; education; English; history, philosophy, and sociology of science and medicine; foreign languages; and writing and editing. Graduate education was to include course work in biomedical sciences, English, management, medical arts, research ethics, production, psychology, statistics and mathematics, scientific illustration, and again writing and editing; graduate electives could be drawn from such fields as management, production, and visual science. In response, Thomas A. Lang [104] proposed a biomedical writing and editing curriculum with seven core courses: An Overview of Biomedical Research and Publications, Medical Editing, Reporting Statistics in Medicine, Data and Visual Displays, Communication Theory and Research, Medical Writing, and Publication Design and Production. Lang also listed electives that could provide further breadth or specialization—for example, courses in journal publishing, book publishing, and aspects of pharmaceutical writing.

Course Offerings

Various visions of optimal training for science editors remain. But what, actually, is available today? Although rare, some academic and other courses specifically in science editing exist. Since 1997, a graduate course in science editing [105] has been given on demand about once a year at Texas A&M University. Topics include general basics of manuscript editing, fundamentals of editing various types of science copy (including science articles for general readerships, scientific papers, and grant proposals), the author-editor relationship, editing of materials by nonnative speakers of English, ethical issues in science editing, and career opportunities in the field. The students use two textbooks: *The Copyeditor's Handbook* [101] and *Editing and Publication: A Training Manual*, which originated as materials for a training course sponsored by the International Rice Research Institute and the International Development Research Center of Canada in collaboration with the University of Toronto Press [106, p. xi]. Although the former book does not focus specifically on science editing and the latter, published in 1991, is now out of date regarding editorial technology ("Imagine a journal without paper. Everyone connected with it has a computer terminal," the author writes [106, p. 371]), both books contain much of relevance. Along with examples of science editing, articles from *Science Editor* magazine and other periodicals round out the reading for the course. During some terms, the course includes a visit to the local university press to learn more about book editing or to a printing company to become better acquainted with print production.

A variety of courses in science editing are available other than for traditional academic credit. These courses tend to be short and intensive. For example, offerings available through the medical writing and editing certificate program [107] at the University of Chicago include "Introduction to Medical Editing," "Advanced Medical Editing," and "Designing and Editing Tables and Graphs"; these continuing-education courses meet intensively for three days and include assignments beforehand and afterward. EEI Communications offers a two-day course in scientific editing [108]. In the mid-1990s, at the request of the editor of the *BMJ* (formerly *British Medical Journal*), an independent trainer established a two-day course in the United Kingdom for editors of medical journals [109]. This annual course, now given by another trainer [110], has attracted editors from many countries. Also, each May, immediately before its annual meeting, the Council of Science Editors conducts one- and two-day short courses [111]. These have long included a course for journal editors, a course for managing editors, and a course for manuscript editors. Recently a statistics course for editors was added. In addition, the many three-hour workshops offered by the American Medical Writers Association [112] at its national and other conferences include some on editing and some on other topics, such as statistics, that can be useful for science editors.

Internships and Other On-Site Learning

Fellowships and internships have served as another means of science-editorial education. Early examples of such science-editorial training through supervised practical experience include the graduate editorial fellowship established in the mid-1970s at the *Quarterly Review of Biology* [113]. In 1977, the *Journal of the American Medical Association* (*JAMA*) established the Morris Fishbein Fellowship in Medical Editing, named for a longtime editor of the journal. Through this fellowship, physicians interested in medical editing and publishing spend a year working and learning at *JAMA*. More than half of those who have held this fellowship have then spent at least part of their careers in medical editing or related realms [114]. The *New England Journal of Medicine* [115] and *CMAJ: Canadian Medical Association Journal* [116] likewise have programs providing physicians with 1-year fellowships at their editorial offices. The editorial fellowship program of the Radiological Society of North America [117, 118] offers radiologists a total of about 1 month's experience observing and taking part in the editorial activities of its journals. The Society for Technical Communication has offered a flexibly structured fellowship program in which each fellow pursues an individually designed program with a mentor who is a journal editor [119]. Also, the periodical of the Council of Science Editors, *Science Editor*, has regularly hosted interns, who serve as staff writers, assist in other ways, and observe the workings of the publication; several of the interns have gone on to science-editorial careers [120].

Some science-editorial internships for students or others are arranged ad hoc. For example, a recent program for Chinese biomedical-editing trainees [121] included individually arranged internships at editorial offices of a variety of journals and institutions. Thus, students and others who wish to learn about science editing and explore career options in it should not hesitate to ask editorial offices about the possibility of an internship. Likewise, science editors should consider offering internships, which can benefit both intern and host; an article in the *AMWA* [*American Medical Writers Association*] *Journal* offers guidance in doing so [122].

Student editorships, student journals, and related endeavors have been other vehicles for introduction to science editing. Some medical journals have included medical students on their staffs, thus serving as "schools for editors" [123]. The many undergraduate student research journals [124]—at individual universities, in single disciplines, or more broadly—likewise acquaint students with editorial processes and issues. Instructive experience also is provided by the National Institutes of Health (NIH) Fellows Editorial Board, through which postdoctoral fellows and others at NIH review drafts of journal papers, grant proposals, and other scientific documents [125].

Much of the training of science editors occurs on the job, either through informal apprenticeship or more formally. Editors-in-chief of scientific journals commonly emerge from the ranks of associate editors or the equivalent. Managing editors commonly orient their successors. Editorial offices at scientific publications and institutions acquaint new manuscript editors with the work. The American Society for Microbiology has a structured six- to seven-month training period for those new to the manuscript editing office that serves its journals [126].

The editorial offices of the American Chemical Society and the journal *Science* have reported training periods of about this length [127], as has the editorial office of *JAMA* [128]. It seems likely that smaller journals tend to have training periods that are less formal or shorter.

BELS Certification

Regardless of the amount (if any) of education and experience in science editing, anyone can call oneself a science editor. Thus, prospective employers may find it especially difficult to determine whether candidates for science-editorial work have the needed knowledge and skills. And unqualified individuals marketing themselves as science editors can damage the reputation of the field as a whole. To help remedy the situation, a group of science editors began working in the late 1970s and early 1980s to develop a means by which manuscript editors in biology and medicine could demonstrate their proficiency and thus receive a credential [129, 130].

The result, officially established in 1991, was the Board of Editors in the Life Sciences (BELS), which offers certification in life-science editing [130, 131]. Individuals who pass the 3-hour multiple-choice examination given by BELS can use the designation ELS (Editor in the Life Sciences) after their names. Those with this credential can later earn Diplomate status, designated by ELS(D), by documenting sufficient experience and submitting an acceptable portfolio. The BELS Roster [132] lists all who have been credentialed by BELS; as of summer 2008, more than 700 people had passed its examination.

ECONOMICS OF SCIENCE EDITING

Although science editors tend not to be very motivated by economic gain, some awareness of the economics underlying their activities can be of use. Funding of those in paid science-editorial roles commonly comes from one or more of the following: publication subscriptions, association memberships (in the case of association-sponsored periodicals), advertisements, and grants, for example to researchers hiring editors. Much unpaid editing, for instance by part-time editors of scientific journals, is subsidized by universities' allowing faculty members to spend part of their time editing or by editors' donating spare time to their editorial work.

The advent of new economic models of scientific publishing—especially open access, in which journal articles are made available immediately on the Internet, at no charge to the reader—raises questions about the continuing economic support of science editing. Thus far in open-access journals, funds that previously would have come from subscriptions have come from publication charges to authors and from subsidies. It remains unclear whether, and if so how, new economic models for scientific publication may affect the availability of resources for editing.

In society as a whole, emphasis seems to be increasing on documenting outcomes and determining whether activities are indeed worth the cost. Although to many of us it seems intuitively clear that the activities of various categories of science editor contribute to the quality of the scientific literature, research to support (or refute) this conclusion seems scanty. For example, the authors of a systematic review article on the effects of technical editing in biomedical journals concluded that "remarkably little is known" [133] on this topic. Growing interest now seems to exist in strengthening the evidence base on which to base decisions about what science-editorial activities to undertake and how. For example, the Council of Science Editors has added a research poster session to its annual meeting and titled its 2009 annual meeting "Show Me the Data–The Science of Editing and Publishing." Meanwhile, the relative proportions of science and art in the varied craft of "science editing" remain subject to debate.

LOOKING AHEAD

As science editing approaches the second decade of the 21st century, what may be in store? Having heard the claims that electronic journals would never succeed, I hesitate to make predictions. However, the following appear likely:

- Additional internationalization of scientific publication and of the science-editorial community
- Further coalescence of the science-editorial community via the Internet
- Continued development of electronic publication technology—resulting in additional changes in how science editors work, increased attention to editing scientific materials that are mainly online, and perhaps emergence of new editorial roles
- Additional efforts to develop or refine economic models whereby scientific content can be readily available, especially to researchers and others in developing countries, but whereby funds will be available for high-quality editorial processes
- Further attention to ethical issues regarding authors, editors, and others involved in scientific publication—perhaps including exploration of new issues that may emerge as the technology, economics, and international character of science editing continue to change
- Additional research on the effects and effectiveness of science-editorial practices and more broadly on science editing
- Perhaps increased formalization of education and training in science editing, and perhaps increased emphasis on the credentialing of science editors

In any case, editing in the sciences seems likely to remain a wide-ranging, challenging, dynamic field, especially well suited for those inclined toward the content of the sciences and the craft of communication. May this chapter help inform the broader technical-editing community about editing in the sciences, and may it contribute to the success and satisfaction of my current and future colleagues in science editing.

DEDICATION

This chapter is dedicated to the memory of my in-laws, Barbara R. and Richard C. Vogel, both of whom died in 2008. They live on in our lives.

REFERENCES

Bibliographic note: Items cited below from *Science Editor* can be accessed via the Council of Science Editors Web site, at http://www.CouncilScienceEditors.org

1. J. A. Hutt, Editing the Sounds of Science: Science Editors at National Public Radio, *Science Editor*, *26*, p. 50, 2003.
2. D. Pineda, Editing a Science Documentary: More Than Words (Literally!), *Science Editor*, *27*, pp. 47-49, 2004.
3. S. Kanel and B. Gastel, Careers in Science Editing: An Overview to Use or Share, *Science Editor, 31*, pp. 18-22, 2008.
4. J. M. White, Editing University Research Magazines: A View from the Top, *Science Editor, 26*, pp. 86-87, 2003.
5. J. M. White, Producing Conference Programs: Tips from Pros, *Science Editor*, *26*, pp. 51-52, 2003.
6. G. M. Smith, The Role of Managing Editor: An Overview, *CBE Views*, *20*, pp. 39-43, 1997.
7. C. Iverson, "Copy Editor" vs "Manuscript Editor" vs . . .: Venturing onto the Minefield of Titles, *Science Editor*, *27*, pp. 39-41, 2004.
8. R. Horton, The Lancet's Ombudsman, *Lancet*, *348*:9019, p. 6, 1996.
9. K. Satyanarayana, Reflections of a Pioneering Ombudsman at an Indian Journal, *Science Editor, 27*, pp. 117-119, 2004.
10. A. Williamson, M. Kidambi, and B. Gastel, The 2008 AAAS Annual Meeting: Some Sessions Related to Science Editing, *Science Editor*, *31*, pp. 124-128, 2008.
11. C. M. Hughes, Project Management Strategies for Medical Writers and Editors, *AMWA Journal*, *22*, pp. 17-21, 2007.
12. J. R. Gilbert, C. N. Wright, J. I. Amberson, and A. L. Thompson, Profile of the Author's Editor: Findings from a National Survey, *CBE Views, 7*:1, pp. 4-10, 1984.
13. M. Tacker, The Creed of the Author's Editor, *CBE Newsletter, No. 21*, p. 7, 1976. Reprinted in *Science Editor, 30*, p. 99, 2007.
14. M. Tacker, Author's Editors: Catalysts of Scientific Publishing, *CBE Views*, *3*:1, pp. 3-11, 1980.
15. M. Kidambi, English-Language Editing Services for Researchers, *Science Editor, 31*, pp. 115-117, 2008.
16. R. Pike, Establishing and Maintaining an Editorial Department Servicing Researchers in an Academic Setting, *Science Editor*, *28*, p. 9, 2005.
17. J. Scales, Editing Grant Applications and Proposals, *CBE Views, 21*, p. 3, 1998.

18. D. Mitrany, Creating Effective Poster Presentations: The Editor's Role, *Science Editor, 28,* pp. 114-116, 2005.

19. T. A. Lang, Physical and Processing Characteristics of Manuscripts Submitted for Substantive Editing, *CBE Views, 19,* pp. 111-115, 1996.

20. T. A. Lang, Assessing the Productivity and Value of a Hospital-Based Editing Service, *AMWA Journal, 12*:1, pp. 6-14, 1997.

21. J. Ancker and A. S. Moore, How to Teach Doctors to Write: 10 Lessons from Teaching a Writing Course at an Academic Medical Center, *AMWA Journal, 16*:2, pp. 17-21, 2001.

22. J. L. Griner, Learning to Listen, Listening to Learn: Developing Scientific Communicators at UAB, *Science Editor, 25,* pp. 61-62, 2002.

23. D. Fuccillo, Teaching Scientific Writing: Early Contributions of the Council, *Science Editor, 30,* p. 80, 2007.

24. F. P. Woodford (ed.), *Scientific Writing for Graduate Students: A Manual on the Teaching of Scientific Writing,* Council of Biology Editors, New York, 1968.

25. F. P. Woodford, *How to Teach Scientific Communication,* Council of Biology Editors, Reston, Virginia, 1999.

26. E. Churchill, Challenges in the Global Classroom: Perspectives of an American Science Editor, *Science Editor, 29,* pp. 39-41, 2006.

27. J. A. M. Eliason, Educating Prospective Authors, *CBE Views, 19,* pp. 125-126, 1996.

28. J. De Gregory, Deciding to Become a Freelance Science Editor, *Science Editor, 28,* pp. 17-19, 2005.

29. S. Lock, *A Difficult Balance: Editorial Peer Review in Medicine,* ISI Press, Philadelphia, Pennsylvania, 1986.

30. F. Godlee and T. Jefferson (eds.), *Peer Review in Health Sciences,* BMJ Books, London, 1999.

31. I. Hames, *Peer Review and Manuscript Management in Scientific Journals: Guidelines for Good Practice,* Blackwell Publishing, Malden, Massachusetts, 2007.

32. Peer Review Congress. Available online at:
http://www.ama-assn.org/public/peer/peerhome.htm

33. T. A. Lang and M. Secic, *How to Report Statistics in Medicine: Annotated Guidelines for Authors, Editors, and Reviewers* (2nd ed.), American College of Physicians, Philadelphia, Pennsylvania, 2006.

34. T. Lang, Common Statistical Errors Even YOU Can Find. Part 1: Errors in Descriptive Statistics and in Interpreting Probability Values, *AMWA Journal, 18,* pp. 67-71, 2003.

35. T. Lang, Common Statistical Errors Even YOU Can Find. Part 2: Errors in Multivariate Analyses and in Interpreting Differences Between Groups, *AMWA Journal, 18,* pp. 103-107, 2003.

36. T. Lang, Common Statistical Errors Even YOU Can Find. Part 3: Errors in Data Displays, *AMWA Journal, 19*:2, pp. 9-11, 2004.

37. T. Lang, Common Statistical Errors Even YOU Can Find. Part 4: Errors in Correlation and Regression Analyses, *AMWA Journal, 20,* pp. 10-11, 2005.

38. T. Lang, Common Statistical Errors Even YOU Can Find. Part 5: Errors in Reports of Diagnostic Tests, *AMWA Journal, 20,* pp. 50-51, 2005.

39. T. Lang, Common Statistical Errors Even YOU Can Find. Part 6: Errors in Research Designs, *AMWA Journal*, *20*, pp. 112-115, 2005.

40. T. Lang, Common Statistical Errors Even YOU Can Find. Part 7: Errors in Conclusions, *AMWA Journal*, *21*, pp. 17-18, 2006.

41. E. L. Fleischer, Editing Across the Sciences: Materials Science, *Science Editor*, *27*, pp. 133-135, 2004.

42. J. D. Baldwin, Editing Across the Sciences: Ecology, *Science Editor*, *27*, pp. 135-136, 2004.

43. J. Hammann, Editing Across the Sciences: Geoscience, *Science Editor*, *27*, p. 137, 2004.

44. J. Ewing, Editing Across the Sciences: Mathematics, *Science Editor*, *27*, p. 201, 2004.

45. C. Iverson, Editing Across the Sciences: Medicine, *Science Editor*, *28*, pp. 30-31, 2005.

46. S. G. Brown, Editing Across the Sciences: Physics, *Science Editor*, *28*, p. 60, 2005.

47. Y. Steiman, Editing Across the Sciences: Chemistry, *Science Editor*, *29*, pp. 60-61, 2006.

48. University of Chicago Press, *The Chicago Manual of Style* (15th ed.), University of Chicago Press, Chicago, Illinois, 2003.

49. Style Manual Committee, Council of Science Editors, *Scientific Style and Format: The CSE Manual for Authors, Editors, and Publishers* (7th ed.), Council of Science Editors, Reston, Virginia, 2006.

50. C. Iverson, S. Christiansen, A. Flanagin, P. B. Fontanarosa, R. M. Glass, B. Gregoline, S. J. Lurie, H. S. Meyer, M. A. Winker, and R. K. Young, *AMA Manual of Style: A Guide for Authors and Editors* (10th ed.), Oxford University Press, New York, 2007.

51. C. Iverson, Manual Labor: The Evolution of the AMA Manual of Style, *Science Editor*, *30*, pp. 191-192, 2007.

52. American Psychological Association, *Publication Manual of the American Psychological Association* (6th ed.), American Psychological Association, Washington, D.C., 2010.

53. A. M. Coghill and L. R. Garson (eds.), *The ACS Style Guide: Effective Communication of Scientific Information* (3rd ed.), Oxford University Press, New York, 2006.

54. International Committee of Medical Journal Editors, Uniform Requirements for Manuscripts Submitted to Biomedical Journals: Writing and Editing for Biomedical Publication, updated October 2008. Available online at: http://www.icmje.org

55. E. J. Huth and K. Case, The URM: Twenty-Five Years Old, *Science Editor*, *27*, pp. 17-21, 2004.

56. M. Kahn, Standards of Reporting Biomedical Research: What's New? *Science Editor*, *28*, p. 4, 2005.

57. D. Moher, K. F. Schulz, and D. Altman, for the CONSORT Group, The CONSORT Statement: Revised Recommendations for Improving the Quality of Reports of Parallel-Group Randomized Trials, *JAMA*, *285*, pp. 1987-1991, 2001.

58. Instructions to Authors in the Health Sciences. Available online at: http://mulford.meduohio.edu/instr/

59. D. Scott-Lichter and the Editorial Policy Committee, Council of Science Editors, *CSE's White Paper on Promoting Integrity in Scientific Journal Publications, 2009 Update*, Council of Science Editors, Reston, Virginia, 2009. Available online at: http://www.councilscienceeditors.org/editorial_policies/white_paper.cfm

60. Committee on Publication Ethics. Available online at: http://publicationethics.org/

61. Ethics and Editorial Policies, Council of Science Editors. Available online at: http://www.councilscienceeditors.org/editorial_policies/policies.cfm

62. WAME: World Association of Medical Editors. Available online at: http://www.wame.org/

63. American Physical Society, APS Guidelines for Professional Conduct. Available online at: http://www.aps.org/policy/statements/02_2.cfm

64. J. C. Bailar III, M. Angell, S. Boots, E. S. Myers, N. Palmer, M. Shipley, and P. Woolf, *Ethics and Policy in Scientific Publication*, Council of Biology Editors, Bethesda, Maryland, 1990.

65. Committee on Science, Engineering, and Public Policy, *On Being a Scientist: A Guide to Responsible Conduct in Research* (3rd ed.), National Academy Press, Washington, D.C., 2009. Available online at: http://www.nap.edu/catalog.php?record_id=12192

66. M. H. Conway, Jerks or Crooks: The Difference Between Ethics and Etiquette in Science, *CBE Views*, *17*, pp. 67-68, 1994.

67. Committee on Publication Ethics, Flow Charts. Available online at: http://publicationethics.org/flowcharts

68. V. Cohn and L. Cope, *News & Numbers: A Guide to Reporting Statistical Claims and Controversies in Health and Other Fields* (2nd ed.), Iowa State University Press, Ames, Iowa, 2001.

69. R. K. Young, Ethical Dilemmas for Manuscript Editors, *CBE Views*, *20*, pp. 15-16, 1997.

70. A. Soffer, Care and Treatment of the Disappointed Author, *CBE Views*, *3*:3, pp. 2-3, 1980. Reprinted in *Science Editor*, *30*, p. 97, 2007.

71. S. Eastwood and D. Liberthson, The Author-Editor Relationship, in *Essays for Biomedical Communicators: Volume 1 of Selected AMWA Workshops* (rev. ed.), F. M. Witte and N. D. Taylor (eds.), American Medical Writers Association, Rockville, Maryland, pp. 79-91, 2001.

72. E. Whalen, The Author-Editor Relationship: Observations and Suggestions, *CBE Views*, *11*, pp. 5-7, 1988.

73. R. M. Pitkin, The Care and Feeding of Reviewers, *CBE Views*, *20*, p. 191, 1997.

74. M. Edington, The Care and Feeding of Reviewers, *Science Editor*, *24*, p. 193, 2001.

75. R. K. Young, How Scientific Editors and Authors Should Work with Scientific Illustrators, *CBE Views*, *15*, pp. 131-132, 1992.

76. M. K. Sahai, Working with Indexers: What, When, Where, Who, Why, and How, *Science Editor*, *24*, pp. 49-50, 2001.

77. Y. Moosy, Editor/Managing Editor Relationships: Management, Policy, Crisis, *CBE Views*, *10*, pp. 62-63, 1987.

78. B. Gastel, Publishing Excellent Conference Reports: Editors and Reporters Share Advice, *Science Editor*, *25*, pp. 118-121, 2002.

79. C. Iverson, US Medical Journal Editors' Attitudes Toward Submissions from Other Countries, *Science Editor*, *25*, pp. 75-78, 2002.

80. C. Cameron, Bridging the Gap: Working Productively with ESL Authors, *Science Editor*, *30*, pp. 43-44, 2007.

81. H. He and K. J. Gan, Advantages of English-Fluent Chinese Editors over Native-English-Speaking Editors in Editing Chinese Biomedical Manuscripts, *Science Editor, 31,* pp. 189-192, 2008.

82. X. L. Sun and J. Zhou, English Versions of Chinese Authors' Names in Biomedical Journals: Observations and Recommendations, *Science Editor*, *25*, pp. 3-4, 2002.

83. B. Black, Indexing the Names of Authors from Spanish- and Portuguese-Speaking Countries, *Science Editor*, *26*, pp. 118-121, 2003.

84. B. Notzon and G. Nesom, The Arabic Naming System, *Science Editor*, *28*, pp. 20-21, 2005.

85. S. Han, Formats of Korean Authors' Names, *Science Editor*, *28*, pp. 189-190, 2005.

86. M. Kidambi, Indian Names: A Guide for Science Editors, *Science Editor*, *31*, pp. 120-121, 2008.

87. E. H. Weiss, *The Elements of International English Style*, M. E. Sharpe, Armonk, New York, 2005.

88. R. A. Day and B. Gastel, *How to Write and Publish a Scientific Paper* (6th ed.), Greenwood Press, Westport, Connecticut, 2006.

89. M. van Naerssen and S. Eastwood, CSE and Teachers of English to Speakers of Other Languages: A Call for Greater Collaboration in Teaching Scientific Reporting, *Science Editor*, *24*, pp. 3-6, 2001.

90. AuthorAID. Available online at: http://www.authoraid.info

91. T. Nading, CSE Helps Manage Partnerships to Enhance African Journals, *Science Editor*, *28*, pp. 106-107, 2005.

92. R. M. Barr, R. S. Benner, P. Erickson, K. F. Heideman, M. Hoffman, and L. Korte, Council of Science Editors International Scholarship Program: The 2007 Recipients, *Science Editor*, *30*, pp. 203-206, 2007.

93. D. Krischer, CSE's First 50 Years: Blazing the Trail for Science Editors Everywhere, *Science Editor*, *30*, pp. 39-40, 2007.

94. B. P. Squires and S. W. Fletcher, The World Association of Medical Editors (WAME): Thriving in Its First Decade, *Science Editor*, *28*, 13-16, 2005.

95. D. L. Armbruster, Training in Scientific Editing, *CBE Views*, *11*, pp. 99-100, 1988.

96. Society for Technical Communication, Academic Programs Database. Available online at: http://www.stc.org/edu/academicDatabase01.asp

97. Directory of Science Communication Courses and Programs. Available online at: http://www.journalism.wisc.edu/dsc/

98. B. Luey, Knowledge, Skills, and Habits of Mind: The ASU Scholarly Publishing Program, *Science Editor*, *26*, pp. 27-28, 2003.

99. V. S. S. Wong, The Training of Physician-Editors: A Call for a More Formal Approach, *Science Editor*, *31*, pp. 75-77, 2008.

100. A. Einsohn, Are Editors Born or Made? *Science Editor*, *27*, pp. 99-100, 2004. Reprinted from *The Editorial Eye*.

101. A. Einsohn, *The Copyeditor's Handbook: A Guide for Book Publishing and Corporate Communications, with Exercises and Answer Keys* (2nd ed.), University of California Press, Berkeley, California, 2006.

102. B. K. Forscher, Preferred Background for Manuscript Editors: English or Science? *CBE Views*, *8*:3, pp. 5-7, 1985.

103. S. Eastwood, Growing a Biomedical Manuscript Editor, *CBE Views*, *21*, pp. 51-52, 1998.

104. T. A. Lang, A Curriculum for Biomedical Writing and Editing: A Second Volley, *CBE Views*, *22*, pp. 3-5, 1999.

105. B. Gastel, A Science Editing Course for Graduate Students, *Science Editor, 30*, pp. 59-60, 2007.

106. I. Montagnes, *Editing and Publication: A Training Manual*, International Rice Research Institute, Manila, 1991.

107. Medical Writing & Editing 2008-2009 Certificate Program & Advanced Program, The University of Chicago Graham School of Graduate Studies. Available online at: https://grahamschool.uchicago.edu/php/medicalwritingandediting/

108. EEI—Scientific Editing Training. Available online at: http://www.eeicom.com/training/dispclas.cfm?classID=10613

109. T. Albert, Learning with Editors: Lessons from a Long-Running Short Course, *Science Editor*, *26*, p. 201, 2003

110. Editing Medical Journals—Short Course. Available online at: http://www.pspconsulting.org/medical-short.shtml

111. Council of Science Editors 2009 Short Courses. Available online at: http://www.councilscienceeditors.org/events/shortcourses09/sc_journaleditors.cfm

112. American Medical Writers Association Education Program Information. Available online at: http://www.amwa.org/default.asp?id=250

113. B. Glass, Graduate Editorial Fellowships—An Idea Whose Time Has Come, *CBE Views*, *3*:2, pp. 3-8, 1980.

114. C. Meyer and R. M. Glass, JAMA's Fishbein Fellowship, *Science Editor*, *27*, p. 202, 2004.

115. T. L. Schraeder, NEJM Fellowship: The Ultimate Journal Club, *Science Editor*, *28*, pp. 141-142, 2005.

116. CMAJ Editorial Fellowship. Available online at: http://www.cmaj.ca/misc/fellowship.shtml

117. M. I. Soglin, The RSNA Editorial Fellowship, *Science Editor*, *25*, pp. 137-138, 2002.

118. RSNA William R. Eyler Editorial Fellowship. Available online at: http://www.rsna.org/Publications/editorial_fellowships.cfm

119. L. Wang, STC Establishes Journal Editor Fellowship Program, *Science Editor, 24*, p. 7, 2001.

120. B. Gastel, Interns, Fellows, and Student Contributors: In Appreciation, *Science Editor, 26*, p. 38, 2003.

121. J. M. White, Training Programs in Scientific Publishing for Distance Learners, *Science Editor*, *23*, p. 155, 2000.

122. B. Gastel, Hosting a Biomedical Communication Intern: From Idea Through Implementation, *AMWA Journal, 21*, pp. 97-101, 2006.

123. S. L. Abrams, Medical Journals as "Schools for Editors," *CBE Views*, *13*, pp. 3-5, 1990.

124. S. Kanel. Undergraduate Student Research Journals: Opportunities to Publish and Learn, *Science Editor*, *31*, pp. 78-80, 2008.

125. R. Al-Hallaq, The National Institutes of Health Fellows Editorial Board, *Science Editor*, *31*, pp. 81-82, 2008.
126. M. A. Reel, Editor Training at the American Society for Microbiology, *Science Editor*, *26*, pp. 137-138, 2003.
127. D. Lang, Editorial Staff: Selecting, Training, and Retaining Copyeditors, *CBE Views*, *19*, pp. 79-80, 1996.
128. J. Walker, Hiring and Training Copyeditors, *Science Editor*, *25*, p. 190, 2002.
129. F. Porcher, Certifying Editors in the Life Sciences, *CBE Views*, *21*, pp. 65-66, 1998.
130. N. Grossblatt and B. B. Reitt, BELS: The First 10 Years, *Science Editor*, *24*, pp. 39-42, 2001.
131. Board of Editors in the Life Sciences. Available online at: http://www.bels.org
132. BELS Roster. Available online at: http://www.bels.org/findeditor/bels_roster.cfm
133. E. Wager and P. Middleton, Effects of Technical Editing in Biomedical Journals: A Systematic Review, *JAMA*, *287*, pp. 2821-2824, 2002.

CHAPTER 9

Editing a Technical Journal

George F. Hayhoe

Although the many activities associated with editing a technical journal certainly include copymarking, copyediting, proofreading, and comprehensive editing, these tasks are essentially no different for a technical journal than for other types of documents [1, pp. 49-81, 107-120, 214-225, 231-246]. Rather than concentrating on these activities in this chapter, then, I will instead consider journal editing at a macro level as the management and operation of all aspects of a technical or scholarly journal.

Relatively little has been published on the topic of editing technical journals since the first one appeared in 1665 [2, p. 1]. The reason for this scarcity of information may be the rather limited audience—the small number of journal editors-in-chief, managing editors, and editorial staff who might have an interest in the subject. However, the audience is bigger than you might think. Thomson Scientific's *Web of Science*, which includes the *Science Citation Index, Social Sciences Citation Index*, and *Arts and Humanities Citation Index*, covers more than 10,000 journals and does not cover all journals in its areas of interest [3]. A much broader listing, *Ulrich's Periodicals Directory*, includes more than 300,000 serials, although the vast majority of those titles are newspapers and magazines [4].

A more likely explanation for the small amount published on this topic is that journals, no matter their size, tend to operate much like medieval crafts. For smaller publications, the knowledge and skills required to produce the journal are handed down from predecessor to successor. For larger journals, that tradecraft is passed among employees in the publishing house or professional society headquarters responsible for producing them.

155

http://dx.doi.org/10.2190/NPOC9

The purpose of this chapter, then, is to explain the concepts, skills, and techniques required to manage a technical journal. The material contained here synthesizes the relevant information in the literature on the subject, supplemented by my 12-year experience as a journal editor as well as my familiarity with the operation of journals published by the Institute of Electrical and Electronics Engineers (IEEE), the world's largest professional organization and the publisher of more than 100 journals.

Although the chapter title might suggest that my focus is scientific, technical, or medical journals, the information here may be readily applied to any peer-reviewed academic or professional journal that exists to expand the knowledge of its field of interest. In the sense that all such publications communicate specialized information, all may be legitimately termed "technical."

Finally, the intended audience for this chapter is broader than the audiences of the other chapters in this collection. Certainly, technical communicators may be interested in pursuing the role of editor-in-chief of a journal in our field or of managing editor for a journal in another discipline, and this chapter contains a significant amount of information about those roles that cannot be found elsewhere in the technical editing literature. However, professionals in other fields of interest should also find this chapter helpful if they wish to pursue those roles.

A VERY BRIEF HISTORY OF THE
TECHNICAL JOURNAL

Like the science they reported, the earliest learned journals were a product of the Enlightenment period in Europe. During the late 17th and 18th centuries, as universities flourished and grew in number, scientists and other scholars began to interact with each other in significant numbers. Organizations such as the Royal Society of London (founded in 1660), as well as the French Académie des sciences and the Royal Society of Edinburgh, provided venues in which eminent scientists, physicians, and mathematicians could meet. Prior to this period, scholars had depended mostly on books written by other experts or on correspondence to share ideas. The rise of these organizations meant that scientists were able to come together regularly, compare their research results and theories, and by learning from each other, grow knowledge in their fields of interest much more quickly than had been possible before.

Shortly after the first of these societies was established in London, the first technical journal appeared. The *Philosophical Transactions of the Royal Society* (1665) not only provided a place where knowledge shared at meetings could be published for the benefit of those unable to attend, but it also served as a permanent record of the knowledge presented at meetings or submitted to the society by those at a distance [2, p. 1].

Membership in these organizations was by invitation from established scholars. In a sense, election as a member, presentation of one's ideas at meetings, and subsequent publication in the *Transactions* served as a kind of peer review. It is important to note, however, that this was review of the individual's reputation, not of a specific manuscript.

The concept of peer review of specific manuscripts was only gradually introduced. By the mid-18th century, the royal societies of London and Edinburgh had begun to ask members to review manuscripts submitted for publication, but only in the past 50 to 75 years has the kind of double-blind peer review that we take for granted today been "widespread and reasonably standardized" in the vast majority of journals [2, p. 1].

As areas of knowledge increased in number as knowledge itself expanded, more specialized professional societies formed in response. These organizations held meetings and published their own proceedings, and so the number of journals—and the expectation that disciplines have their own journals—grew. The result nearly 350 years later is many thousands of journals, most of which are devoted to a relatively narrow field of interest. In some disciplines, depending on the degree of specialization and number of researchers and practitioners internationally, there are large numbers of journals. For example, there are more than 70 journals on orthopedic medicine published around the world [5].

TYPICAL JOURNAL OPERATION

Despite the title of this section, the "typical" journal doesn't really exist. In a sense, each journal is a unique creature that follows the organizing principles of its editor or publisher. It may reflect decisions made decades ago by an editor who has long since retired, or the policies that the professional society or company that serves as its publisher formulated in response to a postal rate increase in the 1990s. It may even derive in part from the vagaries of a typesetting system long since abandoned for the software in use today.

Despite many variations, however, the basic functions of a journal are essentially the same. I describe them here in terms of functions or positions, but the organization charts of two journals that share roughly the same functions may differ significantly depending on the mix of individuals available to fill the positions.

Organization and Responsibilities

The staff of a journal is headed by the editor-in-chief, who is responsible to the journal publisher's governing authority for all aspects of its management. The editor-in-chief is usually free to choose editorial staff as he or she deems necessary, subject to budget restrictions imposed by the governing authority. The production staff is typically hired or contracted with by the publisher. The typical journal staff and their duties are described in Table 1.

Table 1. Typical Journal Staff Functions and Positions

Function/position	Brief description of duties
EDITORIAL STAFF	
Editor-in-chief, Managing editor, Editor	The editor-in-chief, assisted by the editorial board and the rest of the journal staff, provides the vision for the publication. He or she is ultimately responsible for all decisions regarding acceptance or rejection of manuscripts, and for the content of all issues of the journal.
	In the case of large, high-frequency journals, as well as many published by large professional societies or companies, the editor-in-chief may have little direct involvement in the day-to-day operation of the journal. Instead, those duties are performed by the managing editor. The managing editor in such situations is typically responsible for corresponding with authors and reviewers, managing the review process, assembling issues, and sending copy to the production editor.
	Editor-in-chief is sometimes little more than an honorary title, with the managing editor doing the vast majority of the work.
	For smaller journals, these two functions may be combined into the single position of editor.
Guest editor	A guest editor is usually responsible for recruiting and leading the review of a special issue (an entire issue devoted to a single topic) or a special section (a group of articles devoted to a single topic). A guest editor may volunteer specifically for this task or may be recruited by the managing editor or editor-in-chief.
Associate editor	Associate editors are typically delegated responsibility for a topical or thematic area within the journal's field of interest. For example, a technical communication journal may have associate editors responsible for software documentation, international technical communication, editing, and engineering communication.
Department editor	Department editors are responsible for identifying content and recruiting contributors for recurring "departments" such as book reviews, correspondence, and annual bibliography of literature.
Note:	The functions of editor-in-chief, managing editor, associate editor, and department editor may be combined into one or more positions. While some large journals have 10 or more staff members assigned to perform these functions, in other cases, especially small journals, a single person performs them all.
	Essentially, these functions may be seen as part of the duties of the editor-in-chief, who may delegate these duties as he or she sees fit within budgetary limits prescribed by the journal publisher's governing authority.

Table 1. (Cont'd.)

Function/position	Brief description of duties
Review coordinators	Review coordinators may be appointed by the managing editor or editor-in-chief to manage the review of manuscripts. They are responsible for recruiting peer reviewers for particular assignments. Review coordinators are sometimes members of the editorial board.
Editorial board	The editorial board advises the editor-in-chief on vision, policy, and overall direction for the journal. Some journals may have multiple levels of advisory board, a senior board consisting of big names in the field who may have little or nothing to do with the actual operation of the journal, and a secondary board that functions more like the typical editorial board. Editorial board members are often very actively involved in reviewing or coordinating the review of manuscripts.
Indexer	This function is responsible for preparing the volume index for the journal, which usually appears in the last issue of a volume.
PRODUCTION STAFF	
Production editor	The production editor is responsible for managing the process of producing issues from copy supplied by the editor-in-chief or managing editor. Tasks performed or managed by this function include importing or converting word processing files to the journal's typesetting software; ensuring that manuscripts conform to house style; sizing and placing figures and tables; sending proofs to authors and the managing editor to catch errors introduced in typesetting; and making changes identified by the authors and managing editor. For small journals, the tasks of the production editor may be performed by the editor-in-chief or managing editor.
Art director	The art director is responsible for designing and producing paper or digital mechanicals for all figures contained in the issue as well as the cover. He or she also works with the typesetting and prepress operators to ensure that figures and advertising are correctly placed on pages.
Advertising sales manager	The advertising sales manager is responsible for recruiting advertising for the journal and providing paper or digital mechanicals for all ads to the art director.
Typesetting and prepress operators	The typesetting and prepress operators are responsible for composing pages and producing page proofs.
Printing, binding, and mailing operators	The printing, binding, and mailing operators are responsible for printing and binding copies, and mailing them to subscribers
Online issue production and hosting operators	The online issue production and hosting operators are responsible for preparing and hosting the online version of the journal.

Note on terminology: Because for many journals there is not a one-to-one correspondence between positions and functions, in the remainder of this chapter, the term *editor* is used generically to encompass the range of editorial functions and positions described in Table 1.

Correspondence

These days, essentially all journal-related correspondence is conducted by e-mail. The editor is ordinarily responsible for all correspondence with authors and is the author's point of contact for information on a submission's status and the details of its acceptance and publication. The editor may delegate responsibility for correspondence with reviewers to a guest editor for a special issue, to an associate editor for a topical area, or to a member of the editorial board or a review coordinator for a particular manuscript.

In all correspondence, the editor and the editor's designees (guest editors, associate editors, members of the editorial board, and review coordinators) are responsible for ensuring the integrity of the double-blind peer review process by not disclosing the identities of authors to reviewers, and not disclosing the identities of reviewers to authors.

Because of space limitations, it isn't possible to include samples of various types of letters in this chapter—acknowledging receipt of a manuscript, inquiring about a reviewer's availability, notifying an author about a review decisions, and so forth. Fortunately, several sources contain an abundance of such samples [2, 6].

Manuscript Management

For a journal to be successful, it must receive plenty of submissions, and that requirement means that successful journals always have a significant number of manuscripts under review. Since most journals require two or more rounds of review before a manuscript is accepted for publication, the number of reviews under way at any point in time is likely to be large.

To ensure that all manuscripts receive a fair review and that no manuscripts get lost or mislaid in the process, the editor needs a comprehensive method to guide management of manuscripts. The process outlined below has been successfully implemented by many journals.

1. The editor logs the manuscript in the manuscript database (Figure 1) and acknowledges its receipt by letter or e-mail to the author(s) outlining the review process. All subsequent activity in the review process is also logged as appropriate.
2. The editor secures reviewers for the manuscript. (This step may be performed directly by the editor or by an associate editor, guest editor, or review coordinator.)
3. The editor or designee sends the reviewers a copy of the manuscript.

Record Number	371
Author 1 Last Name	Lilibrand
Author 1 First Name	Ernest
Author 1 MI	R.
Author 1 Affiliation	Schoon Software Ltd
Author 2 Last Name	Wehling
Author 2 First Name	Mary
Author 2 MI	W.
Author 2 Affiliation	Schoon Software, Ltd
Author 3 Last Name	
Author 3 First Name	
Author 3 MI	
Author 3 Affiliation	
Street	1243 Kent Crescent
City	Cambridge
State/Province	UK
Postal Code	W2E 1QT
E-mail	lilibrand.e.r@schoon.co.uk
Telephone	011 44 207 2009 2003
Fax	

Article Title	The Online Help File Revision Process in a Software Department Using Recursive Usability Cycles
Date Received	12/18/2008
Date Sent for Review	12/20/2008
Date Revised	
Date Accepted	
Comments	
Review Coordinator	Daphne Smith
Reviewer 1	Joe Kosmo
Reviewer 2	Phoebe Harris
Reviewer 3	
Recommendation	
Soft Copy Submitted?	Yes
Status	Being Reviewed
Rev Acknowledged	No

Figure 1. Record in a sample manuscript database.

4. When the review is complete, the editor informs the author(s) of the reviewers' recommendation. The editor may either attach the comments forwarded by the review coordinator (with reviewers' names deleted) or attach his or her own evaluation of the manuscript that conflates the reviewers' comments. If the manuscript is being returned with a request for revision, the editor asks the author(s) to resubmit by a specified date, allowing approximately 60 days to return the manuscript.

   Note: The editor should give reviewers a specified amount of time in which to complete their work and return their recommendations. There is no excuse for a journal these days to require 6 months or a year to complete the review of a manuscript when electronic copies can be transmitted from one side of the globe to the other in minutes. It is important to follow up promptly with reviewers when they fail to meet their deadlines.

5. If revisions to a resubmitted manuscript are significant, the editor sends the manuscript back to the same review coordinator and peer reviewers for re-evaluation.

6. If a revised manuscript is not resubmitted by the suggested date, the editor contacts the author(s) to determine its status.

7. Once a manuscript has been accepted, the editor requests that the author make any further minor revisions that are required, schedules the article for publication, and secures any necessary permissions and transfer of copyright.

The Peer Review Process

According to the International Committee of Medical Journal Editors' "Uniform Requirements for Manuscripts Submitted to Biomedical Journals," "Peer review is the critical assessment of manuscripts submitted to journals by experts who are not part of the editorial staff" [2, p. xi]. The specific procedure for peer reviewing differs from one journal to another, but the following process is fairly standard.

1. The editor or designee secures agreement from two people with knowledge of the manuscript's subject to serve as peer reviewers. While these reviewers usually work in the journal's and manuscript's field of interest, occasionally it is necessary to go outside that field to find reviewers with the needed expertise in the subject. The editor or designee asks reviewers to complete their evaluations of the manuscript within a designated period. Three or four weeks are usually sufficient.

2. The editor or designee sends to each peer reviewer a blind copy of the manuscript and a copy of the review criteria. Names on the manuscript are removed beforehand to ensure completely anonymous, blind evaluation.

3. Each peer reviewer evaluates the manuscript according to the journal's established review criteria, and each independently makes one of the following recommendations to the review coordinator:

- Accept
- Accept with light revisions
- Ask author to revise and resubmit
- Reject

4. The reviewers send their recommendations, comments, and annotated copies of the manuscript (if applicable) to the editor or designee by e-mail, if possible. If the reviewers recommend that the manuscript be revised or rejected, each provides suitable comments that explain the recommendation to the author(s). These comments need not be extensive but should be reasonably detailed and stated as positively as possible to help the author(s) make the changes needed for the manuscript to be accepted, or to help the author(s) understand why the manuscript's subject or the treatment of it is not suitable for publication in the journal. The comments should use sufficient examples to show that evidence from the manuscript has informed the evaluation. Reviewers may also suggest publication alternatives if they do not feel that the manuscript is likely to be suitable for the journal even in a revised form.

5. If the two reviewers' recommendations do not agree, the editor or designee identifies a third reviewer to evaluate the manuscript. When one of the reviewers recommends acceptance and another recommends revision and resubmission, the editor or designee may bypass the need for a third reviewer by asking the author to revise and resubmit.

6. If the review has been managed by a designee of the editor, when recommendations of two reviewers are the same, the editor's designee informs the editor by e-mail. The letter should summarize the major reasons for accepting, requesting revisions to, or rejecting the manuscript. The editor's designee may either attach the reviewers' comments (with the reviewers' names deleted) or attach his or her own evaluation of the manuscript which conflates the two reviewers' comments.

The Editorial Board

The editorial board's role is to assist the editor in developing and implementing policy and procedures for the journal, to help identify potential peer reviewers and review coordinators, to occasionally serve as peer reviewers and review coordinators, and to help recruit authors for the journal.

The editorial board's size and composition depends to some extent on the journal's size and frequency of publication. Its members are generally appointed by the editor. The board members' terms may be set or not, but it makes sense for the terms to be set and staggered so that all members do not rotate off the board at one time.

In the case of large journals, there are sometimes multiple levels of editorial board:

- A smaller board consisting of very senior people who help set policy (and whose names lend credibility to the journal by their presence on the masthead)
- A larger working board that is more closely connected to the everyday working operations of the journal, especially the review of manuscripts

Production and Distribution (Print and Online)

The procedures for producing and distributing both paper and online copies of a journal differ widely from one journal to another. In many cases, the editor simply hands off the copy for an issue to a production editor and has little or nothing to do with the issue after that point. In other cases, there is interaction between the production editor and editor throughout the typesetting and prepress processes, and perhaps into the printing and binding as well. In some cases, the editor assumes one or more duties of the production editor, taking responsibility for preparing final formatted files for the printer, inserting codes in electronic files that are input to a typesetting system, or preparing SGML headers for the online version of the journal.

Because the responsibilities of the position are so highly variable, anyone applying for the position of editor-in-chief, managing editor, or editor of a technical journal must verify exactly what the duties of the position are and weigh the compensation accordingly.

EDITORIAL PHILOSOPHY AND THE RELATIVE VALUE OF JOURNALS

The editor's approach to his or her role can be immensely influential in shaping others' perception of the journal. It certainly influences to at least a limited extent the attitudes of the editorial staff and those who review manuscripts. It may even affect the assumptions of regular readers and others in its area of specialization regarding the relative worth of what is published in its pages as well as in the competing journals in the field. I'd like to consider two competing philosophies as well as methods commonly used to weigh the relative value of publications.

The Editor as Gatekeeper

The editorial philosophy that seems to be most common envisions the editor as the gatekeeper or guardian of the discipline's body of knowledge, who protects the profession and its practitioners from unsound ideas and determines who should have the cachet of publication in the journal's pages. This approach seems flawed to me in several respects.

First, although the editor wields significant influence, editorial decision-making is shared by a number of people in the process that I have just described. As we've seen, the peer-review and editorial processes may involve the participation of the managing editor, guest editors, associate editors, members of the editorial board, review coordinators, and the peer reviewers themselves.

The editor tends to act only at the end of this process, and his or her decision is most often an endorsement of the recommendations made by those in earlier stages of those processes.

Even if the editor believes that all of the individuals who are involved in the peer-review and editorial processes are clones of him- or herself, it is highly unlikely that they will all react to a manuscript in exactly the same way as the editor. Even those whose training in a discipline has been influenced by the same professors in the same academic programs will differ at times in their thought processes and opinions. Academic preparation is not a cookie-cutter process.

Second, a discipline's body of knowledge is not a treasury that must be protected at all costs from barbarian hordes. Instead, the world of ideas is a marketplace that should welcome a variety of vendors. The relative value of ideas is ultimately determined by the dynamics of the discipline's market. The ideas that are accepted by those in the market are privileged, while those that are rejected are not. And like a market that accepts multiple currencies, a discipline's marketplace may value more than one approach to a subject or more than one way of solving a problem.

To me, approaching the task of editing a journal through the gatekeeper philosophy is about as appealing as being stranded on a desert island for 10 years with a single book. Ultimately, no matter what imagination the reader brings to the text, it remains the same text. Without being exposed to new and even revolutionary ideas, a discipline becomes stale and eventually loses the appeal of a library that is constantly growing its collection to include new authors and their approaches to the problems we face.

The Editor as Mentor

Approaching the task of journal editing as an opportunity to act as a mentor to scholars in the profession, to help them add new ideas or approaches to the discipline's body of knowledge, seems to me a far more fulfilling and important role, and it is the approach that I commend to other journal editors.

Several years ago, an author contacted me to say that he was quite upset that my journal had rejected a manuscript he had submitted. He asked whether I thought that the piece could be revised to make it acceptable. After spending several hours re-reading the manuscript and the reviews, I decided that the manuscript was potentially quite significant. In an hour-long telephone conversation, I went through the draft with the author page by page, suggesting revisions that I thought would respond to the reviewers' objections and result in an accepted article.

The author was very pleased with my response, and even if the story had ended there, I would have been satisfied with the experience as well. I had been able to help the author see beyond the negative comments about a manuscript and envision a revised draft that would better realize what he had hoped to achieve. As it turns out, the author did revise the manuscript, the reviewers responded favorably, and the article was published. It went on to win the award for best article published in the journal that year, and my degree of satisfaction with the mentoring experience increased as well.

Whether the authors involved are submitting a manuscript for the first time or are veterans of scholarly publishing, helping make what could be a very negative experience an opportunity to learn is bound to add value to their perception of the editorial review process as well.

In graduate school, I had the good luck to study with several professors who saw their role as more than passing along knowledge about the subjects of their courses. Instead, they helped me become a professional in the field, learning how to write and deliver a conference paper, revise a journal article manuscript, respond to questions at a presentation, and so forth. They shared insights about publishing in the field that didn't appear in any of the books I had read. This type of professional mentorship apparently seldom happens these days.

It became quite apparent to me early on in my experience as a journal editor that this kind of knowledge was lacking in many of the new scholars seeking to publish in my journal's pages. They didn't have a clue about how journals operate or about what a reasonable length of time for a review should be. Although this kind of mentorship may be above and beyond the requirements for a journal editor, it is certainly information that the FAQ page on a journal's Web site might contain.

For those who have not been lucky enough to have this type of mentor, David Canter and Gavin Fairbairn provide an excellent substitute in *Becoming an Author: Advice for Academics and Other Professionals*, including the very helpful chapters "Writing for Journals" and "The Journal Process," which approach their topics from the author's point of view [7, pp. 117-128, 129-142].

Acceptance Rates

Many journals pride themselves on their low manuscript acceptance rates, and promotion and tenure committee chairs sometimes contact a journal editor to inquire about the journal's acceptance rate. The implication, of course, is that a journal with a low acceptance rate is more selective, that an article published in a journal that accepts only 18% of the manuscripts it receives is worth more than one in a journal that accepts 46% of submissions.

Quite simply, I believe that such an assumption is absurd. Journal editors know that we reject manuscripts for all kinds of reasons, some good and some questionable. If a manuscript contains a misspelled word, it will be rejected by some editors. If it employs qualitative methods, other editors may reject it. Similarly, authors may decide to take their work elsewhere. I've returned several manuscripts with a request to authors to revise and resubmit to make them more appropriate for the audience of the applied journal I edited, only to see the same manuscript appear in another journal a few months later virtually unchanged.

Beth Luey, founding director of the Scholarly Publishing Program at Arizona State University, recently shared some fascinating insights about rejection rates in two very different disciplines.

> The top sociology journals have a rejection rate of 80 per cent. The top astronomy journals have a rejection rate of 20 per cent. Why the difference? First, because astronomy is less divided by ideological and political differences, there is greater consensus about what is important. Second, because astronomy requires expensive instruments, research in the field is funded almost entirely by competitive grants given on the basis of peer review, and is therefore pre-screened. But the third reason is the one that is relevant to our concerns. The editors of journals in astronomy and physics, like their readers, have a very different view than sociologists of what their journals are supposed to do. Astronomers, and their editors, believe that so long as research is done rigorously and the subject is interesting, it should be published. It doesn't have to be the best paper; it doesn't have to be flawless. The assumption is that any research of interest will generate discussion that will, in turn, correct its errors and refine its conclusions. Astronomers and physicists believe strongly in post-publication review. The editor/gatekeeper is supposed to keep those gates open as many hours of the day as possible, rather than to open them grudgingly only to those whose work is deemed, by whatever standard, to be of the very highest quality [8, p. 100].

However we interpret them, it's pretty clear to me that acceptance rates don't really convey any useful information about the quality of a journal or about the quality of the articles it publishes. It does say a great deal about the philosophy of scholarship in the field in question and about the particular editor's notion of the role that he or she plays in relation to that field.

Citation Indexes

Thomson Scientific's *Web of Science* provides information about the frequency with which articles in the indexed journals are cited in other articles [3]. They also calculate "impact factors" that allow users to compare the indexed journals with others in broad categories in an attempt to determine their relative impact or influence on scholarship in those broad categories.

That sounds like a worthy goal, but there are several problems inherent in any attempt to gauge the relative value and importance of journals.

- The existing citation indexes are not comprehensive; they include only a fraction of the journals in most fields. For example, when this chapter was written, the *Social Sciences Citation Index* included only two of the five journals in the field of technical communication.
- Given the specialization common in many fields of interest, the broad categories used to classify the journals that are included make comparisons

difficult. For example, recent editions of the *Social Sciences Citation Index* include technical communication journals in the broad category of communication (covering more than 40 journals in fields as diverse as communications, journalism, mass communication, public relations, advertising, and speech). If one journal in the technical communication field has an impact number of 2 and the other has an impact number of 39, how do we compare them? Additionally, impact numbers can vary widely from one year to the next, making those comparisons even more problematic.

• The reasons for the inclusion and exclusion of journals are not well defined. Neither the age, reputation, nor circulation of the journals seems to be a defining criterion; furthermore, some journals that are excluded might seem to have better claim at being included than some that are. For example, in the field of technical communication, the prestigious *IEEE Transactions in Professional Communication* is not included in the *Social Sciences Citation Index*.

• Although the citation indexes remove articles that have been demonstrated to contain fraudulent or otherwise inaccurate data, the fact that an article has been cited for negative reasons or for the wrong reasons is not reflected in the citation reports. For example, if an article is cited because another author believes its methodology is flawed, that citation is counted. Similarly, if an author misinterprets the applicability of another author's article, that citation is counted. Consider the number of times you have heard or read "The Magical Number Seven" wrongly cited as the reason for limiting the number of menu selections on a computer screen or the number of steps in a printed procedure, despite the fact that George Miller was writing about short-term memory [9].

In short, although citation reports and impact numbers seem to promise significant insights about the relative value of journals, those insights may be worth far less than the promise.

MANUSCRIPT COPYEDITING

In this section I do not discuss the techniques of copyediting for journal article manuscripts, because those techniques are really not any different than for any other manuscript. Rather, I consider two larger issues. The first is the editor's need to decide when clarity and audience comprehension must take precedence over preserving the author's voice in the copyediting process. The second is the increasingly common problem raised by manuscripts from authors whose native language is not English.

Considering the Audience versus
Preserving the Author's Voice

One of the copyeditor's greatest temptations is to rewrite manuscripts so that they correspond with the editor's style. This temptation can be especially powerful in the case of technical journals because many manuscripts accepted by those journals are poorly written despite the quality of the research they report and the insights they contain.

A journal by its very nature is a collection of contributions by a variety of authors with different educations, experiences, and approaches to their discipline. We shouldn't be surprised, then, that the articles within a journal issue exhibit quite significant differences in their authors' styles. These stylistic differences are manifested in the arrangement and naming of the parts of the article when the discipline lacks a conventional arrangement such as the IMRAD (Introduction, Methods, Results, and Discussion) structure used in medical and scientific journals, the authors' selection and marshalling of evidence in arguments, and of course their choice of words and syntactic structures.

The copyeditor naturally notices where an author's style differs from his or her own, but good copyeditors have been trained to maintain the author's voice except to correct errors in grammar, syntax, or usage, or to clarify the author's meaning when needed. Preserving the author's voice avoids stylistic homogenization of the journal's content and ensures that each article retains the author's unique emphasis and expression.

The ideal of preserving the author's voice must be balanced with another value, however. The audience needs to understand the content, and sometimes audience comprehension is inhibited by the author's style. Because we're concerned with technical journals whose audiences are professionals in the journal's field of interest, we don't need to ensure that ideas of subject matter experts are expressed in language that a layperson can understand. However, we often confront the problems of the practitioner reader who must struggle with the academic's choice of words, plodding sentence structure, and urge to refer to every possible work in the literature on the subject, no matter how arcane.

This problem affects many disciplines. For example, an article in an orthopedic medicine journal may be written by a researcher-surgeon who specializes in treating injuries to the anterior cruciate ligament, but that article is likely to be read by physicians in general practice, as well as by nurses, physicians' assistants, physical therapists, athletic trainers, and others. Similarly, an article on the design of a new greywater recycling method may be written by an environmental engineer in academe, but its audience may include practitioners in environmental and civil engineering, as well as architects, city planners, environmental activists, and perhaps even members of citizens' groups.

The editor must identify and describe the major constituencies of the journal's audience. In some cases, especially in non-applied fields, the audience is simply other academics in the discipline. In others, it is both academics and practitioners in the same field. In comparatively rare instances, such as the two cases cited in the previous paragraph, the audience may be much broader, and yet the publication is a technical journal and not a general-interest periodical because the audience is far from general and the content is highly specialized.

Once the editor has characterized the journal's audience segments, he or she must work closely and frequently with the copyediting staff to ensure that they understand the various needs of those segments. The copyeditors must then work with authors to ensure that all of the intended audience members can read and understand the content without expending unreasonable effort.

Note that even in cases where all the audience members are academics within the same narrow discipline, when the audience includes a significant number of readers whose first language is not English, the needs of those non-native readers must be considered. By ensuring that the manuscripts published in the journal preserve the syntactic cues that native writers sometimes eliminate from their speech and writing, the copyeditor will aid non-native readers in comprehending the journal's content [10].

Addressing Second-Language Problems

Globalization means that journals increasingly have not only non-native readers but also contributors for whom English is not their first language. Their manuscripts may require a significant level of copyediting and even wholesale rewriting before they can be published in a reputable journal, even though the technical content is excellent. This problem is compounded because not only is the effort required sometimes quite significant in amount but also because it differs in kind from the copyediting we usually associate with journal publishing.

Several years ago, a team of reviewers for my journal recommended publication of a manuscript by two authors whose first language was French. As usual, I read the manuscript quickly and agreed with their assessment. When I started copyediting the manuscript prior to typesetting, however, I realized that although the authors' mastery of English was generally quite good, it was frequently but subtly unidiomatic. For example, while a native speaker of French might say in English, "it rains," reflecting the French "il pleut," the native speaker of English would say, "it's raining." Multiply such very minor idiomatic divergences by the highly technical subject matter of the typical academic journal, and the result can be significant noise in the transmission of information from author to reader.

Although the authors' English is this case was just barely "off," I spent the better part of a week copyediting their 50-page manuscript and nearly a day on a single word. (I didn't have access to the authors themselves or to their original manuscript that had been composed in French, and I was working against a short deadline for an issue.)

Given the difficulty that such manuscripts can pose (even those that at first seem to have only minor second-language problems), editors can take several approaches.

- **The journal can accept and publish the article as received.** This practice is not advisable because the article does not communicate effectively and risks diminishing the reputation of the journal. In some cases (medical journals, for example), this practice could result in litigation if a procedure is not correctly described.
- **The journal can require the author to seek the assistance of a professional editor** who specializes in helping authors of the same language to produce manuscripts acceptable to English-language journals. The advantage is that this is the easiest alternative for the journal and costs the journal nothing. The disadvantage is that the author may not have access to a professional editor who both is a native-English speaker and possesses expertise in the author's language.
- **The journal can maintain a list of native-English-speaking editors with expertise in various languages** (depending on the journal's discipline, these languages might include French, German, Dutch, Spanish, Italian, Chinese, Japanese, Korean, and Arabic, for example). The advantage to the journal, again, is the elimination of the burden and cost of second-language copyediting, as well as dealing with editors whose quality is known to the journal. The disadvantage is that the author may not be able to afford the services of an editor who lives outside of his or her country.
- **The journal can hire, contract with, or seek volunteers from among native-English-speaking editors with expertise in various languages.** One advantage of this approach is that the journal can rely on the quality and consistency of copyediting provided by these staff or contract editors, and of course volunteer editors have the advantage of no cost. The disadvantage of hiring or contracting with such editors is that few journals have the financial resources to make this kind of investment in non-native-English-speaking authors. The disadvantage of volunteer editors is that quality and timeliness may pose problems, and they may well be difficult to find.
- **The journal can rely on its usual copyediting staff to assist the authors.** The advantage to this approach is that it requires no investment in specialists in the various foreign languages. The disadvantages include the fact that working with such manuscripts is likely to require far more time than copyediting the manuscripts of native speakers, as well as that lack of expertise in the various languages may result in the incorporation of errors that neither the copyeditor nor the author catches.

Whichever approach the journal adopts, the editor should monitor the copyediting process to ensure quality.

EDITORIAL POLITICS

Politics generally enter into the equation of journal editing as the result of the relationship between the editor and the publisher. Although there are inevitably exceptions to any classification system, there are five major types of technical journals based on publisher:

- Organizational journals published by scholarly or professional organizations
- Commercial journals published by for-profit corporations
- Hybrid journals that are sponsored by scholarly or professional organizations but published by for-profit corporations
- Journals published by government entities such as research laboratories
- Independent journals published by neither a company, nor an organization, nor a government agency

Organizational Journals

The editor of a journal published by a professional organization is probably most likely to face political problems. He or she is typically a volunteer who receives a stipend from the society and perhaps released time, research assistance, or additional compensation from his or her "day job" employer in acknowledgment of the recognition that the editorship brings to the company or university. Ordinarily the editor's daytime employer has minimal if any input into the management of the journal, but the editor must ensure that those who are responsible for managing the professional society understand the role of a journal in such an organization and the need for the editor to have a reasonably free hand in managing the journal.

Within a scholarly or professional society, the journal's principal reason for being is to define and expand the discipline's body of knowledge. Because many journals have grown out of newsletters or other house organs, and often exist alongside such publications, the society's management may not appreciate the fact that a technical journal is a different type of publication and that it must be managed differently to preserve the journal's integrity.

Ensuring that the society's managers understand the journal's role and the editor's necessary degree of independence involves a careful balancing act on the parts of all involved. The following principles should be observed.

- **Contract:** The editor should insist on a contract that specifies the duties of the position, the compensation provided by the organization, and the term of the agreement.
- **Policy Discussions:** The editor should be involved in all discussions involving the journal's budget and mission, as well as other decisions that affect the

journal, such as copyright policies, membership structures and fees, and decisions to change publication media.

- **Attendance at Board Meetings:** Because the journal is such a significant part of most professional societies, the journal editor should be invited regularly (at least once or twice a year) to meetings of the board of directors or other governing body.
- **Compensation**: The editor's compensation should be renegotiated whenever changes in the journal's budget or mission affect the scope of the editor's duties.
- **Society Management and the Editorial Review Process:** As long as the editorial review process abides by recognized standards of peer review, the society's management should not insert itself into that process.
- **Disputes:** Should society management believe that the editor has exceeded his or her authority or should the editor believe that society management has interfered in editorial decisions, the matter should be submitted to binding arbitration.

Abiding by these principles ensures that the editor and journal have the needed autonomy and that the organization's needs are also met.

Commercial Journals

In the case of a commercial journal, the editor is typically either an employee or a vendor of the corporation or other entity such as a university press that is the publisher. In this situation, the politics that come into play in the editor's position are not much different than the usual corporate politics. The entire enterprise is typically driven by the need to generate a profit for owners or stockholders from its core business, the publication of technical information. The editor who delivers high-quality issues, observes peer review standards, and adheres scrupulously to production schedules and budgets is not likely to feel much pressure from the corporation regarding content or direction. However, such is not always the case with organizational, hybrid, and government journals because the publication of technical information is not the core business of the publishers of those journals.

Hybrid Journals

In the case of hybrid journals, in most instances, the society appoints the editor and is ultimately responsible, through the editor, for editorial matters—soliciting manuscripts, conducting peer reviews and deciding which manuscripts to accept for publication, determining the content of specific issues, and so forth. The publisher is typically responsible for the business end of the journal—handling subscriptions, advertising, production and distribution of issues, and negotiations and dealings with print and online vendors.

The editor of a hybrid journal is generally much like the editor of the organizational journal, and is most often appointed by the society even though his or her stipend may be paid by the publisher.

As with commercial journals, the publisher of a hybrid journal is not likely to interfere in the editorial process, but the society sponsor may attempt to do so. In any case, the principles outlined above for organizational journals should also guide the editor, the sponsor, and the publisher of the hybrid journal, and the editor's contract should be signed by all three parties.

Government Journals

Some national and local government entities publish technical journals of various kinds. Although many such journals report results of scientific or medical research, in some cases the journals may deal with history, literature, the social sciences, or other fields of interest.

The editor of a government journal is typically a civil-service government employee or the employee of a contractor to the government entity that publishes the journal, not a political appointee. However, a government journal editor may also be subject to political pressure regarding editorial decisions. For example, if the party in power opposes the theory that global warming is caused by greenhouse gas emissions, an editor may be pressured to accept a manuscript that agrees with that premise or to refuse one that disagrees with it. In either case, political pressure exerted on an editorial decision is inappropriate and unethical.

Editors of government publications would do well to establish ground rules with their managers each time the political administration changes or the manager with oversight of the journal changes to define the appropriate roles for editorial staff and for the government entity that publishes the journal. The principles described above for organization journal editors provide a good model for those ground rules.

Note that although the issue of national security is sometimes raised inappropriately, genuine, serious national security concerns are a legitimate reason for a government publisher to intervene in editorial decisions.

Independent Journals

These journals are usually very small, often one-person operations, in that the editor is either actually or effectively the publisher. Therefore, the kinds of political tensions described in the preceding subsections are unlikely.

SUCCESSFUL JOURNAL MANAGEMENT

When new editors begin work, they immediately encounter two problems: Exactly how should the editor manage the journal day to day, and how does the editor ensure a consistent flow of good content for the publication? Some lesser challenges also occur regularly.

Document All Procedures

If you are fortunate, before you begin the job, your predecessor will have provided you three things:

- A backlog of accepted manuscripts, as well as a number of manuscripts in process of review or revision
- A style guide for the journal that supplements a standard style manual such as *Chicago* or *APA* and defines the style for the journal's copyeditors [11, 12]
- Procedures that describe all of the work processes for all members of the journal staff

Okay; I lied. You'll be fortunate to inherit even one of those things. The problem is that few journals have a significant backlog of accepted articles (see the next subsection), and even those that do often lack the style guide and procedures that a new editor needs to train the new staff that are often hired when a journal's editorial home changes—and to train him- or herself as well.

If you have inherited a procedure manual from your predecessor, even if incomplete and out-of-date, consider your luck remarkable and set out to bring it up to date as you and your staff begin work, and maintain it regularly throughout your term. (Make a point to review it annually with the entire staff, and assign staff to bring it up to date.)

Many journal editors who are academics are assigned one or more research assistants by their departments as partial compensation for bringing a journal to the institution. If that is the case, you need to keep these graduate students occupied for 10 or 20 hours per week, and in many cases, you do not have enough tasks to keep them occupied for all the hours for which they are being paid. It's a great idea to put these students to work documenting the journal's work processes as they perform them and interviewing other staff members and documenting their work processes. And because research assistants seldom remain in the same role for more than a year, it is doubly important to have those procedures available for their successors. Peter Vandenberg reflects very helpfully upon the importance of documentation of work processes and other elements of taking over and handing off a journal [13].

Sources of information about workflow and procedures include previous editors and their staffs, as well as editors and staffs of other journals.

Develop a Backlog of Accepted Manuscripts

If you have been fortunate enough to inherit a backlog, guard it carefully and build upon it within reason. Backlogs are a sign of a healthy journal because they indicate that submissions are regular, that the peer review process is working, and that the journal has achieved notice among potential contributors that it is worth their consideration as a publishing venue.

A backlog of accepted manuscripts equal to the content of three to six months' worth of issues will allow a new editor to ease into the job rather than feeling as though he or she desperately needs to get enough manuscripts accepted in time for the next issue's typesetting deadline.

You don't want your backlog to become too large, however. Too large a pool of accepted manuscripts means that the lag from manuscript acceptance to publication is too long. Six months to one year seems to be the ideal target for publication lag. Any less than that and you don't have a real backlog, just a list of candidates for the next issue or so; any more than that risks diminishing the impact of the articles' content, particularly in journals covering the natural sciences, engineering, and medicine.

One way of building a backlog is to issue a call for proposals for one or more thematic issues per year, each of which focuses on a single cutting-edge topic in your discipline. This practice avoids the need for all submissions to come "over the transom" and encourages those who might not have considered publishing in your journal to consider it. D. Barry Lumsden describes this and 13 other methods of increasing submissions in detail [14].

If your backlog becomes too large, you have two alternatives:

- Make the review criteria more stringent to reduce the number of accepted articles. Becoming more selective may seem to be a good thing, but it may have negative effects as well. The more manuscripts you refuse, the more likely you are to discourage potential authors, so you may in fact see submissions drop.
- Increase the number of articles published in each issue. Including more articles per issue is not cost-free, but you might find creative ways to do so without increasing costs significantly. For example, some journals publish abstracts of some articles in the paper editions of their journals, with the full text available online only.

Learn Through the First Few Issues

No matter how well prepared you think you are to take on the job of editing a journal, it is likely that you will encounter some unexpected challenges, especially at first.

Most journals have a predetermined page budget that they must operate within. For example, your budget may be 128 pages per issue or eight 16-page signatures. This page budget is used to estimate and schedule production resources needed to print and mail the journal, as well as to calculate the costs for various services. As with any other commodity, journal printing and distribution services are less expensive per unit for larger journals or monthly journals than they are for smaller ones or quarterlies. Therefore, as editor, you need to be able to estimate how many articles will fit in a particular issue along with the other scheduled content such as departments, correspondence, and advertising.

It is a relatively simple matter to determine how many pages of manuscript translate to a printed page of your journal. Prepare a word-processing file of an article without figures, equations, or tables using the typeface you wish to standardize upon, and compare it to the printed version. In the case of the journal I edited, a printed page was equivalent to 750 words or three double-spaced pages of 11-point Book Antiqua type with 12 points of leading between paragraphs and one-inch margins around.

You will also have to calculate how much space the figures, equations, and tables will use. If you supply camera-ready copy of that material, however, you can easily determine how much space it will require in the printed journal. If your tables and equations are typeset, it will probably take you an issue or two to be comfortable estimating how much space they will require.

If your entire journal is printed in four colors and color is frequently used in figures and tables, determining placement of articles that use color will not be an issue for you. If you use color sparingly, however, then you will need to consult with your production staff to determine where in the issue you can place articles that require color. Those determinations are based on the type of press used to print your journal and the availability of color on certain pages of a signature. In my journal, for example, we ordinarily did not allow color figures unless they were essential to the sense of the article. In those cases where color was necessary, we placed the article in the first signature, where we used color for the table of contents and advertising.

Determining the order of articles in an issue is typically the editor's call, and it isn't necessary to use the same method for every issue. For example, I frequently led an issue with the article that I thought would have the greatest impact on the audience, would prove the most controversial, or would appeal to the largest segment of the audience. I often chose the cover art for the issue based on the same article. The order of the other articles in the issue was similarly determined by impact, controversy, or appeal. In other cases, I simply placed all the articles in the issue in the order that they were approved for publication.

As you encounter questions or problems, remember that if you don't know the answer or the solution, in most cases, your predecessor, the editor of another journal, or your production editor has faced the same problem. Don't hesitate to ask for advice.

SUCCESSION PLANNING AND EDITORIAL TRANSITION

A stint of more than eight years as editor of a major journal is probably too long. Even editors who are comparatively well compensated are not paid enough for the long hours and many tasks that they must perform. In particular, those who edit journals with small or nonexistent staffs to assist with the grunt work burn out sooner rather than later. As a result, most new editors should begin thinking about the process of turning over the job to their successor soon after starting the job, because inevitably the day will come when it is time to retire.

To prepare you for your inevitable retirement, I offer the following suggestions.

Identify Potential Successors

Throughout your term as editor, you will encounter people who could be potential successors. They may include associate editors, members of your editorial board, guest editors of special issues, and even authors who have published in your pages.

It's a good idea to make a short list of potential successors and update it regularly, perhaps in consultation with the editorial board. Although your permanent successor may not come from the list, an interim editor, if needed, may well be included there.

Determine the Transition Process

In some cases, it is impossible to plan the transition of editors optimally. Death, injury, illness, or change in "day job" may require a relatively quick turnover of editorial operations. Usually in such circumstances, an interim editor is appointed to carry on the journal until a permanent successor is appointed. Your list of potential successors or an able managing editor is invaluable in such a situation. An interim editor ordinarily assumes the editorial chair for a limited but fixed term (often 6 or 12 months) during which the search for a permanent editor is conducted.

Most often, however, the editor's resignation is announced far enough in advance for the journal to identify a replacement before the resignation becomes effective.

In some cases, the transition may be relatively easy. For example, in the case of a small journal, especially one in a very narrow field of interest, sometimes the next editor is simply selected from the associate editors or members of the editorial board. For larger journals and those in larger disciplines, however, an open search is the best way to identify the best qualified candidates and to ensure that the journal represents a wide range of points of view within the field.

Complete the Turnover

Once the new editor has been hired, the outgoing and incoming editors should hold a turnover meeting. At that time, the retiring editor should turn over files, report the status of reviews and acceptances of manuscripts in the pipeline, and decide with his or her successor whatever steps remain to complete the transition.

Once the transition is final, the former editor should be available to answer questions, but the new editor should have a good understanding of what is required, especially since the style guide and handbook of procedures were ready before the editorial transition process began.

At this point, it's time for the former editor to get out of the way and find new tasks to fill the hours previously devoted to journal business.

CONCLUSION

Editing a technical journal is a more complex and challenging process than the points presented in this relatively brief space suggest. For someone who wants to help define and develop the body of knowledge in a particular field of interest, serving as editor-in-chief of one of the journals in that field provides insights and opportunities that cannot be matched by any other scholarly enterprise in that subject domain. Although their contributions are sometimes unacknowledged, journal editors often wield significant influence in shaping the direction of scholarship in the field.

Someone who thrives in editorial project management will find serving as managing editor of a journal a very fulfilling and challenging role. This task, of course, poses different challenges and requires different talents than those needed by an editor-in-chief, but those skills are necessary to keep the publication on schedule and to satisfy authors' concerns that their work receives a timely and unbiased review.

For the vast majority of journals where the jobs of editor-in-chief, managing editor, and sometimes production editor are merged, the editor must constantly strive to balance the very different roles of visionary and circus ringmaster. But for those who are able to balance these contrasting demands, the rewards can be significant.

REFERENCES

1. C. D. Rude, *Technical Editing* (4th ed.), Pearson Longman, New York, 2006.
2. I. Hames, *Peer Review and Manuscript Management in Scientific Journals: Guidelines for Good Practice*, Blackwell Publishing, Malden, Massachusetts, 2007.
3. Thomson Scientific, *Web of Science*. Available online at: http://scientific.thomson.com/products/wos/
4. *Ulrich's Periodicals Directory*. Available online at: http://www.ulrichsweb.com/ulrichsweb/

5. FreeOrtho.com, Orthopaedic Journals. Available online at: http://freeortho.com/journals.html

6. G. M. Smith, *The Peer-reviewed Journal: A Comprehensive Guide Through the Editorial Process*, Chatgris Press, New Orleans, Louisiana, 1996.

7. D. Canter and G. Fairbairn. *Becoming an Author: Advice for Academics and Other Professionals*, Open University Press, New York, 2006.

8. B. Luey, A Different Kind of Profession, *Journal of Scholarly Publishing, 39*, pp. 93-108, 2008.

9. G. A. Miller, The Magical Number Seven, Plus or Minus Two: Some Limits on Our Capacity for Processing Information, *The Psychological Review, 63*, pp. 81-97, 1956.

10. J. R. Kohl, Improving Translatability and Readability with Syntactic Cues, *Technical Communication, 46*, pp. 149-166, 1999.

11. University of Chicago Press, *The Chicago Manual of Style* (15th ed.), University of Chicago Press, Chicago, Illinois, 2003.

12. American Psychological Association, *Publication Manual of the American Psychological Association* (6th ed.), American Psychological Association, Washington, D.C., 2010.

13. P. Vandenberg, Handoff, Dropkick, or Hail Mary Pass: Letting Go of an Academic Journal, *Journal of Scholarly Publishing, 38*, pp. 123-133, 2007.

14. D. B. Lumsden, Jump-Starting a Journal's Paper Flow: Fourteen Tested, Effective Methods, *Journal of Scholarly Publishing, 31*, pp. 87-95, 2000.

CHAPTER 10

Annotated Bibliography

Avon J. Murphy and Thomas L. Warren

This bibliography is divided into five sections: General/Background, Procedures, Working with Authors, Tools, and Specific Areas. The following excellent anthologies collect some useful articles on technical editing that will be described under their respective headings:

- Kemnitz, Charles F., ed. *Technical Editing: Basic Theory and Practice.* Arlington, VA: Society for Technical Communication, 1994.
- Rude, Carolyn D., ed. *Teaching Technical Editing.* Lubbock, TX: Association of Teachers of Technical Writing, 1985.
- Shimberg, H. Lee, ed. "Special Issue on Technical Editing." *Technical Communication,* 28, no. 4 (1981).
- Zook, Lola, ed. *Technical Editing: Principles and Practices.* Washington, DC: Society for Technical Communication, 1975.

GENERAL/BACKGROUND

Allen, Lori, and Dan Voss. "Ethics for Editors: An Analytical Decision-Making Process." *IEEE Transactions on Professional Communication,* 41, no. 1 (1998): 58-65. When editors face conflict in loyalties (to the reader, to the author, to the company/client), they need a way to resolve such conflicts. Allen and Voss offer a 6-step approach to navigate various ethical and moral conflicts: (1) Define the issues and stakeholders; (2) determine stakeholder's interests; (3) identify values involved in interests; (4) find values in conflict; (5) rank values based on importance; and (6) select

http://dx.doi.org/10.2190/NPOC10

higher value. They define 10 core values from legal to advancing the profession.

Boomhower, E. F. "Producing Good Technical Communications Requires Two Types of Editing." *Directions in Technical Writing and Communication,* ed. Jay R. Gould. Amityville, NY: Baywood, 1978, pp. 71-75. The two edits are a literary (copyediting) and a technical edit. They both look at the message the paper conveys, but look at different aspects of that message. The literary editor looks at the message from an expression perspective: grammar, usage, punctuation, spelling, etc. The technical editor looks at the material before the literary editor and focuses on the technical nature of the content, assuming the role of the reader and editing for understanding. Both types are important; it is a matter of primary and secondary focus.

Coggin, William O., and Lynette Porter. *Editing for the Technical Professions.* New York: Macmillan, 1993. Textbook that, while targeting technical editing students, can be useful for editing students in other areas such as journalism and business. Covers editing in 10 chapters from defining editing and what editors do to what they need to know, how they work with authors, and editing based on the *Levels of Edit.* Concludes with the editor as contractor. Chapters have exercises and additional readings. Contains a glossary of editing terms.

Corbin, Michelle, Pat Moell, and Mike Boyd. "Technical Editing as Quality Assurance: Adding Value to Content." *Technical Communication*, 49, no. 3 (2002): 286-300. Argues that technical editing, like software testing and technical writing, is critical to quality assurance for information products. Lays out in detail the content editing activities that occur within comprehensive editing, usability editing, and copyediting, all helping to meet users' goals.

Dukes, Eva. "Rules: To Bend or Not to Bend Them." *Technical Communication,* 33, no. 3 (1986): 136-139. Dukes addresses the always vexing question of rigidly enforcing language rules or allowing exceptions. After discussing pros and cons, she concludes that editors should apply language rules situationally in order to help the user understand the communication.

Farkas, David K. "The Concept of Consistency in Writing and Editing." *Journal of Technical Writing and Communication*, 15, no. 4 (1985): 353-364. Convincingly demonstrates the need to understand consistency in documents. Provides examples of how to develop consistency that is logical, evident, functional, resource-efficient, and stable.

Farkas, David K. *How to Teach Technical Editing*. Society for Technical Communication, Washington, DC, 1986. Valuable handbook of 12 chapters characterized by intellectual curiosity and pragmatic suggestions. Gives teachers "a pedagogy of editing" to apply when working with students on such topics as language and computer skills, substantive and rhetorical editing, marking copy, preserving authorial meaning, levels of edit, house style, consistency, managing editing schedules and payment, and class editing assignments.

Kantrowitz, B. Michael. "What Price Technical Editing? Phase I: Reaching a Lay Audience." *IEEE Transactions on Professional Communication,* 28, no. 1 (1985): 13-19. Kantrowitz provides the empirical data for a generally understood truism of editing: If editors do not invest time to clarify a manuscript, the reader will have to. His experiments came as a result of an effort by government and industry to cut editorial costs and publish "quick and dirty" reports. He found that adding editing improves reader comprehension and message acceptability. Another important finding was that readers completed tasks fast when the documents had been edited. Editing becomes increasingly important if reader comprehension and reading time, and message acceptance are important.

Mackenzie, Jo. *The Editor's Companion.* Cambridge University Press, Cambridge, 2004. Written for Australian editors, but most recommendations apply universally. Especially valuable, specific detail on illustrations and tables, proofreading, online techniques, legalities and ethics, and freelancing. Many useful examples.

Mancuso, Joseph C. *Technical Editing.* Englewood Cliffs, NJ: Prentice Hall, 1992. A textbook suitable for classroom or seminar in which Mancuso lays out in 19 chapters what the editor does. He identifies an eleven-step process for editing with a chapter devoted to each: gather reference books; gather implements; mark the manuscript; identify requirements, audience, and purpose; read the manuscript; collaborate with others; edit for organization, conciseness, clarity, and correctness; and proofread and check the manuscript. Provides exercises for each chapter.

Masse, Roger E. "Theory and Practice of Editing Processes in Technical Communication." *IEEE Transactions on Professional Communication,* 28, no. 1 (1985): 34-42. Much of this academic essay is an extensive bibliography on editing theory. Masse's point is to guide teachers to help students develop a theory of editing they can use when editing materials. At the heart of the approach is the levels-of-edit concept that serves as the frame for the student's editing approach.

Putnam, Constance E. "Myths About Editing." *Technical Communication*, 32, no. 2 (1985): 17-20. Repr. Kemnitz, ed., pp. 7-10. Succinctly disproves nine misconceptions about editors, including "Only those trained in technical and scientific fields can be technical editors," "Editors do not need to be skilled writers themselves," and "Every editorial problem has only one solution." Argues for employers' recognition of the complexity of editorial tasks and the need to provide improved training.

Rew, Lois Johnson. *Editing for Writers.* Upper Saddle River, NJ: Prentice Hall, 1999. Textbook/workbook aimed at writers who want to edit their own work. Also for workplace editors who want to learn more. Focuses on proofreading, copyediting, and document editing. Has 19 chapters divided into 3 parts plus glossary and exercise answers. Chapters focus on editing as a process and cover standard topics of grammar and usage, spelling, and punctuation; editing graphics; and document design. Explains working with paper and electronic copy. Introduces the student to international and intercultural editing.

Rude, Carolyn D. *Technical Editing*. 4th ed. New York: Pearson Longman, 2006. Popular textbook for students studying editing. In 5 parts and 25 chapters, covers editing from the big picture to the different types of editing on both paper and electronic copy. Chapters end with applying the knowledge from the chapter, further readings, and discussion topics and applications. Can also serve as a general style manual including chapters on spelling, grammar and usage, and punctuation. Part 5 covers legal issues, production editing, and project management.

Samson, Donald C., Jr. *Editing Technical Writing*. New York: Oxford University Press, 1993. Textbook in 12 chapters intended for both students and professionals wanting to learn technical editing. Focuses on the editor editing technical documents such as final project reports, extending Judd's and Butcher's discussions (see below). Exercises to allow testing progress, including editing and proofreading exercises. Takes the position that there is rarely only one way to edit even though he supplies an answer key.

Tarutz, Judith. *Technical Editing: The Practical Guide for Editors and Writers*. Reading, MA: Addison-Wesley, 1992. Wide-ranging textbook for beginners and advanced editors alike. Covers all phases of editing with special emphasis on her 12 basic rules and 10 lessons in working with writers she had to unlearn. Divided into 3 major parts: Editor's role, job, and career. Includes case studies, exercises with answers, sample style guides, and a glossary. Although dated, still a valuable reference.

Wilde, Elizabeth, Michelle Corbin, Jana Jenkins, and Shannon Rouiller. "Defining a Quality System: Nine Characteristics of Quality and the Editing for Quality Process." *Technical Communication,* 53, no. 4 (2006): 439-446. Quality issues are infrequently discussed in relation to editing, but these authors offer a thorough discussion of what quality is and how it affects the materials editors produce. They define quality information as being easy to use, understand, and find—definitions used at IBM. They then expand the definition through 9 characteristics of quality information. They describe the Editing for Quality (EFQ) process, including metrics.

Zook, Lola M. "Lessons Learned—Not Always by Choice." *Proceedings, 27th International Technical Communication Conference*. Washington, DC: Society for Technical Communication, 1980, pp. W31-W36. Looks back over a long career as an editor and identifies (1) lessons learned, (2) lessons I wish I hadn't had to learn, (3) lessons I wish I had learned sooner, and (4) lessons I never did learn. For the first, the exercise of doing the other lessons is what was learned. For the second, the most important was authors constantly change their minds. For the third, things can and do go wrong. Chief among the fourth category were language problems (spelling *supersede, he/she,* passives, etc.) and incurable optimism. The last category turns into lessons I am still trying to learn and includes trusting the way a sentence sounds.

Zook, Lola M. "Technical Editors Look at Technical Editing." *Technical Communication,* 30, no. 3 (1983): 20-26. One of the few empirical studies addressing questions relating to technical editing. The respondents ($N = 60$) addressed such issues as defining technical editing, problems facing editors, context in which editors work, training, and how the field is changing. Zook concludes that editing has changed over the last 15 years, that more editors are dealing with restricted budgets and that translates into quality issues, and that technology is influencing the job and career.

Zook, Lola M. "We Start with Questions: Defining the Editing Curriculum." In Rude, ed., pp. 3-9. Seeking the right outcome for a technical editing course, focuses on what students should learn: the editing process, the nature of the profession, students' objectives, good technical editors' characteristics, and what working editors do. A major contribution to pedagogical theory.

PROCEDURES

Alley, Michael. *The Craft of Editing: A Guide for Managers, Scientists, and Engineers.* New York: Springer-Verlag, 2000. Bravely attempts to help professionals who are not editors edit colleagues' writing. Especially helpful on the thinking processes in editing for content, style, and form, and on how to deal with authors' responses to editorial changes. Provides checklists, a glossary, and an overly long appendix of style problems.

Armbruster, David L. "Hiring and Managing Editorial Freelancers." In *Publications Management: Essays for Professional Communicators*, ed. O. Jane Allen and Lynn H. Deming. Amityville, NY: Baywood Publishing Company, Inc., 1994, pp. 69-77. Crisply describes, at a high level, the principles, strategies, and steps involved in finding and hiring editorial freelancers and planning and managing their work. Thoughtful recommendations.

Boston, Bruce O., ed. *Stet! Tricks of the Trade for Writers and Editors.* Alexandria, VA: Editorial Experts, 1986. Also *Stet Again! More Tricks of the Trade for Publications People* Alexandria, VA: EEI Press, 1996. Entertaining and informative collections of short and medium-length articles from the newsletter *The Editorial Eye* covering various copyediting dilemmas. Include many short quizzes.

Buehler, Mary Fran. "Defining Terms in Technical Editing: The Levels of Edit as a Model." In Shimberg, ed., pp. 10-15. Greatly expands upon the discussion in Van Buren and Buehler's *The Levels of Edit* to clarify the meanings of such troublesome terms as *editing* and *copyediting*. One of the first published illustrations of the usefulness of the levels-of-edit concept.

Buehler, Mary Fran. "Patterns for Making Editorial Changes." *Proceedings, 14th International Technical Communications Conference.* Washington, DC: Society of Technical Writers and Publishers, 1967, paper 86. Repr. Zook, ed., pp. 1-6. Editors should aim for three goals when editing: clarity, appropriate language style, and appropriate mechanical style. Because of these goals, three groups of editorial activities focus the editor's work: structural changes to promote clarity in presentation, language changes to ensure correctness and appropriate usage, and mechanical changes that relate to the mechanics of the presentation. Buehler explains each of these and concludes that the editor needs to recognize underlying patterns in the material and make changes satisfactory to the author as well as himself or herself.

Buehler, Mary Fran. "Situational Editing: A Rhetorical Approach for the Technical Editor." *Technical Communication*, 27, no. 3 (1980): 18-22. Repr. *Technical Communication*, 50, no. 4 (2003): 458-464. Influential argument that a technical editor best serves both author and reader by going beyond a programmatic approach, which involves applying rules, to take a situational (rhetorical) approach, which demands seeing all elements within a document's context. Rhetorical editing requires a broad perspective, investigative persistence, flexibility, rhetorical knowledge, empathy, and self-confidence.

Bush, Donald W., and Charles P. Campbell. *How to Edit Technical Documents.* Phoenix, AZ: Oryx, 1995. Focus on editing technical content as well as introducing using rhetoric, linguistics, and semantics. Wants to broaden editor's education from style and grammar checking to enhancing communication of material. Editors need to understand what the author wants to say and then help make that clear to the reader. With 13 chapters plus 4 appendixes on special editing, style manuals, and additional readings, the text covers the expected range of topics from the professional's job to getting along with authors. The accompanying workbook of exercises follows the order of the text's chapters and offers a broad range of applications.

Clements, Wallace, and Robert G. Waite. *Guide for Beginning Technical Editors.* Washington, DC: Society for Technical Communication, 1983. Also available from Lawrence Livermore Laboratory, Document LLL-TB-012, 1979. Training materials and reference book for new editors to help them find answers to their questions as they begin their professional work as editors. Describes editing in 11 chapters covering all phases of editing including editing technical manuscripts, working with the author, preparing the manuscript for production, and editing special topics such as mathematics, tables, and illustrations.

Dayton, David. "Electronic Editing in Technical Communication: A Survey of Practices and Attitudes." *Technical Communication*, 50, no. 2 (2003): 192-205. Also "Electronic Editing in Technical Communication: The Compelling Logics of Local Contexts," 51, no. 1 (2004): 86-101; and "Electronic Editing in Technical Communication: A Model of User-Centered Technology Adoption," 51, no. 2 (2004): 207-223. "Survey" reports on the most significant survey on electronic editing to date, using responses of 580 STC members. Among the findings: editors who edit electronically usually also do some hardcopy editing; such variables as gender and age made little difference in editing mode; and only 11% used software with change tracking. "Logics" focuses on 20 editors in 5 workplaces, concluding that each workgroup collectively establishes its logic for preferring online or hardcopy editing. "Model" argues for a user-centered ethic of technological adoption, ingeniously tying the survey research to such theories as Everett Rogers's theory of adoption and diffusion and Christina Haas's theory of embodied practice.

Dragga, Sam, and Gwendolyn Gong. *Editing: The Design of Rhetoric.* Amityville, NY: Baywood, 1989. One of the early books to apply a theory to editing, in this case, rhetorical theory. The authors go beyond the mechanics of editing to demonstrate that it is a creative process made more effective when editors understand rhetorical principles. Aiming at beginning editors as well as experienced editors, the authors begin the 5 chapters with a review of rhetoric followed by chapters applying rhetoric to editing. Heavily illustrated with appropriate examples.

Eisenberg, Anne. *Guide to Technical Editing: Discussion, Dictionary, and Exercises.* New York: Oxford University Press, 1993. Textbook for beginning technical editors. Three parts: Strategies for editing, dictionary of basic technical editing terms, and exercises for editing practice. Approach is to teach readers to sort problems into categories and then be selective in editing within those categories. Encourages use of references, both technical for subject matter and general such as dictionaries and usage guides. Presents problems with before/after examples.

Farkas, David K., and Steven E. Poltrock. "Online Editing, Mark-Up Models, and the Workplace Lives of Editors and Writers." *IEEE Transactions on Professional Communication*, 38, no. 2 (1995): 110-117. An early call to technical editors to encourage the creation of online editing tools that they can easily use. Uses examples to critique various markup models that might underlie the software.

Nadziejka, David E. *Levels of Technical Editing.* Reston, VA: Council of Biology Editors, 1999. Building on such earlier work as Van Buren and Buehler's *The Levels of Edit* (see below), recommends a more realistic, efficient system in which technical content figures into each level. The new levels are rush edit (lowest), standard edit, and revision edit. Lists editors' considerations at each level. Nadziejka provides a credible justification for this approach in "Needed: A Revision of the Lowest Level of Editing." *Technical Communication*, 42, no. 2 (1995): 278-283.

Nelson, Vee. "Sweat the Small Stuff—Editing for Consistency." In *Techniques for Technical Communicators*, ed. Carol M. Barnum and Saul Carliner. New York, NY: Macmillan Publishing Co., 1993, pp. 291-304. An educational how-to article in a classroom textbook. Nelson emphasizes consistency in editing content for style and supplies numerous examples and checklists. An excellent first stop for would-be editors. Has annotated suggested readings. Covers variants (spelling, style, etc.), dictionary and style m rank, and Michael Riordan, eds. *Pocket Pal: A Graphic Arts Production Handbook,* 19th ed. Memphis, TN: International Paper Company, 2003. Complete introduction to the graphic arts including the history of printing, printing processes, type and typography, paper, and a glossary of graphic arts terms. Especially useful is the section on color printing, colors, and photographic screens. A handy size that can fit in your pocket and priced to be one of the best bargains in graphic arts information.

Ramey, Judith. "Educating the Editorial Guess." In Rude, ed., pp. 59-62. Details an approach that teachers can take to build beginning editors' confidence in their ability to edit complex passages. Brief, realistic examples show how to systematically tackle problems of language, logic, rhetoric, and accuracy.

Rude, Carolyn, and Elizabeth Smith. "Use of Computers in Technical Editing." *Technical Communication*, 39, no. 3 (1992): 334-342. The fullest study of the topic before David Dayton's work. Responses to a large-scale STC survey provide a realistic picture of the transitional period. Finds that computers have changed editorial responsibilities more than day-to-day procedures; reminds us that editing will always require human judgment. Despite such difficulties as corporate bans on electronic editing, optimistically concludes that "pleasant surprises" may lie in the future of computerized editing.

Soderston, Candace. "The Usability Edit: A New Level." *Technical Communication*, 32, no. 1 (1985): 16-18. Working from rhetorical theory and success within IBM, proposes adding a usability edit to Van Buren and Buehler's *The Levels of Edit* (see below). Convincingly argues that recursive usability editing ensures quality of the final product.

Swaney, Joyce Hannah, Carol J. Janik, Sandra J. Bond, and John R. Hayes. *Editing for Comprehension: Improving the Process Through Reading Protocols*. Technical Report Number 14. Washington, DC: The Document Design Project, American Institutes for Research, 1981. Reports on a series of experiments testing standard editing techniques and reading protocols as an editing tool. Experiment one tested four documents edited with standard techniques for comprehension. Three of the four were improved and one made worse. In the second experiment, subjects used thinking-aloud protocols. The document was re-edited and comprehension tests showed marked improvement. Sample documents used are included.

Van Buren, Robert, and Mary Fran Buehler. *The Levels of Edit.* 2nd ed. Pasadena, CA: Jet Propulsion Laboratory, 1980. A pamphlet that remains the most influential publication on technical editing practice. Defines the methodology used at JPL to determine the types and amounts of editing to devote to a document. Sees nine types of edits: coordination, policy, integrity, screening, copy clarification, format, mechanical style, language, and substantive. Combines these types into five levels of edit. At the high end, a Level 1 edit involves all nine types; a Level 5 edit demands only coordination and policy editing.

Words into Type. Based on studies by M. E. Skillin, R. M. Gay, and others. 3rd ed. Upper Saddle River, NJ: Prentice-Hall, 1974. Has been a fundamental and essential reference book since first published. Combines how and what to edit with numerous reference lists. Divided into 7 parts: The manuscript, copy and proof, copyediting-style, typographical style, grammar, use of words, and typography and illustration. Considerably out-of-date on technical matters of production, but still useful for other parts. Reflects language thinking of the early 1970s, which should be used with caution.

Zook, Lola. "Editing and the Editor: Views and Values." In Shimberg, ed., pp. 5-9. A stirring appeal to technical editors to formulate their own editorial values. Zook examines her own values: make your editing an art by striving for an ideal, set your own performance standards, build your command of the medium, have an instinctive feeling for order and priorities, and work easily with people.

Zook, Lola M. "Making and Breaking Rules: A Manager's Viewpoint." *Technical Communication,* 33, no. 3 (1986): 144-148. Repr. *Technical Communication,* 50, no. 4 (2003): 465-470. Wittily points up the critical importance of managers' helping their publication staffs develop sound judgment about how to balance the need for both rules and flexibility. Rules encompass basic communication concepts, established precepts of grammar and design, house rules, and managerial guidelines. High quality is possible only when decisions about how to address rules are governed by the question "Does it help communication?"

WORKING WITH AUTHORS

Applewhite, Lottie. "The Author's Editor." *Medical Communications*, 1 (1973): 16-20. An early outline of the roles of an in-house editor who helps authors: language mechanic, teacher, interpreter, author's advocate, and activist for improvement of communications.

Bostian, Lloyd R. "Working with Writers." *Scholarly Publishing*, 17 (1986): 119-126. Offers pragmatic steps for treating writers with empathy and diplomacy while remaining firm. Insightful on writers' egos and female editors' dealing with male writers.

Briggs, Nelson A. "Editing by Dialogue." *Technical Communication,* 16, no. 2 (1969): 10-13. Repr. Zook, ed., pp. 56-61. Briggs furthers the discussion of treating the author-editor relationship as one of sensitivity. He invokes Martin Buber's "I-Thou" rather than "I-It" as the model to follow. While editing by fiat, as he calls it, may be rarely necessary, most author-editor relationships should reflect a mutual respect. Such respect is gained through having dialogues about person, subject matter, improvements, and mutuality. He distinguishes between dialogue and rapport, where dialogue may contain rapport but rapport does not necessarily entail dialogue. Recognizing the otherness in the dialogue of the participants preserves the relationship. He suggests: Show interest in the author's work, prepare notations neatly, avoid subjective changes, remember that corrections and improvements are two different things, avoid red pencils, go to the author, thoughtfully suggest things the author may have forgotten, read about interviewing techniques, and be confident in your knowledge.

Dukes, Eva. "The Art of Editing." *Technical Communication,* 20, no. 3 (1973): 14-17. Repr. Zook, ed., pp. 62-66. Dukes views the relationship between the editor and the author as vital. She discusses several aspects of that relationship including courtesy; communication—oral or written messages— neatly written queries, suggestions, and questions; and apologizing when wrong. Together, these represent the subjective side of editing.

Dukes, Eva P. "The Simple Joys of Editing." *Technical Communication,* 19, no. 3 (1972): 7-8. In this short article, Dukes iterates some of the pleasures of editing. Essentially, it is a working relationship with writers that will allow the writer to trust the editor to help improve the work.

Dukes, Eva. "Some Authors I Have Known." In Shimberg, ed., pp. 27-31. Wisely, entertainingly provides lessons on working with hostile/distrustful, know-it-all, cooperative, vicious, perfectionist, and ideal authors.

Fourdrinier, Sylvia. "The Editor as a Teacher." *Proceedings, 18th International Technical Communication Conference.* Washington, DC: Society for Technical Communication, pp. 55-57. Repr. Zook, ed., pp. 67-70. Editing involves teaching, and good teaching involves not only spotting problems, but also offering suggestions for revision. In addition, the teacher makes clear the principles upon which the comments on problems are based. Fourdrinier provides examples of two editors and their teaching: The supervising editor of a group of writers and a journal editor. Each has different "students," but they have similar responsibilities in the relationship. Explaining principles eases the fragile ego issues of writers. Editors have additional teaching opportunities when they prepare style manuals.

Layton, Edward. "Editor-Author Relationships: Both Can Win." *IEEE Transactions on Professional Communication,* 16, no. 3 (1973): 57-59, 172. Focuses on the journal editor-author relationship with the editor being the reader's advocate. In their initial contact with the author, editors should establish one or two first principles that will govern editing the manuscript. In addition to improving the readability of the manuscript, the editor is also concerned about retaining the interest of current readers and attracting future ones. Editors other than those editing journals can gain from the suggestions Layton makes about, especially, providing the author with aids such as a summary of the assumed reader and author responsibilities.

Mackiewicz, Jo, and Kathryn Riley. "The Technical Editor as Diplomat: Linguistic Strategies for Balancing Clarity and Politeness." *Technical Communication,* 50, no. 1 (2003): 83-94. Convincingly argues that linguistic research offers ways to balance clarity and politeness in dealing with both native and non-native authors. The concluding table is a powerful summary of best strategies.

Shimberg, H. Lee. "Editing Authors' Style—A Few Guidelines." In Shimberg, ed., pp. 31-35. Cautions not to alter writers' style unnecessarily. Suggestions: Do not exceed your limited right to alter authors' style, detect and help correct extreme styles, edit for readability, and take special care to remain unobtrusive when editing non-native writers.

Smith, Herb. "Methods for Training the Technical Editor in Interpersonal Skills." *IEEE Transactions on Professional Communication,* 28, no. 1 (1985): 46-50. Smith interviewed 20 professional writers and editors about interpersonal relations and skills. He asked about their training in interpersonal skills. Many (65%) indicated that the edited work was better when author and editor collaborated. And that involved good interpersonal skills. Academic preparation as well as workshops should stress the editor developing appropriate interpersonal skills. Finally, Smith stresses the goal of editors is to improve writers' manuscripts.

Speck, Bruce W. "Editorial Authority in the Author-Editor Relationship." *Technical Communication,* 38, no. 3 (1991): 300-315. Recommends categorizing editors by their organizational status. This approach can help editors gain more authority, important especially when they must edit incompetent authors.

Whalen, Elizabeth. "The Editing Equation: A Reply to Authors Who Ask, 'How Come You Changed My Stuff?'" *Technical Communication,* 39, no. 3 (1992): 329-333. Why do copyeditors change what others have written? This article is one reply based on the editor's relationship with the author and the reader. But Whalen adds a third entity: the company or journal as a stakeholder in the material. After presenting the usual advice about working with authors and readers, she introduces the company or journal interests. The author and reader issues become magnified when considering the company or journal because the stakes are so high. Authors may receive criticism for faulty prose, but companies and journals can lose customers and business if the message is not clear and correctly expressed.

TOOLS

American Psychological Association. *Publication Manual of the American Psychological Association*, 6th ed. Washington, DC: American Psychological Association, 2010. The main style guide for publications in the social sciences, especially psychology; used in other disciplines as well. Detailed guidelines on all facets of publication, including online work. Updated by APA on http://apastyle.apa.org/ (retrieved December 5, 2009).

Bright, Mark R. "Creating, Implementing, and Maintaining Corporate Style Guides in an Age of Technology." *Technical Communication*, 52, no. 1 (2005): 42-51. Gives research-based recommendations for creating style guides. Most useful tips concern choices of media and ways to achieve accessibility.

Coghill, Anne M., and Lorrin R. Garson, eds. *The ACS Style Guide: Effective Communication of Scientific Information*, 3rd ed. New York: Oxford University Press, 2006. The main style guide for the American Chemical Society and other chemistry publications. Good, general discussion of ethics. Most valuable is Part 2, an in-depth presentation of ACS style guidelines on such topics as numbers, compound names, and chemical symbols.

Dictionaries. Print dictionaries often required of technical editors include the current editions of *Merriam-Webster's Collegiate Dictionary* (Springfield, MA: Merriam-Webster, Inc.); American Heritage Dictionaries, *The American Heritage Dictionary of the English Language* (Boston: Houghton Mifflin); and *The Oxford Dictionary for Scientific Writers and Editors* (Oxford: Clarendon Press). The Web sites OneLook (http://www.onelook.com/) and Dictionary.com (http://dictionary.reference.com/) link editors to the online versions of these and many other dictionaries. In addition, editors within the many technical and scientific disciplines must use appropriate field-specific dictionaries.

Duffy, Thomas M. "Designing Tools to Aid Technical Editors: A Needs Analysis." *Technical Communication*, 42, no. 2 (1995): 262-277. Rigorously analyzes feedback from expert editors to describe their technical editing environments, their editing problems, and computer-based editing tools that might be designed. Calls for tools that would later be developed, such as networked document-management systems and commenting features.

Gibaldi, Joseph. *MLA Style Manual and Guide to Scholarly Publishing,* 3rd ed. New York: The Modern Language Association, 2008. Extensive style manual and primer on scholarly publishing aimed at advanced undergraduate and graduate students in literature and languages. Sections cover scholarly publishing; legal issues in scholarly publishing; basics of scholarly writing; preparation of manuscripts, theses, and dissertations; documentation style; and abbreviations. Appendix offers information on specialized style manuals. Extensive examples. An important reference for editors.

Hale, Constance. *Wired Style: Principles of English Usage in the Digital Age.* San Francisco: HardWired, 1996. One of the earliest and the most spirited style guide of Internet usage, using data gathered by *Wired* magazine. In tone witty and wise, celebrates the colloquial voice in online style. Witness the definition of *techie*: "Garden-variety nerd, geek, gearhead, propellerhead." Each of nine main chapters (for example, "Go global" and "Acronyms, FWIW") opens with stylistic guidance, followed by several terms and their definitions, in dictionary format. The index lists all terms defined.

Howell, James Bruce. *Style Manuals of the English-Speaking World: A Guide.* Phoenix, AZ: Oryx, 1983. Annotated bibliography of over 200 style manuals written in English, at least 5 pages long, and published between 1970 and 1983. Excludes style manuals found in and for individual periodicals. Includes listings for manuals and author's guides from 10 countries. A historical note at the beginning traces the evolution of the style manual from printer's manuals (earliest in Germany, 1608) to author's guides and style manuals.

Iverson, Cheryl, Stacy Christiansen, Annette Flanagin, Phil B. Fontanarosa, Richard M. Glass, Brenda Gregoline, Stephen J. Lurie, Harriet S. Meyer, Margaret A. Winker, and Roxanne K. Young. *AMA Manual of Style: A Guide for Authors and Editors*, 10th ed. New York: Oxford University Press, 2007. The standard guide for medical writers and editors in the U.S.; also much used by scientific communicators. Five sections contain 25 detailed chapters. Outstanding discussions of visual presentations, ethical and legal issues, indexes, nomenclature, preferred usages of common words in medical contexts, and statistics. Provides many examples, tables, and graphics.

Lipson, Charles. *Cite Right: A Quick Guide to Citation Styles—MLA, APA, Chicago, the Sciences, Professions, and More.* Chicago: University of Chicago Press, 2006. Focuses on citation differences among 11 subject-specific styles of citation. Covers why to cite references and the basics of citation. Divides the different approaches into 11 chapters—one each for a specific style plus a FAQ about reference styles. Includes examples of over 60 citations in each chapter as well as brief discussions about less obvious points of citation style. Highly useful, especially at the economical price.

Microsoft Corporation. *The Microsoft Manual of Style for Technical Publications*, 3rd ed. Redmond, WA: Microsoft Press, 2004. Developed to help Microsoft writers and editors create consistent documentation; other organizations use it heavily. The first part presents 12 chapters on general topics; the second part is an alphabetized usage dictionary. Especially strong on coding, specific technologies, indexing, and interface design. Many correct-incorrect examples, tables, and screen shots.

Murphy, Avon Jack. "Technical Editing," in *Technical and Business Communication: Bibliographic Essays for Teachers and Corporate Trainers*, ed. Charles H. Sides. Urbana, IL: NCTE, 1989, pp.75-93. Although somewhat dated, this essay still is an excellent starting point for researching technical editing. Murphy divides the 96 books and articles into 8 categories: books and bibliographies, outlooks, editor as a person, doing the job (macro- and microviews), editing nonprose and other materials, and editing pedagogy. His style is fluid, making a potentially pedestrian topic interesting to read.

Nichols, Michelle Corbin. "Using Style Guidelines to Create Consistent Online Information." *Technical Communication*, 41, no. 3 (1994): 432-438. Presents research on style, screen design, online documentation, and user models to establish the need for guidelines when developing online information. Concludes that rather than stifling creativity, guidelines push technical communicators to create more consistent, usable online information.

Ritter, R. M., ed. *The Oxford Style Manual*. Oxford: University Press, 2003. Consists of two previously separate books: *The Oxford Guide to Style* and *The Oxford Dictionary for Writers and Editors*, historically the first books of their types published anywhere. Widely adopted not only within the Press but throughout the UK and worldwide. The 16 chapters in the *Guide* provide in-depth detail—often learned but always practical—on all matters relevant to book publishing. Authoritative especially on languages, punctuation, numbers, and reference formats. The *Dictionary* includes terms from *A* to *zythum* that might be problematic, indicating such information as acceptable abbreviations, internal punctuation, spellings and U.S. variants, and definitions if necessary for clarification.

Rude, Carolyn D., and Rex W. Castle. "Technical Editing: A Selected, Annotated Bibliography." In Rude, ed., pp. 173-204. Selective listing of 313 books and articles significant for editing teachers published 1970-1985, with a subject index. Some attention paid to quality as well as content of items. Remains an invaluable place to start research.

Speck, Bruce W. *Editing: An Annotated Bibliography*. Westport, CT: Praeger, 1991. Also Speck, Bruce W., Dean A. Hinnen, and Kathleen Hinnen. *Teaching Revising and Editing: An Annotated Bibliography*. Westport, CT:

Greenwood Press, 2003. Together, cover the literature of roughly 1960 to 2000. Despite significant omissions and weak indexes, provide over 1,400 useful summaries, with usually accurate author and subject indexes.

Style Manual Committee, Council of Science Editors. *Scientific Style and Format: The CSE Manual for Authors, Editors, and Publishers*, 7th ed. Reston, VA: Council of Science Editors, 2006. The most authoritative style guide for communicators in all scientific disciplines. The 32 chapters are gathered in four parts discussing fundamentals of publishing, general style conventions, conventions of 12 specific scientific genres, and publication elements. The lengthy bibliography lists many style guides, dictionaries, and other guides. Of special interest are the recommendations on such specific areas as chemical formulas and disease names.

Sun Technical Publications. *Read Me First! A Style Guide for the Computer Industry*, 2nd ed. Upper Saddle River, NJ: Prentice Hall PTR, 2003. Although developed within Sun Microsystems, has a less in-house tone than Microsoft's style manual. Discusses most topics within 14 chapters. Particularly helpful on indexes, online style, legal guidelines, and interfaces. Many tables and examples, often in illustrations.

United States Government Printing Office (GPO). *United States Government Printing Office Style Manual, 2000.* Washington, DC: United States Government Printing Office, 2000. Standard manual used for editing government documents. Originally published in 1894 and updated many times. Covers topics authors and editors need such as rules for capitalization, spelling, compounding, punctuation, etc. Also contains material for visualization and enhancement of text (tables, type enhancement, etc.). Suggestions for Congressional publications such as reports and hearings. Helpful advice on countries and geographical division.

University of Chicago Press. *The Chicago Manual of Style,* 15th ed. Chicago: University of Chicago Press, 2003. Substantial revision of 14th edition. Generally, each section reflects the influence of computer technology to some extent. The editors consulted a broadened range of experts regarding changes from the 14th. In addition, new areas added include new sections on electronic publications including citation styles added to major sections; updated and expanded material on copyright and permissions; and typographic conventions for American Sign Language. To make access easier, they added run-in headings for each paragraph announcing the subject matter of the paragraph. They eliminated "For Further Reference" in favor of an expanded bibliography. The editors added a new section from Bryan Garner on grammar and usage. Standard rules for grammar and other such matters were reviewed and changed only when current practice suggested a needed change (for example, retaining the *n* in 2nd). Revision not as extensive as was done in the 12th, but still considerable.

SPECIFIC AREAS

Amsden, Dorothy Corner. "Get in the Habit of Editing Illustrations." In *Publication Production*, ed. Anthony H. Firman. Arlington, VA: Society for Technical Communication, 1993, pp. 118-125. Wisely and enthusiastically recommends using a working approach, not a formula, when editing illustrations. Even if the many black-and-white illustration examples are dated, the specific advice on content editing remains valid.

Anderson, Steven L., and others. "Editing a Website: Extending the Levels of Edit." *IEEE Transactions on Professional Communication*, 41, no. 1 (1998): 47-57. Creatively adapts Van Buren and Buehler's *The Levels of Edit* (see above) to an orderly three-level editing process for Web sites. Outlines new requirements for editors at each level.

Bishop, Claude T. *How to Edit a Scientific Journal*. Philadelphia: ISI Press, 1984. Aimed at editors of physical science journals; applicable to other scientific editors. Genially explains how to set policies, maintain procedures, and troubleshoot problems of running a journal. Excellent on ethics, referees, and recordkeeping. Does not touch on the editing of writers.

Bostian, Lloyd, and Barbara Hollander. "Technical Journal Editors and Writing Style." *Journal of Technical Writing and Communication*, 20, no. 2 (1990): 153-163. Finds that because editors of technical journals value scientific quality much more highly than writing style, articles have poor style. Dares to suggest that editors reject all poorly written articles.

Bush, Don. "Content Editing, an Opportunity for Growth." In Shimberg, ed., pp. 15-18. A stirring call to action. Urges technical editors to enhance their careers by looking beyond mere error-finding and stylebook editing to create technical accuracy, clarity, English correctness, and consistency. Doing so will not only solve the real writing problems, but also persuade staff and employers to value language skills.

Butcher, Judith, Caroline Drake, and Maureen Leach. *Butcher's Copy-editing: The Cambridge Handbook for Editors, Copy-editors and Proofreaders*, 4th ed. Cambridge: Cambridge University Press, 2006. Widely used by UK copyeditors, especially at CUP. Pays special attention to CUP house style, proofing, parts of a book, science editing, and online editing.

Cheney, Patrick, and David Schleicher. "Redesigning Technical Reports: A Rhetorical Editing Method." *Journal of Technical Writing and Communication*, 15, no. 1 (1985): 317-337. Looking at the whole report rather than individual lines, Cheney and Schleicher construct a five-step process: identify the audience and purpose, analyze the ideas in the draft report, synthesize the ideas into a focused revision, interview the author, and finish the report. An environmental impact report nicely demonstrates the approach.

Einsohn, Amy. *The Copyeditor's Handbook: A Guide for Book Publishing and Corporate Communications, with Exercises and Answer Keys*, 2nd ed. Berkeley: University of California Press, 2006. The most useful handbook for working U.S. copyeditors; also excellent as a textbook, with challenging end-of-chapter exercises. Fifteen chapters provide thorough details on the nature of copyediting, editorial style, and language editing. Smart advice on such topics as levels of copyediting, spelling variants, style sheets, variants among U.S. style manuals, typecoding, and numbers. Summarizes the backgrounds of many grammatical, usage, and other controversies.

Gilad, Suzanne. *Copyediting & Proofreading for Dummies*. Hoboken, NJ: Wiley Publishing, Inc., 2007. Informal and enthusiastic in tone, written for beginning copyeditors and proofreaders. In addition to the overall whys and how-tos, provides especially sound advice about finding work (particularly for freelancers), style sheets, and electronic editing. Offers many extended examples.

Judd, Karen. *Copyediting: A Practical Guide*. Menlo Park, CA: Crisp Learning, 2001. Includes material on both copyediting text and handling the physical manuscript. Written for both the beginner and experienced copyeditor. Thirteen chapters follow process from definition of copyediting to proofing and then getting a job. Describes what publishers look for in a copyeditor as well as some of the specialized copyediting tasks such as coding texts and proofreading. Concludes with listing of essential references.

Lanier, Clinton R. "The Implications of Outsourcing for Technical Editing." In *Outsourcing Technical Communication: Issues, Policies, and Practices*, ed. Barry Thatcher and Carlos Evia. Amityville, NY: Baywood Publishing Company, Inc., 2008, pp. 147-161. Focuses on five edited authors' responses to electronic editing using Microsoft Word within a government laboratory. For the most part, such editing successfully resolved problems of unnecessary editing, changes in meaning, and an excessive amount of time required to review edited documents. Notes that authors reporting negative feelings had not learned how to use Word's reviewing features.

Leininger, Carol, and Rue Yuan. "Aligning International Editing Efforts with Global Business Strategies." *IEEE Transactions on Professional Communication,* 41, no. 1 (1998): 16-23. Editors, as well as writers, must be aware of cross-cultural implication in the work they do. Leininger and Yuan focus on how editors should treat cross-cultural communication issues. They begin with 4 categories of editing, explaining each with examples—linguistic (readability for non-native speakers), socio-cultural (the role the document plays in the other culture), political (political implications in business and government), and technical (substantive editing). They then address 3 global strategies editors can employ—ethnocentric (what works here works there), polycentric (accommodates needs of specific cultures), and geocentric (balance between the two).

Malone, Edward A. "Learned Correctors as Technical Editors: Specialization and Collaboration in Early Modern European Printing Houses." *Journal of Business and Technical Communication*, 20, no. 4 (2006): 389-424. An excellent historical study of "editing" in early modern European printing houses using specialists in the content of the material as editors. In reality, they were more proofreaders than editors as we know the term.

McGinty, Stephen. *Gatekeepers of Knowledge: Journal Editors in the Sciences and Social Sciences*. Westport, CT: Bergin & Garvey, 1999. McGinty, in his 8 chapters, provides an excellent introduction to journal editing for young and would-be editors. He not only gives an overview of journal processes, but also offers sage advice on handling the people issues such as those related to reviewers and authors. Each chapter is filled with examples that serve to help the editor establish his or her own communications. As the subtitle suggests, he concentrates on the sciences—soft, hard, and social. Editors in the humanities would also find the materials quite useful. An annotated bibliography provides additional resources.

Morgan, Peter. *An Insider's Guide for Medical Authors & Editors*. Philadelphia: ISI Press, 2002. Explains to medical authors of all levels of experience what a medical editor does and why. Features a running narrative with entertaining characters. The two chapters most relevant to editors discuss how editors work and how authors can work with editors. Insightful on improving weak manuscripts, handling disagreements among reviewers, and rejecting manuscripts.

Philbin, Alice I. "Editing Statistics." In Rude, ed., pp. 72-88. A wake-up call to editing teachers to show their "math illiterates" how to format mathematical and statistical information. Uses definitions, classifications, examples, exercises, and a solid glossary.

Plunka, Gene A. "The Editor's Nightmare: Formatting Lists Within the Text." *Technical Communication*, 35, no. 1 (1988): 37, 42-44. Repr. Kemnitz, ed., pp. 50-53. Offers guidelines for properly and consistently preparing and editing lists. Focuses on miscellaneous errors, such as faulty parallelism; run-in lists; and vertical lists. Pays much attention to the troublesome issues of bullets in lists and introductory colons.

Stainton, Elsie Myers. *The Fine Art of Copyediting*. New York: Columbia University Press, 2002. A concise introduction to copyediting practices. The short chapters touch on such matters as the job, legal aspects, personal relationships, editorial procedures, computer strategies, style, and special problems. Although chapters do not go into complexities or alternative strategies, the advice is valid, the annotated bibliography surprisingly full.

Weeks, Robert A., and Donald L. Kinser, eds. *Editing the Refereed Scientific Journal: Practical, Political, and Ethical Issues*. Piscataway, NJ: IEEE

Press, 1994. An anthology of 29 articles divided into 10 chapters that serve as a proceedings for a 1992 conference of editors of scientific journals. The format was to have papers followed by a discussion in each of the 90-minute sessions. The discussion transcripts are included with each chapter. Chapters of interest to editors include one on an editor's responsibilities (4 papers), ethical concerns for editors (4 papers), and guidelines for editors (3 papers). Chapter 10 summarizes the conference presentations focusing on the functions of scientific journals and editorial ethics and practices.

Williams, Thomas R., and Deborah A. Harkus. "Editing Visual Media." *IEEE Transactions on Professional Communication*, 41, no. 1 (1998): 33-46. The authors argue that to properly edit both text and visuals, you need to understand the weaknesses of both. They compare and contrast visual and verbal media to give editors practical guidelines for editing and using visuals. They present many examples with comments that they analyze focusing on both as systems. The central editorial decisions they address are how to use visuals once they decide to use them, and then what kinds of visuals to use.

Contributors

MICHELLE CORBIN is a senior technical editor and information architect at IBM. She has been a technical communicator for 20 years. She is an associate fellow in the Society for Technical Communication (STC). She holds a BA in English and an MS in Technical Communication, both from North Carolina State University. She can be reached at corbinm@us.ibm.com

ANGELA EATON is an Associate Professor of Technical Communication and Rhetoric at Texas Tech University. She studies professional and technical communication practice, pedagogy, and professionalization. She teaches courses in editing, grant and proposal writing, and introductory and quantitative research methods. She owns Angela Eaton & Associates, which specializes in technical editing and grant proposal preparation. She is a senior member of STC, belongs to the Association of the Teachers of Technical Writing (ATTW), and received the 2005-2006 STC $10,000 Research Award. She can be reached at angela.eaton@ttu.edu

BARBARA GASTEL coordinates the graduate program in science journalism at Texas A&M University. A physician specializing in biomedical writing and editing, she also edits the Council of Science Editors periodical, *Science Editor,* and is Knowledge Community Editor for AuthorAID@INASP, a program to help researchers in developing countries to write about their work. Her publications include *Health Writer's Handbook* and, with Robert A. Day, the 6th edition of *How to Write and Publish a Scientific Paper.* The Board of Editors in the Life Sciences has named her an Honored Editor in the Life Sciences. She can be reached at b-gastel@tamu.edu

GEOFFREY J. S. HART, a fellow of the Society for Technical Communication, has worked as a scientific and technical editor, technical writer, and translator for more than 20 years. For the past 5 years, he has specialized in international clients for whom English is a second or third language, and he has clients on every continent except Antarctica. He is the author of *Effective Onscreen Editing,* the only book currently in print that focuses exclusively on editing using a word processor. Visit him online at http://www.geoff-hart.com

GEORGE F. HAYHOE is professor of technical communication at Mercer University. A fellow of STC, he edited its journal, *Technical Communication,* from 1996 to 2008. He is also a senior member of the Institute of Electrical and Electronics Engineers and the IEEE Professional Communication Society, and is a past president of that society. He holds a PhD in English from the University of South Carolina. His professional interests include product and document usability, research in technical and professional communication, and core competencies of professional and technical communicators.

AVON J. MURPHY is a technical editor based in western Washington. He owns Murphy Editing and Writing Services, specializing in the development and editing of Web sites, articles and books on computer technologies, and mystery fiction. A former college professor and government technical writer, he is an STC fellow and, since 1993, the book review editor for STC's quarterly journal, *Technical Communication.*

CAROLYN RUDE teaches professional writing and chairs the Department of English at Virginia Tech. She is author of *Technical Editing* (Allyn & Bacon), in its fourth edition (2006). She is past president and fellow of ATTW. She is also a fellow of the Society for Technical Communication and winner of its Jay R. Gould Award for excellence in teaching.

THOMAS L. WARREN is professor emeritus of English and former director of the Oklahoma State University Technical Writing Program, and has taught technical writing since 1972 in universities and industry in the United States and Europe. He developed the BA, MA, and PhD technical writing degree programs at OSU where he taught editing, information design, and document project management. He is also a guest professor at the University of Paderborn (Germany). He is a Past President of INTECOM and is both an ATTW and STC Fellow, recipient of CPTSC's Distinguished Service Award, and STC's Jay R. Gould Award for Excellence in Teaching.

JEAN HOLLIS WEBER has worked as a scientific and technical editor and writer for over 30 years, specializing in software documentation. She has also taught short courses and workshops, lectured in technical writing and editing at several universities, and spoken at professional conferences. Jean has written nine books, including the award-winning *Is the Help Helpful?* For many years she was active in the Australia Chapter of the Society for Technical Communication and the Australian Society for Technical Communication. Jean maintains a Web site for technical editors, http://jeanweber.com/

Index

For details on these titles from Baywood's Technical Communications Series, visit http://baywood.com.

For details on these titles from Baywood's Technical Communications Series, visit http://baywood.com.